MW00908459

BORN
AT
REVEILLE

BOOKS BY COLONEL RED REEDER

West Point Plebe
West Point Yearling
West Point Second Classman
West Point First Classman
2nd Lieutenant Clint Lane: West Point to Berlin
Clint Lane in Korea
Attack at Fort Lookout
Whispering Wind
The Sheriff of Hat Creek
The Mackenzie Raid
The Story of the Civil War
The Story of the Revolutionary War
The Story of the War of 1812
Pointers on Athletics
Sheridan: The General Who Wasn't Afraid to Take A Chance
The Story of the First World War
The Northern Generals
The Southern Generals
Ulysses S. Grant
Medal of Honor Heroes
Born at Reveille
The Story of the Spanish-American War
The Story of the Mexican War
Dwight D. Eisenhower—Fighter for Peace
The Story of World War II (in two volumes)
Omar N. Bradley—The Soldier's General
Heroes and Leaders of West Point
The Story of the French and Indian War
Bold Leaders of the American Revolution
Bold Leaders of World War I

WITH NARDI REEDER CAMPION

The West Point Story
Bringing up the Brass

BORN AT REVEILLE

The Memoirs of an American Soldier

by
Colonel Red Reeder

VERMONT HERITAGE PRESS

A SUBSIDIARY OF CABER PUBLISHING LTD.

Quechee, Vermont

Manufactured in the United States of America

Library of Congress Cataloguing-in-Publication Data

Library of Congress Catalog Card Number 94-068026
ISBN 0-911853-08-1

To
Dorothea (Dort) Darrah Reeder
My beloved wife and best friend.

My father said, "Read autobiography because if the author tells the truth the book is valuable." In this book I try to tell the truth although at times it is inconvenient

Red Reeder

COLONEL RUSSELL P. "RED" REEDER
U.S. ARMY RETIRED
USMA 1926

ATHLETE, OFFICER, LEADER
COACH, AUTHOR, FRIEND

In appreciation for decades of inspired service to USMA, the U.S. Army and his Country . . .

In recognition of a unique Army Baseball legend who, through his actions on the baseball diamond and battlefield, and his influence upon generations of graduates, has become an American Hero in his own time . . .

To this magnificent soldier, sportsman and friend, the Doubleday Society humbly present this, the first Doubleday Society Distinguished Service Award . . .

19 November 1991

Preface

THIS IS THE COMPELLING TALE of one of the finest human beings I've ever known, a man bigger than life. A loveable soldier with a grand smile, a still grander heart . . . and with passions—

for a game played with ball and bat
a school on the Hudson that he lived for
a country he proved willing to die for

. . . and for a beautiful girl named Dort—who made it fun all along the way. This is the moving story of those passions . . . and what they have meant to our Country.

Rod Vitty
The Publisher

Acknowledgments

YOU WOULD THINK that when a man writes about his life he would need no assistance except possibly from a spelling teacher or two. When I started to write this story, I knew my wife Dort would stand by me in every way possible, and she spent many hours sharpening the manuscript. I also enlisted the aid of two other literary persons, Nardi Reeder Campion and BG Jack Whitelaw. All three worked faithfully, but they should be held blameless for errors.

I expected their help and my notes would suffice, although the first memorandum I pulled from its shelter startled me because it was a sketch of the battlefield at Stony Point, an engagement slightly before my time. I began to write, and I had hardly described Chaplain Easterbrook when I was asking questions of the following so I could fill in chinks of my memory:

COL John Billingsley, COL George Bixby, General of the Army Omar Bradley, COL P. D. Calyer, Mr. Tom Campion, GEN Bruce

Clarke, Mr. J. O. Christian, COL E. C. Cutler, Jr., Mr. Tim Cohane, Chaplain Jim Ford, COL Harvey Fraser, Mr. Lorenz Freyermuth, MG Jerry Galloway, Mr. Ted Glowa, Mr. Abel Green, Miss Nancy Harlow, BG Vald Heiberg, Mr. Harry Hershfield, COL John Harvey Kane, Mr. Carney Laslie, Mr. George Lewis, BG Steve Mellnik, Memphis Area Chamber of Commerce, MAJ William L. Mills, Jr., Mr. Willard Mullin, MG Ray Murphy, Music Division of The New York Public Library, GEN Emmett O'Donnell, Mr. John Parker, Mr. Kenneth Rapp, COL William Ray, Rear Admiral Fred Reeder, BG Jack Renfroe, GEN M. B. Ridgway, BG William Ludlow Ritchie, MG George Smythe, Miss Charlotte Snyder, Southern Bell Telephone and Telegraph Co., BG James Stapleton, COL and Mrs. C. P. Summerall, Jr., *The New York Times*, Mrs. Forrest E. Williford, Mrs. C. E. Whitehouse, and BG James K. Wilson.

I am indebted to the following authors and their works for refreshing my memory: COL Gerden F. Johnson, *History of the Twelfth Infantry Regiment in World War II*; Omar N. Bradley, *A Soldier's Story*; Robert L. Eichelberger, *Our Jungle Road to Tokyo*; Dwight D. Eisenhower, *Crusade in Europe*; Daniel Blum, *A Pictorial History of the American Theatre, 1900 to 1956*; Marjorie Farnsworth, *The Ziegfeld Follies*; Abel Green and Joe Laruie, Jr., *Show Biz from Vaude to Video*; Henry Blackman Sell and Victor Weybright, *Buffalo Bill and the Wild West*.

I acknowledge gratefully the use of photographs taken by Signal Corps, U. S. Army; International News Service; Mr. Morry Luxenberg; Mrs. Mary Wade Reilly; and Mrs. Charlotte Rumsey.

Wendy and Russell Philip (Rusty) Reeder exceeded expectations by steering this republication away from a reef.

Mrs. Dale E. (Dodie) Hruby, a winner, skilled writer and teacher, left the bench for the mound to give new chapters invaluable direction.

RED REEDER

Contents

CONTENTS

CHAPTER ONE

The "Old" Old Army

THE DOORBELL RANG in our home at Fort Worden, Washington, and I answered it. The lanky soldier standing on the threshold had no tie. He wore blue trousers with red stripes down the sides, a campaign hat, and an olive-drab shirt open at the throat.

"Tell your pa I want to see him," he said. "In a hurry."

This was 1909 and I was only seven, but I knew soldiers did not come to our house and talk like that.

My father, the post adjutant, appeared behind me. He was almost as tall as the soldier and heavier. My father's mouth was set in a firm line, the way he looked when things displeased him.

"What do you want?" he asked.

"I want a pass."

"How long have you been in the army?"

"Two days."

My father, the soldier and I walked out on our front porch, and a crowd of soldiers on the porch of the barracks, two hundred yards away across the parade ground, slid indoors.

"Those fellows over there sent me," the soldier said. "They said you're the gazabo who gives out passes, and I want to go to Port Townsend."

"You go back over there and wait for your company commander and ask him. A soldier does not come to an officer's house unless there is an emergency, and you're not in right uniform. We have a number of customs and you have to learn them."

A number of customs! In 1909 the United States Army had a barrel of customs.

This was a world to itself, a world long gone. In the "Old Army" an enlisted man had to ask his company commander for permission to get married. There was a reason for this. A private was paid $14 a month and married ones got into trouble even though they were clothed, fed and housed. Young officers did little better. The pay of a second lieutenant in 1926, the year I graduated from West Point, was $143 per month, so low that we first classmen received a lecture warning against marriage, entitled "A Second Lieutenant's Pay Divided by Two."

In the Old Army enlisted men addressed officers in the third person unless the soldier knew the officer well: "Sir, does the lieutenant want his horse saddled?" When an enlisted man desired a particular favor he might begin, "Sir, Lieutenant, sir . . . " and for a moment you felt like a knight. Or maybe two knights. A soldier who wanted to talk to an officer on official matters saluted smartly and began, "Sir, Private Kane has the first sergeant's permission to speak to the lieutenant."

The United States Army I saw as a boy had soldiers who had served the country in Cuba and the Philippines. There were retired soldiers around who had fought in the Indian and Civil Wars. I saw army teamsters, cavalrymen, packmasters, and riflemen who shouldered Krag-Jorgenson rifles while they spent long hours on the parade ground practicing "on right into line!" and other complicated Zouave maneuvers, holdovers from the Civil War. I saw artillerymen who manned disappearing guns, horse-drawn cannons, twelve-inch mortars, and submarine mines intended for harbor defense.

My boyhood I kept in my head. When I became an officer I kept notes, for I didn't want to forget the people I lived with, some wise, some foolish, and some brave. Many of the brave ones I knew in the "Combat Club"—as a British general of World War II called the forward area of the battlefield.

In writing this autobiography I will, to paraphrase Mark Twain, talk about some of the giants I met, rejoicing when they make

RR surrenders food to Tige, 1904—Fort Caswell, N.C.

themselves useful as beacons, "but for real business I depend upon the common herd."

Boys who lived on old army posts made their own fun but we small Reeders had special help from our mother, a southern belle from Little Rock and Memphis. She played baseball with us, but I did not like it very much because, with her long skirt, she could stop grounders better than I could. When she would build a fireplace of bricks near the rear of our house, we had cookouts. Sometimes the wind would almost snuff out the fire, but at the same time it tossed the smell of bacon about and made you hungrier.

In the summer of 1909 at Puget Sound, the fourth army post I had lived on in seven years, my mother was also occupied with my sister Julia, five years old, and my brother Fred, three years, and Nat, nine months.

My father looked like both a football player and a doctor; in his youth he played guard on the University of Michigan football team, and later earned the M.D. degree. He did not follow the medical profession but became a soldier in the best sense of the word, starting his career, after the battleship *Maine* went down, as an aide de camp to President McKinley in the White House. High society, however, was not for him with a war going on, so he asked to be relieved from his aide duties and fought as an infantryman in Cuba. Now he was a coast artilleryman.

I loved him, but sometimes he upset me because he was so busy with his job. I knew he knew baseball because he had once been Michigan's first baseman, but when I suggested we play catch he put me off. "I haven't time," he would say. "Have to go to the office."

Because I was bitten by the baseball bug, a nick that developed into a virus from which I have never recovered, he let me break one of his orders. "Stay away from enlisted men," he said in his firm voice. When he gave an order he snapped it out.

This order puzzled me, but I know now why he gave it. Many of the enlisted men in the Old Army were rough. Numbers of them at Fort Worden had been raised on ranches, or in small western settlements, in an era when there was scant emphasis on refinement.

But one day a corporal who was a ball player gave me a cutdown baseball uniform with "Fort Worden" across the chest. I have never been more excited. My father frowned, but my mother talked him into letting me be the team's mascot, even though all the players were soldiers. She amazed me, because she came to the games not to see Worden win but to see me take care of the bats.

Fort Worden was a small post. It had a level parade ground lined on one side by the officers' row and on the other by two-story barracks. Behind the barracks stood a hill that was almost a mountain—a tree-covered mass that rose eight hundred feet above the parade ground. There were mortar batteries on that hill. The ball diamond was in the center of the parade ground.

The star of the team was a powerful batter, my hero, "Jumbo" Henry. When he walked up to bat the Worden fans, sitting in bleachers about four rows high, greeted him with screams. He was picturesque—a natural off-hand cusser. No one took offense. Once I crossed the bats in front of the bench and he said that no damned good would come of it. I leaped to uncross them but the damage had been done. We lost late in the game to Fort Flagler. I felt terrible, personally responsible.

Jumbo Henry thought he was rough on umpires, but the post commander, Lieutenant Colonel G. N. Whistler, with 43 years' service, could be worse. He had permission from the War Department to wear his hair long, down over the stand-up collar of his blue uniform. He was a cousin of the artist, and looked it. He was a thin and prim man, about five feet eight, but he seemed six feet. A colonel of an army post in 1909 had more power than many generals a half century later. Colonel Whistler, a kindly man, seldom cursed, but when he wanted to he could scorch any object he aimed at.

Once when Fort Worden was getting a raw deal in a game, Colonel Whistler stepped down from the bleachers. Everybody quieted. He had a straight back, as if he were always on parade. His blue uniform, with a broad red stripe down each leg, was immaculate, and he wore his small, stingy-cut, flat-top officer's cap jammed down over his Buffalo Bill haircut. He stalked over to home plate. He did not cuss the umpire direct, he blistered all around him.

When Colonel Whistler marched himself off the field, his long hair blowing in the breeze, the umpire turned to our catcher and said, "Who was that?"

"Colonel Whistler," the catcher said.

"My!"said the umpire. "I thought he was the major prophet from the Old Testament."

The other man at Fort Worden who cursed in championship style was a civilian teamster who worked for the quartermaster, a "mule skinner" named Strawberry McKenna. He was about thirty, with a contagious grin and a face sprinkled with freckles. He drove a team that hauled up supplies from the Seattle boat. McKenna enjoyed his own private cuss words, and maybe his mules did, too. When he sat on the box of his escort wagon, rattling the reins and roaring, the mules snapped into a fast trot.

Sometimes, when the wagon was empty, he would stand behind the seat as if he were driving a Roman chariot. I knew where to catch him, and he would stop and let me climb up over a front wheel to the seat. It was nice up there. You could see all around. When the mules broke into a trot you gripped the iron railing that bordered the seat and hung on for all you were worth. For excitement, riding with Strawberry McKenna even beat roller coasters.

When he sent his long blacksnake whip over the mules' backs, it unrolled with a crack like a pistol shot. If he snapped the whip three or four times, the mules would lay their ears back and gallop down the road, the wagon rattling as if it were coming apart, a funnel of dust behind. At times like this I used to pray that my friends would see me.

When Strawberry saw my mother he would shift the reins to one hand, wave his hat and yell. Once when I was with him he roared the two mules to a stop, snatched off his sombrero, and said, "Ma'am, how 'bout a ride?"

She thanked him, but preferred not to deliver kindling and coal with us.

McKenna had been a cowboy on a ranch. He disillusioned me by saying, "Punching cows did no damned good. I got sick quick of ropin' mired-down cattle. That's why I'm here."

He could outcuss anybody. He cursed poetically. Down at the corral, rounding up his mules, he would say, "Why you lily-livered, sweet-scented dandy! You hammer head, you! How come you so goddamned dirty? Come here, Pontius Pilate, you lop-eared bastard. *Back in there!*" And in a minute, "Dainty Marie, you lift a foot at me and I'll take a piss elm club and beat out your damned brains. I'm sick of nursing Rocky Mountain canaries that don't know right from wrong. You're the worst excuses for gov'ment jarheads this side of Seattle."

I was at the corral one day when Strawberry was harnessing his teams. Suddenly, as if she meant it, Dainty Marie stepped on his foot. The air seemed to change color. Strawberry hopped around on one foot, howling and grabbing his mashed toe. He climbed up and down Dainty Marie's ancestors. In a few minutes he yelled to Dainty Marie, from the top of the box, that he would get even later.

Every day when I came to the corral, I expected to see Dainty Marie hanging from a tree or stretched lifeless near the watering trough as a result of the awful tortures Strawberry said he would perform on that mule. He was by far the best cusser I ever heard, and that includes such masters as John J. McGraw, brimstone manager of the old New York Giants, old Sergeant Marty Maher of "The Long Gray Line" fame, and a West Point professor named Colonel Harvey Fraser.

One day the talk I had heard at the stables generated trouble. "Tip," my dog, trotted into the house wringing wet, tracking mud all over the kitchen. My mother jabbed at him with a broom. I helped by calling him a pet name of Strawberry's.

Mother switched from Tip to me. She shouted, "Russell!" and marched me by the ear to the laundry room in the basement. She grabbed a worn bar of yellow G.I. laundry soap, jammed it into my mouth and swished it around. The soap tasted thick, sour, and awful. I gagged. Then she felt sorry for me, got down on her knees and wiped my face, put her arms around me and kissed me.

She said, "I hated to do that, but you must *never* use that word again. It's a bad word. I put the soap in your mouth so you will always remember." She looked at the laundry soap and said it was the best kind for the job.

I felt confused and hurt. Late that afternoon a crisis occurred. Just before supper my mother came into my room and said, "Russell, Chaplain Easterbrook is downstairs in the parlor. He wants to see you."

This was the most startling news I had ever had. I was astounded and went downstairs wondering what could make the famous and adored Chaplain Easterbrook want to see *me*. He was Jesus' personal representative on the post, and later became Chief of Chaplains for the Army.

He was wearing his blue uniform and was seated on the sofa. A coal fire burned in the grate. Its red reflection danced on the silver crosses pinned to the high collar of his coat. The firelight heightened the ruddiness of his cheeks. His wavy hair, just turning gray, crowned a noble face.

"Sit down," he said. "How are you, Russell?"

"Fine." I sat gingerly on the edge of a buckskin chair.

"Russell, I hate to hear of little boys who swear. It's not a good thing. It's very, very bad indeed."

"Swear? You know some boy who swears?"

"Yes, I do. Don't you?"

"Maybe."

"Russell, do you know what happens to little boys who swear?"

"No, sir."

"Well, when they die, they go to a bad place. Down to the devil. He's a very hard man to get ahead of."

He let that sink in.

"Then," Chaplain Easterbrook continued, "the devil heats up a steel pitchfork until it is sizzling red hot. He sticks it into boys who swear and broils them over a slow fire. Then he dips them into a vat of boiling oil. Finally, he pitches them headlong into the fire itself."

"Why," I said, "that son-of-a-bitch!"

CHAPTER TWO

A Bad Ending to 1909

MOTHER WAS GIVING us four children a late breakfast. It was good to eat oatmeal because it neutralized the soap. My father had gone to work before the reveille gun, and we were having fun at the table. Manners by the board. Little Nat, propped in his high chair, was laughing and banging his table with a spoon. He had oatmeal all over his face. Out in the kitchen, cooking rice cakes, was our Japanese butler, Ube.

Ube dressed the part. In the mornings he worked about the house in faded blue denims that had been laundered until they were gray and threadbare, and in the evenings when he served dinner he wore a black silk coat that buttoned on the side and had a high collar that *was* a high collar, because it hid his throat and neck. He barely tolerated children. He was taller than most Japanese, prim as a New England deacon, efficient and cold. I did not like Ube.

Suddenly the doorbell rang and I tore to answer it, then leaped back. On the threshold stood three Siwash Indians, two men and a girl. The center Indian gripped a bow and some arrows. The two men were squat and powerful. Their braided black hair, knotted at the ends with telegraph wire, hung down over buckskin vests. The girl wore a knee-length buckskin skirt and trousers. The center Indian had a red-tipped feather in his hair that made him seem tall and important. I thought we were attacked, but I noted they lacked hatchets. The head Indian thrust the bow and three arrows at me and said, "Twenty-five cents."

I invited the Indians in and my mother invited them out. I begged her for twenty-five cents.

She said, "We don't have a penny in the house. You'll have to go see your father. He's up on the hill at the mortar battery."

I was afraid the Indians would leave. I explained to them as best I could that I had to run to the top of the mountain to get the money. "Please wait," I begged. "Be right back. I run fast."

The Indians sat down on the steps of the front porch. I flew across the parade ground and ran up hundreds of wooden steps that were built along the slopes of the big hill. I was afraid the opportunity would vanish. When I located my father, at a range-finding station, I was out of breath.

"Daddy! Indians!"

"What?"

"Three of 'em."

"Where?"

"At the house! Bows and arrows. I need—help."

He grabbed his cap and yelled upstairs. "Corporal! Come here, In a hurry!.

"Wait," I said. "Twenty-five cents."

He was so relieved to learn there was only purchasing trouble, he gave me thirty-five cents. *More arrows*. I thought. "Thank you very much."

I ran back. The Indians I was certain would be gone, but they were in the same spots on the front porch. I spent the rest of the day shooting arrows at pirates who were threatening our home.

Near evening I went down to the quartermaster corral to find Strawberry McKenna. Most of the teamsters were hosing down their wagons or saddle-soaping harness, in preparation for tomorrow's Saturday inspection. The activity in the stables was entrancing. Two soldiers, just back from a hunting trip, were nailing a deer hide to a stable door. The hairy hide felt soft and warm. A teamster was throwing a "wedding ring" with a lariat, making a wide, horizontal loop with his rope while he stood in the center, the ring floating around him. Strawberry McKenna and a man named Fleagle were perched on top of the corral fence. I climbed up beside them.

Strawberry barely grunted. He and Fleagle had been talking. "All right," Strawberry said to him, "let's have at it."

In a minute the two teamsters stood about thirty feet apart, glaring at each other, long blacksnake whips at the ready.

"I'm going to cut you into pieces," Strawberry said.

"You couldn't whip a kitten," Fleagle said. "If you were gagged and couldn't spray tongue oil at your knobheads and had to depend on your whip, there wouldn't be a scuttle of coal delivered on this post. You're about to get the whippin' of your life."

I hated to see Strawberry hurt. Fleagle was taller and had powerful arms. He must have outweighed Strawberry by twenty-five pounds. The two men had their blue-denim trousers thrust into canvas leggings that laced on the side.

A crowd gathered but stayed well back.

"Your first cut," Fleagle said. "I whomped you so bad last time you can lead out."

Strawberry flicked his long whip to the rear and stood poised. Suddenly his whip lashed at Fleagle's ankles. Fleagle jumped into the air as the whip popped up a burst of dust where he had been standing.

Fleagle sent his whip at Strawberry. Strawberry's jump into the air saved him.

Both men laughed. This was the first I knew it was a game.

In a minute Strawberry's whip bit Fleagle's shoe. Fleagle dropped his whip and hopped around on one foot. He grabbed his hurt foot. "Goddam, that stung!" he said. Then his face tightened. He picked up his blacksnake and squinted at Strawberry.

"Whoa, boy. No more tonight," Strawberry said. "You'll have to wait a week. Me and Red Reeder's going to chew the cud."

He sat with me on the corral fence. Below us some fifty fine-looking mules milled about the muddy corral. It was near their feeding time. Over in the far corral a light rider was breaking in a rat-tailed horse. The animal sunfished and jackknifed but the rider stayed in the saddle, swaying with each violent buck.

"Renton's a pretty good rider," Strawberry said."Out of A Battery. He got six months in the guardhouse for kicking a mule while his bunkie, Wagon Wheel Williams, got three months for sassing Cap'n Norton. Shows they think more of the mule than they do of the cap'n."

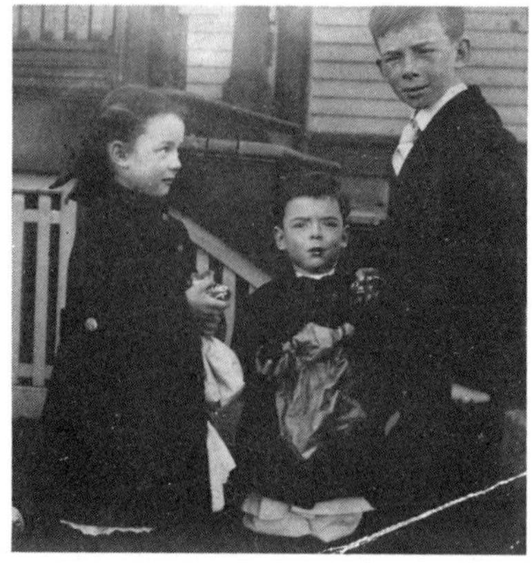

RR with brother Fred and sister Julia at Ft. McKinley, ME., 1914

An arrow of ducks flew over the stables, soared above the dark pines, and headed toward the Strait of Juan de Fuca. The late afternoon sun highlighted the peaks of the Cascade Range a hundred miles away. Fort Worden was a beautiful place and its air, tinged with salt, made your lungs feel good.

Strawberry sprinkled Bull Durham tobacco on brown cigarette paper, tugged the string of the tobacco sack shut with his teeth and a jerk of his head, rolled the cigarette, and struck a match with a flourish on the sole of his shoe. I told him about Chaplain Easterbrook, the devil, and the laundry soap. Strawberry puffed on the cigarette.

Fleagle climbed up and perched on the high fence with us. He passed a bottle over my head and said, "Berry, a little red disturbance?"

I do not know why he called it that. The fluid was milky white.

"Not on your tintype," Strawberry said. "I had several heists last Sat'dy night and my boiler's just recovering." Strawberry turned to me. "Now, Red about your ma. She's trying to civilize you. She's the grandest lady on this post—her and Mrs. Whistler combined. Not upstage, and genuwine thoroughbred. Your ma helps ever'body. She always has time for a pleasant word and a smile, no matter what you are, and she keeps her dignity. You got to learn that there's times when you swear and times when you don't. Take my gov'ment jarheads. I couldn't start 'em without a good cuss all around. But when I'm over at the canteen around those pretty fillies that work there, I mind my manners and speak perfect English by the book. You have to learn when you can swear."

When I got home Gladys Easterbrook was there, taking care of Fred and Nat while my mother shopped at the commissary. Gladys was taller and slightly older than I and beautiful. She wore hair ribbons on her braids that matched her eyes. I was in love with her, but this is the first time I have ever said so.

Several hours after my mother returned, the commissary wagon delivered the groceries she had selected, and Ube put them away. There was no fun being around Ube because he hated a boy like a snake. He never smiled except when my father spoke to him. He was the first yes-man I ever saw.

Mother let me pack a suitcase and visit a friend named Lawrence Barroll. He lived quite a distance—about two hundred yards.

When I got back to the house the next morning, my father met me at the head of the stairs near his bedroom. He had a strange look on his face. I thought he had discovered that I had been hanging around the corral. I knew he did not care for McKenna.

But that was not the reason for my father's more than unusual solemnity. "Russell," he said, "your brother Nat died this morning."

I was stunned. "Dead?" I said. I did not even know he was sick.

My father looked older. "Stomach trouble," he said. "Probably."

This became one of the worst weeks of my life, and certainly the loneliest. They treated death differently in 1909. Julia and Fred were bustled out of the house to a neighbor's. I stayed.

The next morning they placed little Nat in a white casket that had white gingerbread work about its top. He looked like wax. His golden-blond hair was combed more carefully than it ever had been in life. I was frightened. When Mother put an arm across my shoulder and led me to the casket, she cried. "Kiss him good-by!" I was petrified, I could not touch him. My mother's consuming grief and the look of Nat lying in the white casket filled me with a horror of the dead that took long years to overcome, and even now I am not hankering to see any dead people.

At his funeral in the tiny cemetery cut out of the Douglas firs, we obeyed the custom of the times by standing on the brink of the grave while the casket was lowered. Dirt rattled on it like a lonely wind in the shutters. I became afraid that my mother would not survive. This was the lowest point of my entire life.

Afterwards Mrs. Whistler took me to their home, and her bubbling nature rescued me from shock. If you stayed at the Whistlers' you had to pay attention to them. She showed me my room and removed a three-masted glass boat from a shelf and gave it to me. Then she asked me to feed their two Mexican hairless Chihuahuas. While I was doing this she told me how she had taken one of them to Seattle and how she had climbed aboard a streetcar with the dog in her arms.

The conductor said, "No dogs allowed, madam."

"Dogs?" she asked. "I see no dogs." She held up the puppy. "That's the second time today it's been taken for a dog, and if it happens once more I shall never take it out again." This was too much for the conductor, and when she took a seat he allowed her and her dog to remain.

She talked with a rich Charleston accent. The soldiers who worked at the canteen liked to tell how she ordered a case of "bee-ah."

"Now, Russell," she said, " you think you have your problems. Everyone does. For me, I have to live with a genius. You know, Colonel Whistler invented the Whistler plotting board, a new way to fire big guns. He's absolutely crammed with math. A very kind man, but he thinks I am part of his command. When we moved here from Fort Caswell, North Carolina, I had to do all the work. He just marched downstairs wearing his blues and his saber and said, 'Madame, *you* will pay, pack, and follow.' When we were on our honeymoon forty years ago, he handed me a piece of paper and announced, 'Here are the rules and regulations by which you, as my wife, will abide.' "

My aunt, Mrs. Forrest E. Williford, later gave me a set of "Colonel Whistler's Rules for Wife Behavior." Here they are:

1. You will see that meals are served on time.
2. You will not come to the table in a wrapper.
3. You will smile at breakfast.
4. If possible, you will serve meat at least four times a week.
5. You will not move the furniture without my permission.
6. You will present the household accounts to me by the fifth of the month.
7. You will examine my uniforms each Tuesday and if they need repair you will take the necessary action.
8. You will do no work in the evenings. You will entertain me.
9. You will not touch my desk.

10. You will remember you are not in command of anything except the cook.

Rule Number 8 would have challenged the comedian, W. C. Fields. Once Colonel Whistler came home and found Mrs. Whistler sewing, and she kept on sewing in violation of the rule. The fashion in women's neck-ribbons called for raveled ends that formed a fringe.

"Umph!" Colonel Whistler said. "You know the rules. Please put that down and pay attention to me. I want to be entertained, madam!"

Mrs. Whistler cocked her head at her sewing and glared at it through her steel-rimmed spectacles—and worked on.

"Nellie!" Colonel Whistler blared. "What *are* you doing?"

"Frazzling, Garl, frazzling."

Colonel Whistler drew himself up as if he were on parade. "Very well," he said. "I shall go to the club, and I will remain there until you are finished."

Mrs. Whistler pointed to the door. "Depart! But when you return I will still be frazzling."

When Colonel Whistler came home from work, Mrs.Whistler stopped talking to me. He shook hands, and we talked about how Jumbo Henry could wallop curve-ball pitching. The colonel told about what made a curve ball curve, and drew several diagrams. It seemed strange and I took little stock in it. Then he said. "I'll make some music."

He unbuttoned his high shoes and slipped them off and sat down at an old player piano. He inserted a roll of music,pumped away, and the music tinkled out. It sounded like water flowing over a dam and splashing on rocks.

"I can get better expression," he said. "with my shoes off."

A fine-looking Negro butler in a white coat popped in, bowed, and said, "Sir and Madam, dinner is ready." This was Isaac, a happy man with a mile-wide grin and a beautiful set of teeth. I liked being around Isaac far more than I did Ube, for Isaac had time to laugh.

After a week at the Whistlers' I went home and found excitement. Ube was gone. My father had been told by a Secret Service agent that Ube should leave.

We had a most unusual Christmas present—a photograph of Ube wearing the full-dress uniform of a lieutenant in the Imperial Japanese Navy. The package was postmarked Tokyo and autographed, "To Captain R.P. Reeder and fine family*from friend Ube*."

My father explained to me what a spy was, and for a while I looked upon every stranger with suspicion, even the kindly Siwash Indians.

It was terrible that we could have had a man in our home for almost six months who had been trying to harm the United States.

"This made a bad ending to the year," Mother said.

But the next year had a great beginning. "In the spring," my father announced, "you're going to visit your grandparents. You're going to Memphis, Tennessee."

CHAPTER THREE

Gideon Fred Martin of Tennessee

THIS WAS THE GREATEST trip I ever made. We ate fried chicken all the way to Chicago. As soon as we emptied one white shoe box, my mother produced another. We did run out of deviled eggs near Butte, Montana. It was my job to go to the diner for milk, and on the third day I suggested that we go there and eat. "No," Mother said, "wait until there's no more chicken."

After we left Chicago on the Central Illinois Railroad, she gave the porter the last of the chicken and we marched into the diner. It was wonderful in there. You ate on stiff white tablecloths and watched the scenery slide by. The train would whistle long and low for a crossing, and you thundered over it while a bell clanged outside. Then the train would stop at a small town and you ate slowly so the people outside could see and envy you. I had not been raised in society, but when the waiter brought finger bowls, I noticed a man across the aisle dip his fingers into one. Fred wasn't so observant or didn't care; he drank his and asked for more.

Once a day Mother purchased ham sandwiches from a "butcher," a boy who walked up and down the aisles carrying a long basket by a strap slung about his neck and filled with things to eat. The job of "butch" seemed great to me. You rode on trains with food chained to you.

When the train rattled into Tennessee, the weather turned hot. The porter forced open the window, and cinders and a warm breeze poured in. My job was to keep Fred from tumbling out of the window, and it wasn't easy. Whizzing along at thirty-five miles an hour in our wooden Pullman was miraculous. We listened to the roar and clank of the wheels on the rails: "Gotyour trunk! Gotyour trunk! Gotyour trunk!" Then they rattled over a crossing. "Going to Memphis. You can't catch me!"

I began to watch for the big Bull Durham signs in the fields and along the right of way that pictured a huge red bull against a white background, his head erect, with part of it and his horns above the top of the board. Crowning the billboard was a sign: 110 MILES TO MEMPHIS. Farther down the track we would find another sign imploring you to smoke Bull Durham and its message: 95 MILES TO MEMPHIS. Mother read them to me, and these signs filled me with desire to read better.

"Memphis, next stop!"

There was some excitement, We had been on the train six days. Mother moistened a handkerchief and tried to remove a smudge of soot from Fred's Buster Brown collar. "I want you to look handsome for your grandfather," she said. She combed my hair and adjusted Julia's hair ribbon so that it fanned out like the wings of a huge butterfly.

In the Memphis railroad station we looked for Grandfather Martin while the huge engine puffed and labored, sending up clouds of black smoke and hissing white steam. A medium-sized man ran up, threw his arms around my mother, and cried, "Lordy! Lordy! Have you really come?" This man had a neat white mustache, blue eyes and white hair. A horseshoe stickpin ornamented the center of his tie. He picked up Fred and tossed him into the air. "I'm your grandfather. So this is little Fred Martin?" He left off the "Reeder." " Say 'Grandfather,' " the man said.

Fred, who didn't like to talk, managed, "Bocker,"

Fred Martin bellowed. "*Bocker!* That's my new nickname!"

My grandfather soon had me entranced. He was pacing his snug office in the Eureka Livery Stable, Memphis, Tennessee, after giving me a tour of the place and an illustrated lecture on the sex life of horses.

"How old are you?"

"Eight and a half."

"That half's very important. At my age it ain't. Now 'member all I told you. I don't want any of my helpers taking for the kitchen when it comes to business. And don't let on about what I've learned you when you get home. It belongs here in the stable."

I felt important. In on the know. Up until this time I thought they all were just horses or mules.

"I'm steppin' down the street to get *The Commercial Appeal,*" he said to me. "You answer the phone."

It was 1910. William H. Taft was President. Maine, Kansas, North Dakota, Georgia, Oklahoma, Mississippi, North Carolina, and Tennessee had adopted prohibition. Charlie Chaplin was performing in vaudeville. The Camp Fire Girls were being organized, and the telephone was just beginning to make a nuisance of itself.

A red sun was outlining the buildings across the street. It was the best time of day. Grandfather Martin tiptoed into my bedroom before five and whispered, "You awake, Russell? In the kitchen I got fried ham and eggs for you and a slice of watermelon."

While we walked briskly the half-mile to the stable, if I tried to talk, he shut me off, "Too early for conversation."

Through the office of the Eureka you could see and hear the hustle and bustle as his crew of twenty blacks worked to harness horses and mules and to get out saddle horses and delivery wagons. Shortly carriages and surreys clattered after them into the July morning.

The Eureka Livery Stable was a marvelous place. It was whitewashed on the outside and occupied almost an entire block at 343 Madison Avenue. It contained a maze of box stalls, with a blacksmith shop, a corral, and a wagon park tucked around the sides and back. It was important to the life of Memphis.

I had only been visiting Bocker a couple of weeks, but I realized that he was one of the best-known men in town. I loved him. He was *my* grandfather.

Cousin Rufus Polk, the stable manager, stepped into the office. He grabbed the crank of the wall phone and turned it angrily. With him came the smell of the stable and the noise of the confusion.

He shouted a number into the mouth piece. Then, "Line busy? Dang it, operator. This is important! Please give me a ring when I can talk to Mrs. Crump."

Cousin Rufus had a red face covered with stubble, fingernails that looked as if he had been laying sod, and a kindly disposition that was strained by playing second fiddle to Bocker.

"Russell, where's your grandfather?"

I told him.

"He's the irritatin'est man in Memphis. Never here when I need him. I'd rather depend on a raccoon. There's as many sides to him as there is to a politician."

I disliked the stable manager. He owed his livelihood to Bocker but never skipped an opportunity to run him down.

He rattled on. "Your grandfather is an unreconstructed Confederate. He never draws a natch'l breath. If he had taken the stage, George M. Cohan would never have been heard of. Genteel, most of the time. Can hypnotize a hog. He walks around like he had a noseful of nickels. Thinks he's on a level with Boss Crump, only he ain't. Gambling was born in him, but he looks on money he wins as sort of a receipt, a proof that he can gain a victory.

"Your grandmother, a perfect lady, has her trials with him. Just imagine how she felt last year when out of a clear sky he comes home and blurts,' Help me pack. I'm leaving in four hours on the six o'clock for Chicago.' He'd been bragging to some of his poker-playing pals how easy he can make money. First thing you know he bet he could land in Chicago broke and make a hundred dollars in a month. What a shock to *me* and your grandmother."

"Did he make it?" I was breathless.

"His pals took him to the railroad station. Searched him to make sure he had no money. The sports even took away his diamond stickpin and his valuable gold cufflinks."

"Why?"

"So he couldn't pawn 'em. They gave him twenty-five cents for a sandwich and a cup of coffee and a one-way ticket. They had a high old time at the railroad station. But back home, me and your grandmother was worried sick. I had ast him for orders –'What about the stable?' 'Use your own judgement,' he said."

The stable manager refreshed himself by pouring a cup of chalky-looking coffee from a glass milk bottle. "When he got to Chicago, he hurried around to Swift and Company. Identified himself as former president of the Arkansas Packing Company and showed 'em he knew how to butcher. He was a farm boy. Back here–not even a postal or a telegram.

"He came home in two weeks with the hundred dollars, a new suit of clothes, an alligator grip, and a theater ticket stub to prove he'd been in Chicago. He had lived on a shoestring and played poker with his wages. The worst of it was his bragging. Man! I listened to the damned details five hundred times."

My respect for Bocker skyrocketed. When he pranced into the office and perched on the safe, I looked at him with new admiration. He handed me a box of Zu Zus and stuck his nose into the newspaper.

He was small, immaculate in a Palm Beach suit. The sun had dotted his face red, but a trim white moustache made him look distinguished. He resembled Mark Twain, only flashier. A diamond-studded gold horseshoe stick pin bolstered a blue tie matching his eyes. Tiny ruby eyes in his Medusa-headed gold cufflinks sparkled as he editorialized on the news to me, and to an unseen audience of at least fifty. Suddenly he put down the paper and changed the subject.

He clicked his heels against the safe to emphasize certain words, phrases, and sentences. "I tell you I'm sick and tired of *leadership.* The everlasting details coming at me week-on-week give me the wobbles. *You're the best stable manager in Memphis!* Dedicated. Meet people well. But I got to remind you—*nothing operates by itself.* Oh, I know I gave you off to go to the Masonic picnic yestiddy, but you got to compose yourself. I come down here after church, and what do I find?"

Bocker squirted a stream of tobacco juice at the potbellied stove, the juice forming a pattern like the outline of a devilfish. He hopped off the safe and glared.

"I got some of the best stock here in Shelby County. The race horse would be *im*-possible to replace. I arrive here at 'leven-thirty. Of the four hands supposed to be on duty, there were just two, and one of 'em was suffering from too much Beale Street Saturday night."

Bocker bent his knees and staggered around the office, slopping imaginary water out of two imaginary buckets.

"I had to help water and feed," he said.

The phone tinkled. Bocker dropped the water buckets. "Hello," he shouted. "Get the hell off the line! This is the Eureka Livery Stable speaking! Oh, hello, Bessie, I hear you perfect, you wonderful woman. Your voice is carrying the sun right into this office."

Rufus said softly into Bocker's open ear, "Tell her her man drove out of here with the surrey fifteen minutes ago. I've been trying to get her on the phone to warn her and the Boss their hosses need exercise."

Bocker delivered the message and listened. "They did? Well, I'll take care of this end. Lallie and I'll see you and Ed Saturday night. I can't wait. Goodbye, dear."

Bocker turned on me. "Mrs. Crump says you and Eddie have been throwing stones at the peacocks. Stop that. And I want to inform you, you bring home another damned peacock feather, I'll give you all the hickory limb oil you can stand. Worst thing you can do in the world. Peacock feathers bring bad luck." In a second, "How many of 'em did you hit?"

Bocker whistled a few bars of W.C. Handy's "Mister Crump" and said to the stable manager. "You should have tooken that call. I want you to run this place."

A man stepped in, one coat sleeve tucked into a pocket. He said through his nose, "My horse ready?"

Bocker ignored him. He hopped back on the safe and opened *The Commercial Appeal*.

"They're saddling him now."

When the man left the office, I asked, "Who's that?"

Bocker closed the door. He glowered at me and snapped. "A damned Yankee soldier. Lost his arm at Shiloh. You can bet I'd never keep his hoss here a minute 'cept they put pressure on me. I can't stand Yankees."

"Why?"

"Because of the way they treated the South. The Constitution said nothing about a state withdrawing. In the years before the war, the power-hungry Yankee politicians violated every rule for their own ends. The New England hypocrites called us 'Southern slave hounds.' Heck, slavery was on the way out. From about 1820 on the North oppressed the hell out of us. They must have thought us people without pride."

I was confused. Before we left Fort Worden, Puget Sound, Washington, to visit in Memphis, my Grandmother Reeder, from Cincinnati, had come to see us. My father was a U.S. Army captain at the post. At a retreat parade, just after the guard detail lowered the flag against the breathtaking backdrop of Mortar Battery Hill, grandmother had pointed at the reviewing officer, Colonel Garl

Whistler, United States Army, and exclaimed, "Colonel Whistler stands out there so. He reminds me of General U.S. Grant, one of the saviors of our nation."

When the blue ranks swept by in review, Grandmother Reeder said, "Russell, I wish you could have known your ancestor, Nathaniel Reeder. He served as a lieutenant in our navy, and when the Civil War burst on us he left retired life at sixty-one-years of age and got a commisssion in the Ohio Infantry. Think of it. At sixty-one it's rough carrying a pack and sleeping on the ground in the rain. It is men like Nat and other loyal Yankees who kept our Union together.

"And your cousin Will Thomas! He fought in a Massachusetts infantry regiment at First Bull Run. When they got jumped by Confederates at the Stone Bridge, Will *says* he ran all the way to Washington, through the city, and halfway to Baltimore." Grandmother Reeder laughed to show me it was a joke. A Reeder wouldn't run.

"You want to keep in the front of your mind always the sacrifices made by our boys in blue. That's why we have a United States."

In Memphis it was different.

When the one-armed Yankee came back to pay his bill and departed, Bocker dropped the money in the cash drawer and took out a plug of tobacco. He bit off a chew and said, "I'm glad that bastard's gone. I don't like to do business with any Yankee son-of-a-bitch."

Bocker's blue eyes flashed. The more he talked the more excited he became. He talked of the past as if it were yesterday.

"Where was the next meal coming from? We ten children didn't know. Six of my brothers fighting in the ranks for what they believed. George was closest to me, and he was batt'ry commander for Nathan Bedford Forrest." Bocker shook his head mournfully. "George never came back. You know who General Nathan Bedford Forrest was?"

"No, sir."

"What the hell they teach you in school? He was the world's greatest cavalryman, Could *he* kill Yankees! He should have got a better chance.

"When our boys came reelin' back after the Battle of Nashville, my brother Joseph, he was one of Forrest's scouts, was in our house, Mercer Hall over at Columbia, gettin' something to eat when the

Yankees ransacked it. Your great grandmother saved his life by hiding him in the capitals of one of the big columns on the porch, up in the top of the column. Did your mother tell you about Mercer Hall?

"It was beautiful. On a hill. Pastures all around. I thought it was heaven until one day–I was twelve–Mother said, 'Fred, I can't feed you anymore, You have to go.' Can you imagine her feelings? And mine? Hardest day of my life.

"So I could live, I got a job in the Yankee camp, cleanin' boots and saddles and polishing pots and pans. I hated 'em. My brother Branch. He was a boy, too. We tried to make some money. Picked blackberries, and Mother made us some pies. Took 'em down to the railroad station where the troop trains was rumblin' through. When a train stopped, we held the trays of pies up to the windows–for a sale. Yankee soldiers reached down and took everything. We never got a red cent."

The way Bocker told it you could shut your eyes and hear the Yankees laugh as the train chugged out of the station.

"They grabbed most of Tennessee. You ever hear of Sam Davis? Personal friend of mine. We were boys together in Pulaski. I judge he was five years older."

"No, sir."

Bocker addressed the wall. "Think of it! He never heard of Sam Davis.

"He was a young soldier in the First Tennessee Infantry, on scouting duty behind the Yankee lines, in uniform. He wore a dirty gray military jacket and a Yankee overcoat with brass buttons that had been captured. He dyed the coat from blue to brown. The blue bellies picked him up in Giles County. They found in his saddle a map and information about Yankee forts around Nashville. They charged Sam Davis with being a spy. He was no more spy than you are. He was a soldier doing his duty."

Bocker sent a stream of tobacco juice at the cuspidor near the safe and missed. "They hauled Sam Davis up before General Grenville Dodge. Never forget that name. *General Grenville Dodge!*"

Bocker became Sam Davis, his hands bound behind him by a phantom rope. He fixed his eyes on the shotgun in a rack over the door. "General, sir, I cannot tell you who gave me the information."

Bocker stepped across the office into General Dodge's place and put a whine in his voice. "Sam, you *got* to tell me. If you don't, I'll have to have you executed."

Bocker switched places again. "Sir, I'll never tell on a comrade. If I have to die, I'll be doing my duty to God and my Country."

I could hardly breathe. The old man looked at me hard. Then he continued.

"They got the drums and formed a *pro*-cession, Sam sittin' in a wagon on his coffin. They stopped in that little grove near the town square. Captain Chickasaw came galloping up. 'Hold everything,', he shouted. 'Sam! The general's giving you one more chance. Who gave you the information?"

"I'm not a traitor,' Sam said. And they hung him."

It was hard to breathe. I could see Sam Davis on the scaffold.

"General Dodge was bad enough, still he couldn't hold a candle to Grant and Sherman. You heard of them?"

"I know about General Grant," I said weakly. I hoped that I wouldn't have to relay Grandmother Reeder's information.

"That butcher was bad enough, but Sherman!"

"What did he do?"

"He set fire to the states of Georgia and South Carolina."

I turned Confederate. Besides it made it easier around the stable and the house.

But a few days later Cousin Rufus cracked a joke. His jokes ground you down. They made *him* happy. "Russell, after your mother and father were married in Little Rock, there was a great send off. A big to-do. They rode to the railroad station in a surrey. I *personally* decorated it."

Rufus crinkled his red face and smiled at the memory. "When they drove off, your grandfather said to me, 'We Martins suffered during and after the war. I saw enough of the blue bellies to last me forever. Now here is my own daughter Narcissa married to one—a goddamned Yankee!' "

I slid out of the Confederacy. I loved Bocker, but I loved my father more. I was becoming unstable. When I had a chance, in the little office, I asked Cousin Rufus about the Yankees versus the Confederates, and all I got was a lecture on how General Lee resembled Jesus. Rufus was well on the way to the causes of the war when Bocker burst into the office with another man. "Rufus," Bocker interrupted. "Get me Dave Jackson."

When the huskiest of his stable hands walked into the office, Bocker said, "Dave, I bet this gentleman you could lift a side of beef in your mouth. How do you feel?"

"Poorly, thank God." Dave Jackson flashed a mouthful of beautiful teeth and laughed.

Dave's tattered clothing let you see his strength. Biceps as large as footballs and powerful legs. He had the neck of a champion wrestler.

Two men struggled into the office carrying something under a bloody canvas. They unveiled a side of beef. Bocker handed each a quarter. "Thank you, boys."

"I want a referee," the stranger said.

"How about Rufus Polk here?" Bocker said

"No siree Bob! No offense to you, Mr. Polk. You may be as honest as the day is long, but I want a neutral official."

Bocker intercepted a man from the sidewalk. He wore twotone, high button shoes, a celluloid collar fastened with a gold collar button, and a serene expression.

Dave Jackson carved at the beef until a sinew stood out. Something told me he had done this before. He got down on his all fours. Bocker gave the referee a ruler to hold against the meat. "Now," the referee said, "I'll clap him on the back if the beef rises four inches.

Dave placed his mouth over the sinew. The office was mouse-quiet. We all lay down on the floor. The telephone tinkled. "Take that damned thing off the hook," Bocker snapped.

"Go!" shouted the official.

The veins in Dave's neck and face looked as if they might burst.

His palms and fingers turned the color of cocoa. The beef swayed. Dave's nostrils widened. He gasped like a steam engine pulling up a grade.

"You're doing fine," Bocker shouted. "Come on, Dave!"

Sweat popped out on Jackson's forehead. His eyes were closed, but they bulged. The side of beef rose higher, It swung against his forearms. The referee said, "Two and one-half inches," and then in a minute he slapped Dave on the back and yelled, "Four inches."

Dave Jackson collapsed on the meat.

The stranger swore, handed Bocker a roll of bills, and stomped out of the office. Bocker peeled off five dollars for Dave, and said, "Great work, great work, Dave. Take the rest of the day off."

The phone rang and Bocker answered it. "Well, we've been busy, I'll be glad to, glad to, Honey." When he hung up, he reached for the shotgun above the office door and turned to me.

"Your grandmother wants six squab. Run back there among the stalls and don't get kicked. I'll knock 'em down to you."

He fired. Feathers flew from a small pigeon under the roof. The bird tumbled in that awful winds-askew way it does when it is shot from a height. The rest of the flock, of about ninety, flew around the stable in a wild cloud. Five more shots, and we had our dinner.

"Bocker," I said, "won't the shot that hit the roof make a hole?"

He looked at the roof as if he'd never seen it before.

" Oh, I might knock off a shingle or two, but what's a little water on the back of my animals?"

He relayed my remark to Cousin Rufus, and they both laughed as if I had gotten off something witty. When Bocker laughed, Rufus bellowed.

One evening at dusk, back of Bocker's home on Court Street, I was taking my turn riding a pony he had given my sister Julia. A gas light, hitched high on a pole, gave the alley an eerie look. A light-blue evening pierced by yellow rays of light. When I had my last ride, I went inside and found Bocker, then walked down into the parlor.

"Is your grandfather out with the pony?" Grandmother asked.

"No. He's lying up on the roof of the front porch with a shotgun."

Lallie tore upstairs, me on her heels. She threw open a window. "Fred Martin, what on earth are you doing?"

Bocker turned his head. He was lying on his stomach, peering into the gloom. "Hush, Don't spoil everything."He aimed the gun at a figure across the street. "No. That's old man Thompson. Don't want to wing him. I'm out here doing the neighborhood a good turn. I get me one sneak thief, and they'll all leave."

"Come in this house. It's better to have thievery than blood on your hands. Last time you killed a man you were in serious trouble."

"What was that?" I asked.

" Reconstruction," Bocker said. "It wasn't trouble. It was self-defense. Now, I got a special load of rock salt in this gun. Wouldn't kill a mockin' bird. It'd just sting him bad."

Bocker stayed on watch for four evenings with his shotgun. We ate supper on the edge of our chairs expecting to hear an explosion, but it never came. On the fifth day, he ate with us.

"They may have spotted me and moved to another part of town," he said.

One morning, at the Eureka, a black rushed into the office, eyes wide with excitement. "Mr. Martin," he shouted, "Mr. Ben Peters gave it to Dave Jackson in the laig."

We hurried up a stable aisle to the back reaches. The light was dim but you could see a sign daubed in red on the whitewashed planks of a stall:

MR. BEN PETERS DANGER

The huge black man was lying in the dirt, hugging his leg and crying, "Mr. Martin," he moaned, "this is the wildcattest nag in Memphis! I was cleanin' in there, and he cracked me. My laig's broke." He unleashed a string of the most magnificent curses I had ever heard.

I peeked through the cracks at the wild animal. A magnificent stallion, sorrel coat and wide eyes full of distrust. He saw me and banged his hoofs against the boards. I moved back.

"Rufus," Bocker said, "Get Dave to the hospital and send me the bill. Spread the news for people to be careful entering this stall. Ben Peters is a war horse."

After Dave Jackson was driven off in a buggy, I found Bocker in the office talking to a group of men. He was almost riding Mr. Ben Peters. "Gen'men, I give you my word this hoss cost me a fortune. I really don't know much about him yet. Up on the farm they said under a mile he's the fastest hoss in the world." Bocker loved superlatives.

A man said, "Mr. Martin, can you give us an idea as to his times?"

"Well, I was at his early mornin' workout yesterday and clocked him in the mile and a quarter, but that ain't his race. The time was two minutes and eight seconds."

"Great scott!" a man said. "That's faster than Wintergreen won the Derby."

"Did I say eight seconds? I meant eighteen. Now he's pretty good in the sprints, providing he gets a good start. He has to get off the post. I'd give my soul to see him in the short furlongs on a cardboard track."

There was a buzz of talk about a Mr. Swartz and his horse "Volcano."

Bocker switched the talk to fishing. He described a trip we made on a steamboat to his secret lake in Arkansas *down* the Mississippi. Actually, it was *upstream,* inland from a town named Tomato. We stayed a week, sitting in a rowboat on a swampy pond while he hauled in largemouth black bass. I caught the bottom and became restless. I had enjoyed listening to him extol Confederate generals whose pictures decorated a faded lithograph tacked to the kitchen door of his shack and eating hoecake, anointed with molasses, that he cooked in the ashes. He told the listeners that I would be the best fisherman in the world if I would just stay at it.

When Bocker and his friends left the office, I asked Cousin Rufus, "Is Mr. Ben Peters a great race horse?"

"You aren't the only one in town who'd like to know. What your grandfather's doing is stirring up interest. I'll tell you a secret. He's out to trap a rattlesnake named Andy Z.Z. Swartz. He owns Volcano. Swartz played it low down on your grandfather last summer in a hoss trade, and he's skinned others. If Bocker can snare this lousy Swartz it would be better for him than champagne watermelon on a hot day."

"How's he going to trap him?"

Rufus shook his finger at me and said in his odd drawl, the only one I ever heard that squeaked, "The underground secret is that Ben Peters is red hot **in the mile and a quarter**, and that's how Bocker wants to race him. The rumor is that Volcano is best in the mile and a sixteenth. You let this out, and you'd better head for Seattle, or wherever the hell you came from."

The secret ate into me at night. I was afraid that I'd spill it. I wished I had never heard of it.

On the day of the race, Bocker drove me to the track in a buckboard. He was strangely quiet although he had reluctantly agreed to race his horse in the mile and a quarter.

His brother, Branch, who looked like a distinguished Confederate officer, trotted alongside on a bay saddle horse. We found about twenty other horses and rigs tied to a hitching rail near the huge grandstand at the old fairgrounds.

Mr. Swartz, a greasy-looking, square-built man wearing a derby came up. He removed it and said, "Good morning, Mr. Martin. Great day for a race."

Bocker introduced me and made Swartz acknowledge that I was on earth before he'd talk about horses.

Swartz stepped to the head of our horse and forced its mouth open. He said, "Mr. Martin, I also bet my horse and buggy on this race against your horse and buggy."

"Where's your rig?"

"At the end of the hitching line."

Bocker stood and gave it a careless glance. " Agreed. Let Russell be the witness. Now let's get the race going."

I was frightened. I asked myself, "How in the world will we get back to Memphis if we lose?"

I told Cousin Rufus about the extra bet. "Typical," he said.

"What's a witness have to do?" I asked.

"Just shut up."

About fifty men climbed the fence in the infield near the finish line. Bocker and I pulled ourselves up on a higher fence on the uphill side of the finish. A judge on a fat horse bellowed through a megaphone, "Clear the track."

Swartz's horse bore a jockey wearing purple and white. I had never seen the little man with an orange stocking cap and work clothes who sat on Mr. Ben Peters. Our stallion pranced sideways. I thought, "It's five miles back to Memphis."

Suddenly there was a shout. The two horses broke for the bend in the track. Volcano tore away from Ben Peters. I had tears in my eyes from the excitement. But on the far side I saw the orange stocking cap overhaul the blur of purple. They pounded into the stretch. A cavalcade of about twenty howling horsemen now swept down from the high side of the track and galloped behind the race horses. When the two principals passed us, Ben Peters was about four yards ahead of Volcano. Bocker almost fell off the fence laughing.

Swartz trudged up. He looked inches shorter. "Congratulations, Mr. Martin. Will you please give me a ride back to Memphis?"

Bocker's eyes became slits. "No. Walk, you damned son-of-a-bitch!"

I was thunderstruck. The joy of winning vanished. How could Bocker talk like that to a man he had beaten?

By the time we drove into the Eureka, the telephone had given the news to his stable crew. They greeted us with wild yells. We were conquering heroes. Bocker stook up and held up his hand. "Sunday schedule and double pay for everybody today!" Inside the office, he put his arm around my shoulders. "You love me, don't you?" he said.

"I sure do."

"You're gettin' a new suit of clothes. Now don't think I was rough on that hound Swartz. He's a hoss thief who cheats widows and ever-body. He beat me in a trade by telling a dozen lies. Learn this. Never trust a scalawag."

Later, Bocker came to visit us at Fort McKinley, part of the coast defenses of Casco Bay, a few miles off Portland, Maine. He made friends easily, and in a week he knew almost everyone in that beautiful army kingdom. Sergeant Snook, in my father's Coast Artillery company, was his particular pal. Both loved to fish.

I was subpoenaed to go after flounders with them—at four on a September morning. The tide would be "right" then. Long before dawn Bocker tiptoed into my room and whispered, like days in Memphis, "Come on down. I got bacon and eggs."

I was dressing in a trance, and he stayed to superintend. I staggered around after my clothes and tossed my hat on the bed.

Bocker grabbed the hat and hissed, "Never do that! Worst thing in the world. Bad luck. I'll be surprised if we catch a single fish."

We met Sergeant Snook and walked a pine needle path to the Old Mine Dock. They rowed a yawl across the race, and we tied up to the ancient, decrepit Cow Island dock.

The air was nippy. The sun rose out of the blue water, way out there. The wind ruffled the race and kicked up white caps. The waves slapped, slapped, slapped against the yawl. Nothing else happened. It looked as if the flounders knew about my hat. But after a while they began to bite. We hauled them, hand over fist. Bocker was in heaven. In an hour and a half I tired, and began to eat the bait, succulent clams, tasty and sweet.

"Damn it! Fish!" Bocker commanded.

We had the floor of the yawl swimming in flounders. It became a problem as to where to put your feet.

In the early afternoon Sergeant Snook borrowed a horse and wagon and we delivered fish to my father's company kitchen and to every back door on officers' row. At home we enjoyed the succulent flounders until I almost tired of them.

I was sorry to see Bocker's visit end, and on his last night, at dinner, I unintentionally brought on trouble. I said, "We studied in school today about Robert E. Lee."

"One of the world's greatest generals," Bocker said, "but give me Stonewall Jackson. He captured five Yankee armies. If he hadn't been killed in an accident, the Stars and Bars would certainly be flying over this fort."

The north wind began to blow. The temperature of our dining room dropped thirty degrees. "Why—the winner was U.S. Grant," my father half-shouted. "We should all study to see why that great man succeeded."

"Great cats and little fishes," Bocker exclaimed, "You don't mean it."

My mother said, "Who'll have some more roast beef?"

After dinner Mother and Dad left to go calling, the curse of American army life before World War I. "Dropping cards at people's doors, hoping they're not home," General Douglas MacArthur later described it.

As soon as they stepped out. Bocker took over. He turned the living room lamp off and stood in front of the coals glowing in the grate. His thinning gray hair was trimmed, his white moustache as neat as ever, but his gray suit a bit worn. He had had a run of bad luck. Experiments he had conducted in freezing meat hadn't worked out, and he had staked an inventor for two years to perfect a machine that played a stack of musical discs. The inventor died. There was no written agreement. Bocker settled for two hundred and fifty dollars. The automobile was closing the Eureka Livery Stable. His diamond stickpin was gone, but the ruby-eyed Medusa cufflinks still winked at you.

Soft reds and yellows lit the room. We three Reeder children stretched out on the rug. "Tell us about when you were a boy," I said.

He told of hunting deer ". . . down on the level in Arkansas. I saw five thousand head trot out of the forest at one time." (This was an increase of a thousand over the last time.)

He switched to a ghost story. The wind began to moan and snort. The wind can talk, up in Maine. The fire flickered and smoldered down. He bubbled on, with gestures, sometimes acting out a part.

I was scared and wondered about Fred. He was only seven. He was lying with his eyes shut, not even breathing. I wasn't worried about Julia, nine; she had enough courage for a tribe.

When Bocker killed the ghost, his mood changed. "Ever hear of Ol' Dan Tucker?"

He began to sing in a low melodious voice:

> "Ol' Dan Tucker, he got drunk.
> Fell in the fire and kicked out a chunk.
> A red-hot coal got in his shoe.
> God Almighty, how the ashes flew.
> Get out of the way for Ol' Dan Tucker.
> You're too late to get your supper."

CHAPTER FOUR

Bocker Sees the Ku Klux Klan

I VISITED BOCKER and Lallie Martin for a week in Memphis, Tennessee, arriving on the Fourth of July, 1910.

Except for fireworks, cracking and booming, it was just like Sunday. People wore their best.

Bocker, Lallie, and I sat on their front porch watching a Negro funeral a block away. Its procession on Fourth Street crossed Court Street, a brass band leading and moaning "Nearer My God to Thee."

Down Court Street, headed for the funeral, rushed a runaway automobile. It had no top. The driver, standing up, worked feverishly at the controls and honked his horn. You could see through his goggles that he was frightened. His linen duster fluttered out behind. He was making at least twenty miles per hour.

When he neared the procession, he zigzagged, then crashed into the hearse. The noise reverberated through the neighborhood. The music stopped. The mourners swarmed toward the auto.

I started for the wreck, but Bocker stopped me. "Don't go. Nothin' but trouble there. I don't think the hosses were hurt. There ought to be a law against these danged automobiles."

"No," said Lallie. "You should think about selling the Eureka and find out about automobiles. Not too far away, it's going to retire the horse."

Bocker frowned. "Honey, we usually see eye-to-eye, but that time's a hundred years away." He shot a stream of brown tobacco juice at a petunia. The little flower crumpled and lay flat in its window box. He tried to revive it with his hankerchief, but it had had enough. "I'm sorry," he said.

"I wish you would stop that filthy habit." Lallie said as she walked into the house.

Bocker shook his head. "I love tobacco. I've been chewin' stand-up Burley since I was fourteen. If I had the last piece of tobacco in the world in my hand and it fell into some manure, I'd wash it off and chew it. Some doctors allow it ain't good for you, but what have they proved? Tell you what. If you don't smoke, drink, or chew until you're twenty-one, I will give you the *most handsome* gold watch money can buy."

That's easy, I thought.

We went down to the Court Street Fire Station. The chief was running out the flag on a pole jutting from the building. I saluted. Bocker waved his Panama hat.

"What are you going to be when you grow up? Livery stable owner? Fireman or what?"

"A soldier."

"Well, you were born at reveille, right after the salutin' gun was fired , your mother told me."

Bocker introduced me to the chief. "Here's the boy I told you about, my grandson Russell Reeder. This is some boy! I've never seen a boy like him." Bocker made you feel good. "Chief, can you give him a ride on the hook 'n ladder?"

"That's against regulations, strictly," the chief said. "We're going out to the Fourth of July parade. But I will let him ride as far as Court Square, where the parade begins."

Soon a bell clanged. Firemen in red shirts slid down brass poles and hurried into red rubber raincoats. Doors to box stalls inside the firehouse opened, and four magnificent horses backed out of their stalls into position alongside the tongue of the hook and ladder truck, two horses to a side. The bell still clanging, added to the excitement. The harness descended from the ceiling and firemen quickly buckled it. I climbed aboard. A fireman passed me a red helmet, but it was too big. Firemen jumped on the running board, and the four powerful animals pranced out of the station drawing the powerful machine. Up at Court Square I dismounted and walked home unfrocked.

After a noon dinner, Andrew, a footman from the stable, and Bocker, Lallie and I went riding, just like Sunday, in a surrey with a fringe on top behind two matched sorrels whose coats glistened. Andrew himself was a study: blue-black suit, white shirt, and a shiny, black top hat. He held the reins in black gloved hands, his red tassled whip stood ready in a holder affixed to the dashboard. When we passed people they knew, Lallie waved a lace gloved hand, Bocker lifted his Panama hat. They were aristocrats.

After friends passed, Bocker made observations. "Why doesn't Mitchell get rid of those two spavined mares?" "Those Duffy horses need exercise. Too fat." "Smith ought to make that lazy man of his clean the mud off the spokes of his surrey." And with pride, "Bob Cahill keeps his rig and hosses at Eureka. What a handsome outfit!"

When we got home, Bocker tipped Andrew and thanked him. To us he said, "I'm going down the block to find out about the jaybird who smashed into the hearse. I hope they have him in jail."

It was an hour before Bocker returned, and when he did he sailed his Panama toward a hat tree in the hall and missed. "This is the end," he said. "I am unglued."

I had no idea what this calamity was about. I imagined I had caused it by bringing home the peacock feathers.

"What's wrong?" Lallie said.

"Out in Reno, Nevada, Jim Jeffries disgraced the entire white race. He . . ."

"How much did you lose?" Lallie said.

He ignored her. "He let a big black prizefighter, Jack Johnson, become champion of the world. I never thought it would happen. Rufus Polk is delighted. He won two dollars and says no man can stand up to Johnson's attack. That he fills the air with boxing gloves. It went fifteen rounds."

Lallie said again, 'How much did you lose? "

Bocker said, "I feel like a brass door plate that's been out in the weather fifteen years. I don't want any supper. Excuse me."

The next morning he said, "Lallie, honey, I'm taking Russell on a steamboat ride. It'd do us both good."

I was delighted.

While we waited down at the wide cobblestone landing, at the river, where four steamboats were moored, we watched Negroes unload one of them. They came off in step in a long line, down a wide gangplank, backs bent under sacks of corn-I found out. The line going aboard sang in low key. The line carrying the sacks was grunting, and the two lines harmonized.

We sat in wicker chairs as the sidewheeler thrashed the muddy Mississippi. The river looked lonely, beautiful. No houses in sight, just countless trees. When a Negro boy in a white coat walked the deck ringing a dinner bell, Bocker said, "It isn't a question of money. We could eat below, but up here, where the breeze makes you a new man, it's better. I got ham sandwiches comin'. Tell me about your school. How do you get along with the books?"

I thought of Dave Jackson's "Poorly, thank God." "Just fair," I said.

"Well, bear down. In this modern world learnin's very important. My two oldest brothers went to Chapel Hill, in N'oth Ca'lina. Then the war hit, and all of a sudden it was survival."

Bocker took off his white Panama, and the wind tossed his white hair. He fell asleep. He looked older than his fifty-eight years.

Back in the Eureka Livery Stable the next day, he handed me two tickets to B.F. Keith's Theater. "I'd like to go with you, but I can't. Rufus says I have to go over the ledgers. If there's anything I hate in this world it's a damned ledger."

I knew that Bocker received four front row tickets to B.F. Keith's each week in return for billboard space on the side of the Eureka. I told him once that the billboard was the most valuable thing our family owned. He thought this very funny and repeated it to his friends until I was sick of it.

"Go to the show," Bocker said. "This week they got Japanese acrobats. They fly through the air. Ben Franklin Keith, personal friend of mine, told me it's the best dumb act in America, curtain raises for Blossom Seely."

Cousin Rufus said–"Boy, when she sings 'Put Your Arms Around Me, Honey,' I want to leave home." He closed his eyes at the prospect.

While we were waiting out in the street for a buggy to be hitched up for Bocker, a well-dressed man drove past the stables. He sat in a neat wicker cart pulled by two pert ponies whose hooves beat a tattoo on the pavement. He flipped his whip in a half-salute as he glided by.

"Look at that!"I said. "Oh, Bocker, won't you please buy me two ponies and a cart like that?"

"Certainly. I'll buy that very outfit for you if you can get him to sell."

I took off through the Memphis traffic. After five blocks, at an intersection, I caught him. I jerked off my cap.

"Sir," I gasped, "I'm Fred Martin's grandson. He said he'd buy these ponies and cart for me. Won't you please sell?"

"Fred Martin!" the man snapped. "I wouldn't sell him the dirt on these wheels."

I walked slowly back to the stable. I felt crushed. When I told Bocker what the man said, he roared with laughter.

"Who was that?" I asked.

"The meanest man in Memphis."

When Bocker drove off on business, I asked Rufus to have a horse saddled so I could ride in the stable aisles. I told him about my chase through the traffic.

"Typical," he said. "Fred Martin loves a practical joke. At Christmas time he used to get up on the roof and talk down the chimney to make his three young daughters think they were hearing Santa Claus. But being a friend of B.F. Keith's, he doesn't know him any more'n I know President Taft."

When I finished my ride Bocker had returned. He handed me a postal from my aunt Susie Mayfield who lived in Alabama. Bocker said with pride, "My three daughters, Susan, your mother Narcissa, and Frederica, stamp me as the most illustrious sire in the world."

The week raced by. Lallie went out to visit a friend. Bocker and I enjoyed supper in their neat kitchen. We demolished a delicious meal prepared by their black cook: black-eyed peas and ham hocks, cornbread, and buttermilk. Bocker thought he heard a noise in the back yard and went out to investigate. He returned laughing. "In the twilight, that white sheet hanging on the line startled me. I thought for a second it was a ghost."

"Did you ever see one?"

"Well," he drawled, "I don't believe in them at all, but I saw one once. It was right after the war and we were having trouble with carpetbaggers down in Pulaski. That's were I was born and raised."

"What's 'carpetbaggers'?" I asked.

"Thieves from the North in respectable clothes. They were skinning Southerners and were protected by occupation rules. I was riding our gelding, Stonewall Jackson, home from calling on a girl in west Pulaski, past the buryin' ground. It was moonlight, a little after eleven. I 'member the moonbeams shining through the pines. I slow trotted by a clearing, and in the middle of it was a gang of Ku Kluxers."

"What was that, Bocker?"

"A gang of men out to settle trouble in their own way without a nod to the law. They hid behind the sheets they dressed in. They had a fiery cross burnin' near a tree, and a good-sized caldron squatted on a fire. Near it three or four men I knew were carpetbaggers were tied to some saplings. I reined in Stonewall and jiggled my reins so he wouldn't neigh. Hanging around those Ku Kluxers wasn't particular healthy, but I wanted to see what those scalawag carpetbaggers were going to get. While I was 'in observation,' as the scouts used to say, a weird bugle call sounded and a horseman in white, on a white horse, glided by me into the clearing. I thought it was part of the Klan act, but the horse didn't make no noise, nor nothing. The Klansmen cleared out, leaving the carpetbaggers. I galloped the long way home. I wished I had a clock on Stonewall. We wasted no time. Perhaps it was a ghost I saw."

When time came for me to leave for the railroad station, Andrew drove the Martin surrey around. He was dressed for Sunday except for his shiny black, top hat. He had on an off-white cap, slouched over one ear.

I liked Andrew. Bocker and he, expert horsemen, were my riding instructors, and both always had time for me.

At the station, Bocker and Lallie walked me by the wooden cars so I could see the cowcatcher on the engine. The planks on the station's floor were stained black with oil and were flush to the tracks. The engine was wheezing, blowing up clouds of gray smoke, waiting to pull its train away.

Bocker introduced me to the conductor who wore a blue suit, a conductor's cap, a blue vest with a gold watch chain sagging across it. I hated to go.

"Mr. Wilson, shake hands with my grandson Russell. A wonderful boy. I guarantee he will be heard from." (Bocker filled you with confidence.) "Please take care of him. His father, a captain in the Yankee army, will get on when you hit Nashville. He's been there on official business. He, Russell, and his mother, my daughter Narcissa, live in my favorite dislike state, Massachusetts."

"I certainly will," the conductor said.

I kissed lovely Lallie goodbye. I never saw her again. When I kissed Bocker, I braced myself. His neat, bristly, white moustache stabbed you.

It was all aboard for the North.

CHAPTER FIVE

The Wild East and the Wild West

IN THE SUMMER OF 1912 my father and I were marooned with a ham.

We Reeders were living in Arlington, a small town near Boston, Massachusetts. Mother set the stage for the trouble when she took Julia and Fred to visit the Willifords at West Point, New York. This left in our home in Arlington only my father, me, a Swedish cook, and a ham.

Olga, our cook—almost every middle-class family had one in 1912—had it easy. All she had to do when Dad left for work in Boston was to find my baseball glove and accomplish what housework she could think up. She had no marketing because before Mother left on the trip she had bought a large ham.

We had fried ham with eggs for breakfast, I had cold sliced ham at noon, and we had warmed-up ham with may be a potato at dinner. This did not bother me because I had not heard that meals might be varied. All I wanted was to put on my high shoes that Mother had let me fix by screwing baseball spikes into them and to get up the hill with the Monk boys, a tribe of baseball players.

My father and I arrived at home at the same time one evening from our respective work to discover a note on a chair from Olga.

"My night off." On the dining table sat the ham all by itself, just part of its north end gnawed off.

"Damn it!" my father snorted. "We've had ham morning and night now for four days. What do you have for lunch? Ham?"

"I can't remember."

"Go upstairs, clean up, and put on your Sunday suit. We're heading for Boston."

We rode the streetcar, then the subway, and came up in the middle of Boston. We marched into the Parker House. People bowed to my father. He was a big man, and in his dark-blue suit, vest, and brown hair tinged with gray he looked like a millionaire out for a night on the town instead of an escapee from a ham. We sat under a huge chandelier that sparkled with hundreds of lights and had an elegant dinner with Parker House rolls. I do not know what else the dinner was but I know what it wasn't.

After dinner he bought tickets to the Ziegfeld Follies. This was the first time I had been to this kind of a show. There was a blacked-up man, Bert Williams, who drove a broken-down cab onto the stage drawn by the most woebegone horse you ever saw, only the horse wasn't real. Williams could make you laugh just by wiggling his toe, covered with a white sock, that stuck through his shoe.

There were beautiful girls everywhere. One was dressed as a clown in thin black lace, another as Pocahontas—we had learned about her—and there was a girl who flounced out representing the twentieth century. She had on a lemon-colored skirt, a coat of fiery orange, and a flaring black hat. This girl would appear every now and then, and when she came out, the rest of the girls backed up or moved to the side. "That's Lillian Lorraine," my father said. "She's the star."

They even had a girl in a golden aviator's suit, goggles and all, fly out over the audience in an airplane while a man sang a song I knew, "Come, Josephine, in My Flying Machine." I almost wore myself out applauding.

Then the stage became a dock down at the harbor. Two men wearing police caps with the words "Customs Inspector" above the visors came out and said that smuggling had gotten out of hand. They said that jewel thieves from Europe were hiding their loot and bringing it into the United States and that this was against the law, that even President Taft in the White House was worried about it. This was the first time I knew of this trouble.

A ship eased up to the dock on the far side of the stage and there was lots of excitement, people aboard shouting to men and women on the stage who had come to greet them. The inspectors backed everyone up who came down the gangplank and started searching their suitcases and bags. The way the customs inspectors threw things around made you ashamed that government officials would act that way. The last person off the ship was the prettiest girl I ever saw. She was dressed all in pink and was carrying a pink parasol. She was just about to walk off the stage when the inspectors called her back and whispered among themselves. You could hear the whispers but the girl couldn't. One inspector said that this girl was supposed to be the head of the ring of smugglers and that she ought to be examined. I couldn't believe that this lovely girl could be guilty of anything. I began to hate the inspectors.

One of the inspectors spied the end of a pink ribbon hanging out of the throat of her dress and he gave it a yank. About two yards of ribbon came out. Then the other inspector started to help, and they hand-over-handed the ribbon as fast as they could, pulling it out of the girl's dress. A great heap of ribbon began to stack up on the stage. I was on the edge of my seat.

Soon the girl wore no dress, just a pink petticoat. The way her dress had unraveled made me suspect that she might be guilty after all. When they began to haul out more ribbon, the girl hid her face in her hands.

Suddenly, when the girl was almost naked, all the lights in the theater went out. I thought, *This is the most unfortunate thing! They went out at just exactly the wrong moment.* I stood and looked back, hoping an electrician could get them fixed. My father and the rest of the audience laughed and applauded.

When, Mother, Julia and Fred returned at the end of the summer, we moved to Fort Andrews, an island army post in Boston Harbor. My Grandmother Reeder came from Cincinnati to visit us, and she was my champion. She wore a little bustle that made her black silk dress stick out behind and a black cap that tied under her chin. I thought she was one of the greatest ladies I ever saw because she always took my side. Everything I did was right. She took me to the Botanical Gardens in Boston, to the Red Sox baseball park, anywhere I wanted. I really wanted to go back to the Follies but somehow it didn't seem right to ask her.

There were not many things for us small boys to do on the island, but there was a seventeen-year-old boy there who was preparing for West Point. He gathered the smaller boys about once a week and told us what to do. "Today," Matt Ridgway would say, "Let's hold races." Next week it would be group fishing, or digging for clams, or target shooting. He had a friendly, compelling air. I wanted to do what he suggested.

He owned a .22 rifle and this added to his prestige. Once he said to me, "Russell, do you want to come up to my room and help me grease bullets?"

I was too ignorant to know what this meant, and I am not sure if I know yet, but I answered, "Yes."

Up in his room we smeared vaseline on .22 bullets and replaced them carefully in their boxes. Then he gave me instructions in sighting and aiming. He shouldered the gun, pointed it at the ceiling, and said, "When you fire be sure you are in a good position." Then he pressed the trigger. *Bow*! The .22 sounded like the saluting gun. The bullet knocked out a hunk of plaster. It showered dust. I streaked down the back stairs and tore for home. I never learned how this came out.

This seventeen-year-old leader, Matthew Ridgway, made his mark in the United States Army, rising from West Point plebe to combat general to chief of staff. He became "Supreme Commander" for the United States in more places than any other American. Wearing four stars in the Korean War, he staved off defeat by turning the war around.

We were living in Weston, Massachusetts, because my father was on militia duty in Boston. In Weston I was the general manager, field manager, captain and shortstop of the Red Devils baseball team.

We played near the Weston cider mill, where you waited your turn, and for two cents, drank cider from a grimy leather cup. Sanitation had not reached Weston in 1911. The owner of the mill placed a camp stool under a tree in deep left field for Grandmother Reeder, where she sat while I dropped an easy pop fly. The mill owner examined my glove later, pointed out cracks in its leather, saying, "This old glove needs a soakin' of olive oil." Not only did I soak it with grandmother's help, but I played in the game with a capped bottle of olive oil, about four ounces, in my pocket so

I could bathe it constantly. A pop fly slipped out of my glove, and I caught hell from the ump for ruining the only ball on the field.

Grandmother Reeder said to her son, "Russell, I think we ought to take the family to Boston to see Buffalo Bill. He's sixty-six now and the children ought to see him and his Wild West."

My father chuckled. "He's part fraud. If Buffalo Bill has done half of the things he says he has—who can prove he was a scout with Kit Carson? How many farewell appearances is he going to make?"

I was wild with excitement. I knew about Buffalo Bill and his adventures on the plains with the Indians and how he shot buffalo to feed men building the cross-continental railroad. My father pooh-poohed Buffalo Bill, but we caught the boat for Boston and went to the show.

It was held in a long, rectangular, roofless tent which enclosed a dirt arena. Outside were picket lines with ponies tied to them. Indians in feathers and war paint, soldiers with red stripes down blue trousers. Cossacks, cowboys and cowgirls. A band inside the big tent was playing "There Will Be a Hot Time in the Old Town Tonight," but I was not anxious to go inside the big tent: life was entrancing around it.

The "Wild West" opened when Annie Oakley, one of the best women rifle shots of all time, billed as the "peerless lady wing-shot," started firing at glass balls that were tossed into the air for her. Then cowboys played pushball on horseback, using a ball as high as the horses. The game was shortened because field artillery-men dashed in on horses that drew guns and ammunition carts. I could barely hear the commands over the clatter of the carts. The artillerymen unlimbered the cannon in a twinkling, wheeled them so they pointed toward the open end of the tent, and fired. The bitter smoke flooded the grandstands. "This is the real thing," my father said. "Most of these fellows are artillerymen on furlough from the army."

There were pony races. I wished for Bocker. Then in galloped cowboys yelling like on Saturday night in a border town. They showed how they picked up handkerchiefs off the ground with their teeth. Arabs, Hawaiians, Filipinos, Mexicans, Rough Riders of '98, and Plains Indians milled around. The Deadwood stagecoach was held up and the U.S. Cavalry thundered to the rescue in the nick of time. Things looked pretty good, but suddenly in dashed the Sioux Indians, riding bareback, and when it seemed as if the cavalrymen were losing, United States infantrymen ran in as skirmishers and shot the Indians out of business. All the while two bands crashed out martial music.

A squad of Civil War cavalrymen swept in, escorting a horse soldier who carried a guidon staff mounted in his stirrup. From the staff flew the Stars and Stripes. As they galloped by, Grandmother Reeder stood and applauded. "Our boys in blue!" she cried. I wondered what Bocker would have said about that.

The performers cleared the arena for an announcer on a horse who put a red fiber megaphone to his lips and shouted, "Ladies and Gentlemen! Your attention, please! Buffalo Bill will now show how he gives his horse a drink of water when he is on the plains."

The scout galloped in on a white horse. He wore a fringed white buckskin jacket, buckskin trousers thrust into black boots, and a white sombrero, its rim ornamented with silver discs, and he cradled a rifle in his arm. A mounted cowboy band at the far end crashed out a patriotic air.

Buffalo Bill trotted to the center of the long arena and held his sombrero overhead while his horse bowed to the crowd. I went wild. Even my father applauded. The sun highlighted the virile scout's white hair, which hung to his shoulders. You could tell just by looking at him that he was noble.

An attendant placed a wooden box of water in the center of the arena and Buffalo Bill was left alone. "That wooden box is the spring," my father explained to me.

At first I thought that the scout was not going to find the water, because he cantered right by it. I could imagine life on the plains with miles to the next creek. The horse seemed to stagger. Finally Buffalo Bill turned his mount to the spring and swung out of the saddle. He took off his sombrero and dipped it into the wooden box, filled it with water, and lifted it to the horse's mouth. The animal drank long and deep. The applause was tremendous.

It took twenty-five years before I wondered. "Why didn't Buffalo Bill let the horse drink out of the spring?"

CHAPTER SIX

Corporal Karm's and My Father's Problem

THERE WAS A SENTRY STANDING in our house underneath the cellar stairs. I thought he looked funny there because he was dressed for sentry duty and the weather: muskrat hat, fur mittens, boots, and buffalo coat, and a web belt of ammunition gripped his waist. His rifle leaned against the cellar door and he looked frightened. We were living at Fort McKinley on Great Diamond Island, part of the harbor defenses of Portland, Maine, and sentries did not belong in homes.

An hour before Fred and I had been out on snowshoes, running the bases on the ball diamond, or at least where we thought the bases were. The wind sweeping across the bay threw bursts of snow and particles of ice that cut us almost like a knife. We came home early because it was dark at four, and icicles kept forming on Fred's nose. It was so cold that buffalo coats were issued to the men on guard, and soldiers on pass could walk to Portland and back across the sea ice on Casco Bay.

As soon as I saw the man, I tore upstairs and said, "Mother, there is a sentry inside our house. Down in the cellar."

"I know it," she said quietly. "Their regulations say they have to walk, but out in *this* weather? It's fifteen below, and they'll catch their death of cold. I telephoned the guardhouse and just told the corporal of the guard that I would leave the cellar door unlocked all night so the poor sentries can get warm. Don't tell your father. He wouldn't like it. Besides, he's busy studying how to blow up ships."

Father was one of the Coast Artillery's experts in submarine mines, a rating he obtained by hard work. In his company were one hundred and fifty soldiers, and they labored long hours at his order, learning how to load the spherical mines with TNT and to plant them in the bay from a mine planter accompanied by motor boats."Mine practice," as they called it, was difficult and sometimes hazardous. My father also commanded a battery of six-inch disappearing guns on nearby Cow Island—guns that could, in time of war, protect the mine fields from hostile mine sweepers.

He was one of eight captains under a colonel at Fort McKinley. This was an island kingdom of about fifteen hundred people. Most of the soldiers hailed from the State of Maine, but one in our 37th Company did not. He was the best athlete on the post, Private Pete Dussen.

When I asked my father about him, he frowned and said, "Dussen is a spoiled child. Absolutely undependable. He's twenty-one and has never grown up. Ran away from home. Comes from a rich family of Dutchmen in upper New York State., and because he caught one season for Buffalo (in the old International League) he thinks he's a privileged character. He's not. He's a ne'er-do-well."

"A what?"

"A person who never does well at anything."

Pete Dussen did not look like a ne'er-do-well. He was a top catcher in baseball, with an arm like a rifle, and a clutch hitter. Also, when he hurled his husky frame at an opposing line from the fullback position, he averaged almost five yards a carry. He was the idol of every private on the post. Besides, he was my friend.

I knew why my father was angry with Dussen. He did not like to work. When the 37th Company was at mine practice, Pete Dussen discovered that if he fell overboard, he would be rescued quickly and sent below to spend the rest of the day in the engine room. The engineer warmed him up with coffee and fed him cake.

The water in Casco Bay is always cold, and if you are in it very long in late November, you are in danger of freezing. Once again, near the end of that month, while hauling an electric cable on the mine planter, Peter Dussen fell into the sea.

"Man overboard!" everyone yelled.

A man's head in choppy water is a small object, but the coxswain of the accompanying motor boat spied Dussen, steered for him, and thrust out a boat hook for Pete to grasp. In fifteen minutes he was back on the deck of the mine planter. A sergeant said in disgust, "All right, Dussen. Go below before you freeze to death."

My father, up on the bridge of the mine planter, shouted, "Dussen! Come up here!"

When Dussen stood before him, shivering and dripping water, Captain Reeder said, "I saw you go overboard. You didn't fall, you jumped! Don't go to the engine room. This time you work in your regular position in wet clothes."

There was no more falling overboard the rest of that season.

When I heard, at football practice on the big parade ground, how Pete Dussen had been disciplined, I felt ashamed. I did not see how my father could punish a hero, and I did not look forward to meeting Pete. I was embarrassed. But Pete came out early and said, "Come on, Red. I want you to learn how to feed the ball to your foot. You'll never be a punter unless you learn."

"My father—"

"Nuts," he said. "Nuts to all officers."

I was relieved he let my father off that easily.

Once, before Casco Bay water became too cold for swimming, in August of 1913, my mother took a group of kids to swim off the old mine dock that stood near the race of water between Great Diamond and Cow Islands. We were having fun, diving off the roof of the boat house, going down in fourteen feet of water for the bottom. It was cold, bottle-green, and creepy down there. After a while we tired and dressed. The tide was on the way out. There were some soldiers over on the beach. We were about to start home when we stopped to watch Georgie McMullin, fat and six years old. Georgie, who could not swim, was in a rowboat moored to the dock, amusing himself by pushing away from the pier. When the rope tightened it acted like a spring and tugged the boat back to the pier. Georgie was not in our party, but I remember my mother's calling to him. "Don't do that, Georgie!"

"Why?"

"Because it is dangerous," Mother said.

Georgie stood up this time and shoved the rowboat away from the dock. The tide helped him and the rowboat cut the water for

(PHOTO COURTESEY OF MRS. CHARLOTTE RUMSEY)

RR, 37th Co. Mine mascot with James M. Bevan in front of the Reeders' home, Ft. McKinley, ME, about 1913.

about twenty feet. When it reached the end of the rope the boat stopped with a forward jerk, and Georgie McMullin was flipped into the air, turning a backward somersault like a gymnast and popping into the icy water. He made quite a splash.

He came up, thrashed his arms, and sank. I yelled directions to him. He couldn't carry them out. When he fought his way up again, he was a bit farther out.

My mother commanded, "Go get him, Russell!" just like you might say, "Go fetch it, Rover!"

I plunged off the wharf and swam after him. It was the first time I had ever been swimming with my clothes on. Water flooding into my high-topped shoes made them feel like anchors. I looked for Georgie and when he battled his way up again, wide-eyed and gasping, I swam to him. He grabbed me. I did not realize he was so strong. He felt as heavy as a boulder. The sweep of the tide dragged us. I gasped salt water and dog paddled as hard as I could. Georgie rode my back. I was frightened. His hands gripped my neck in a death hold. Mother awaited us, perched on the bottom rung of a wooden ladder, nailed between two piles.

When I woke up, I was back home in bed with the shades drawn. My father walked in, took my pulse and temperature and said, "There's nothing wrong with you. You just swallowed too much salt water. Stay in bed."

Pete Dussen came over the next day and rang our doorbell. This took courage. Privates did not ring officers' doorbells in 1913 ordinarily. I went to the door and Pete wrapped his paw about mine and gave me his big grin. He said, "Red, you're my boy." This was one of the warmest greetings I ever received.

Mother got some photographers over from Portland and my father said for me to wear my Sunday suit. Several months later a silver medal and a letter from the Treasury Department came through the mail, and Father pinned the medal on me. There were photographers again and pink lemonade all around. After the party Julia said, "I'm glad you won the medal. I know how happy you are—especially having Pete Dussen come to see you." Smart girl, my sister Julia.

She was an unusual girl, the best pupil in Sunday school. Knew all the answers. Mother was our teacher, and I have never seen a Sunday school teacher who could explain the Bible in her own words as she could. "Gideon asked for volunteers to go fight the Midianites . . ."

I had no idea who they were. I was for Bocker. His name was Gideon Fred Martin, and the more she talked, the more it seemed to me she was talking about *him*.

"Gideon was in trouble. To help him, 32,000 men volunteered. When they came to a stream, some of them knelt and lapped the water up like dogs, but 300 of them scooped the water up one-handed. Gideon said to himself, 'These are my best men. These are the ones I want. I am taking them with me because they are dependable.'"

That afternoon after Sunday dinner I went down in the woods behind our house where a stream bubbled over the rocks and practiced drinking one-handed. I wanted to be sure that when the time came they could count on me.

The bronze medal of the Massachusetts Humane Society arrived, but this time there was no ceremony. All hands were thankful, especially me, that Georgie and I had been spared. I treasure these two medals and the memory-picture of Mother on the bottom rung of the seaweed-green ladder, just above the water, waiting to help us.

The next summer my father and Pete Dussen upset the whole post—especially me.

We had in the 37th Company a stern first sergeant named Wilson. The men did not like him. I warned my father about this and he said, "That's because Sergeant Wilson's a very fine first sergeant." I went to the big beechnut tree beside our house and tried to think that out. It was impossible.

The trouble was caused by an exciting baseball season that ended in a Fort McKinley World Series. For almost three months the eight company baseball teams had battled for the red pennant that hung outside the colonel's office at post headquarters. It was fringed in yellow and across its center in gold letters was printed:

> POST CHAMPIONS, FORT MCKINLEY, 1914
> WON BY

I was very anxious that that "won by" be followed by "37th Company."

The week before the season ended, the 51st Company slumped badly. Our 37th Company, finishing with a rush, tied them on the last day of the season The excitement was out of this world. The colonel said that the championship would be decided in a three-game play-off. I could not sleep. I knew we *should* win because we had the best battery. With Shine Pear, curve-ball pitcher, on the mound, and Pete Dussen behind the bat, we had a combination that had proved unbeatable. Pete was the best player on the post.

But the 51st Company was led by a crafty catcher, Tommy Sherlock, who made catching look like a picture in an art gallery. They had a well-balanced team and all of their officers were actively backing it. But my father still had his nose in that red book on how to blow up ships.

The tension over the play-off affected almost everybody. On the day of the first game, my mother came home at noon angry.

"Guess what!" she said to me. "Mrs. Mosteller's neutral! I thought she was my friend. She's not going to root for either team." This seemed pure treachery.

After lunch I climbed into my cream-colored baseball suit that had "37th Co., C.A.C. (Mine)" across the chest and streaked for the 37th Company barracks. Only three hours remained until game time.

I found the company in deep gloom. Corporal Sid Karm, the money lender, sat almost on the back of his neck in one of the leather Morris chairs in the company's day room, his blouse open and his chin on his stomach. His mouth was turned down. Above him hung an eight-sided clock with a brass pendulum. Gold letters crowded the clock's face, making it hard to tell the time. They said:

GIFT OF
SID KARM
A FRIEND

When that clock was put up, there was a lot of talk. Some said that Karm should have given two clocks. Corporal Karm had a barrel of money somewhere. He lent soldiers ten dollars when they needed it in the middle of a month and they gave him fifteen on payday.

On the far wall, above the pool and billiard tables, hung a row of pennants the 37th Company had won on the diamond in previous summers. Soldiers crowded the day room, most of them staring at the floor.

No one said, "Hey, Red!"

Corporal Karm jerked his thumb at Corporal Chick Sebago, crack third baseman. "You tell Red Reeder, Chick," Karm said. "I ain't got the heart. Red, we are ruint."

Chick Sebago and I went outside and perched on the top of the pipe railing on the porch. "We have a corker of a problem," Chick said. "I think your father thinks we're makin' a mountain out of a mole, but he don't know the trouble we're in, even though most of it's been *explained* to him."

I felt my face growing red.

Chick continued to unfold the bad news. "Last night when I left to visit my folks over in Portland I was as happy as a clam at high tide. The series looked Jake. We had took care of what we thought was the only problem, Shine Pear, by having him locked up in the guardhouse to keep him from that rotgut booze. We don't want him to even smell a cork at the Headache House at the other end of the island. It was a cinch to stick him in the lockup because our company was on guard, though one of the corporals said that confining Shine without charges was against the Constitution of the United States. He was overruled. There won't be a whisper of it in the guard book, and what the officers don't know won't hurt 'em."

I thought this was a great idea. I had seen Shine try to pitch after a payday. I raised my chest slightly, happy that Chick had enough confidence to let me in on a secret.

"Then the bottom gave way," Chick said. "Sergeant Wilson put Pete Dussen on kitchen police! Holy gee, he should have knowed better!" All the enthusiasm left Chick's voice. "Pete made a scene. He slammed his hat down on the day-room floor and told off a corporal. Thank the Lord Sergeant Wilson didn't hear that. Pete swore that if he had to do K.P., he would not play."

I said innocently, "Was it his turn to go on K.P.?"

"Of course," Chick said, "but Pete thinks he should have special treatment. Looks like we've lost him because he won't meet your dad halfway. This makes the outlook for the series as black as the king of hell's ridin' boots."

I could not talk.

"And," continued Sebago, "a committee was formed, headed by Corporal Karm. I was on it. We got Sergeant Wilson's permission to speak to your old man. Your dad listened. Corporal Karm wound up and said he would be glad to do Pete Dussen's K.P. 'No,' your dad said, 'N.C.O.'s do not do no K.P. for nobody. Dussen will do his own duty.' Your father snapped his jaw shut, you know."

I knew.

"But your dad said, 'He may be excused from his duty durin' the game, and as soon as it's over, he will return at once to the kitchen.' We came out and explained this to Pete. He slammed down his hat again, took off his fatigue jacket and stamped on it. He said he wasn't putting up with any quick hitch like that there."

My throat felt narrow and tight. I went back to the kitchen with Chick Sebago and Corporal Karm. The great man was sitting on a stool along with other K.P.'s peeling potatoes for Chief Cook Red Hawk's slumgullion. The pile of peelings looked as big as the pile of potatoes.

The fat Penobscot Indian smiled at me. He looked distinguished. Gray hair peeked under the edge of his white chef's hat.

"Any news?" Karm said glumly.

Pete said, "Hello, Red," with but a trace of a smile.

"I got five dollars bet," said Red Hawk, "but this big boy here," he pointed a finger decorated with a bloodstone ring at Pete, "this big kid—no play. I can't run this kitchen without kitchen police. Pete wants Cap'n Reeder to make his case special, and I told Pete he might as well wait for Doomsday. I guess it's good-by five bucks."

I just wished my father could understand how serious this was.

"I wish I only had five dollars riding" Karm said. "I got half a fortune. Pete, won't you *please* play?"

Pete sliced a potato in half, then flipped his knife into the pile of potatoes as if he were playing mumblety-peg.

"That won't do the potatoes any good," Red Hawk said.

"Nuts to everybody," said Pete.

Chick Sebago tried flattery, only it was the facts: "Pete, you're the only four-hundred hitter on this post. Willie Snodgrass can't begin to catch Shine Pear in this world, and you know it. You're our main spring. Without you we're in the soup."

Pete had his lips stuck out so far you could hang a tea cup on them. "I'll play in the third game," he said, "but I won't today or tomorrow if I have to do this goddam K.P."

"There won't be no third game," Corporal Karm said. "It's the best out of three."

Pete whittled at a potato.

We were caught up in a calamity. "I'll see my father," I said. "He doesn't understand."

Pete called after me, "I'm sick of dragging my fanny around this dump. I'm going to buy out of this goddam place and go to Fort Monroe, Virginia, where they like athletes." This was the worst news of the day. I felt *I* was the one in trouble. I felt bad about my father.

I walked into the orderly room, past First Sergeant Wilson, who was working at his desk, and into my father's office.

"Daddy," I said, "I came to see you about something important. We can't win the pennant if Pete Dussen's on K.P."

My father said quietly, "I made it perfectly clear that Private Dussen may play, but he has to return to K.P. immediately after the game. The privates are not running this company."

I went out of his office feeling that I could walk under the door.

Down at the ball park in the hollow beneath the pine- and hemlock-covered hill, the 51st Company's team was warming up, yipping like Cree Indians. They were on fire. With Pete Dussen out of action, they smelled victory.

I helped our jittery substitute catcher, Private Snodgrass, find his mask, and while he put on the rest of his equipment I went to the plate and caught Shine Pear's warm-up pitches. I was happy that I could do this. He was as sharp as a knife; the night's rest in the guardhouse had helped him put a real bend in his curve.

I hated to see the game begin.

Pure miracle got us by that first inning. Snodgrass dropped every other pitch. Shine Pear struck out a batter, but Snodgrass let the third strike roll away from the plate and the batter was safe at first. There was one out. When the 51st Company had runners on first and second. Chick Sebago trotted in from third to buck up Catcher Snodgrass, but it was easy to see that Snodgrass wished he were back in the day room. The next batter, Tommy Sherlock, cracked a liner right at Wop Triano, our second baseman, who caught it and doubled the runner off first.

We came in and went out one, two, three.

Suddenly there was a roar. The only sound I ever heard on an athletic field that approached it was in the Yankee Stadium years later when Knute Rockne, Notre Dame football coach, sent his first string backfield, destined to become the "Four Horsemen," into the game against Army.

Pete Dussen, in baseball uniform, dashed onto the diamond like a big pony. I ran alongside shaking his hand. He had decided to play ball and to continue his turn on kitchen police after the game. I helped buckle on his red-fiber shin guards; my fingers seemed like thumbs.

Shine Pear threw his pretzel twists and Pete caught them perfectly. In the middle of the game Lieutenant Alden Strong, my father's top assistant, lined out a double. Sunny Ladue walked. Pete Dussen came up. He looked like a giant, and he was a giant. He ground his spikes into the clay and glared at the pitcher. I caught a glimpse of Corporal Karm in the bleachers back of the wire behind home plate. His hands were clasped, eyes on the sky.

Pete Dussen took a cut at the ball and it streaked over the left fielder's head and rolled into a drainage ditch sixty feet behind him, back where the hemlock forest began. There was a roar. Pete trotted around the bases for a homer. I was jumping up and down on home plate waiting for him. That was the game.

Afterwards I carried Pete's chest protector and shin guards back to barracks in a flock of 37th Company rooters. Morale was cloud high. Everything was funny. Pete went to the showers and changed into his fatigues. He carried himself like a young prince.

Chief Red Hawk's kitchen smelled and looked wonderful. The floor had been washed with lye and holystoned until it looked like the deck of a yacht. You could eat off it. Lined up on tables were forty mince pies. Slum bubbled in huge iron pots on the stoves. Pete came in laughing, and his laugh always made others laugh—this time especially.

Corporal Karm waltzed in with an imaginary partner, humming. He dropped her and squeezed Pete's hand and said, "My buddy! In appreciation, even though a corporal ain't supposed to do no K.P., I am personally coming in here after supper to help you swab up the dishes."

Red Hawk cut pie for us and for the four men on kitchen police. He removed his cook's hat and mopped his brownish-red face. A great man, but far too heavy.

"Pete," he said, "they say you hit that ball a mile. Good work. You know, I think you very great ball player, but Cap'n Reeder is growing you up. What do you think?"

Pete's face looked blank, as if he were asleep.

A light dawned for me. I liked that Chief Red Hawk.

At Ft. McKinley we had only nine boys of baseball age, so it was vital that all show up for games. We were playing boys from Portland one Sunday, when our second baseman, a wonderful boy named Harrison Todd, arrived wearing a crisp white linen suit.

His mother, a large lady, gesticulating with a parasol, appeared just as Harrison slid into third and came up covered with dirt. She broke baseball rules by entering the playing field and by marching our player home.

But we won when Sgt. Hecker ferried us in his motor boat across Casco Bay to Ft. Williams. Soldiers' drill there had just been dismissed so we listened to about two hundred enemy rooters. Years later Rogers Hornsby, one of the best players ever, said, "A baseball team is like an army. If it doesn't win, it's no good."

CHAPTER SEVEN

A Wedding Present for Sergeant Snook

AFTER WE WON the next game in a landslide, we hung up the pennant in the day room near the clock. I started to enjoy Red Hawk's kitchen. Not only was he a good man to be around, but I liked his food. He could always produce a piece of pie: mince, apple, or lemon. The odors in that kitchen made your mouth water, especially when the chief and his assistants were baking. The cellar was almost as interesting. Down there he had barrels of home-made sauerkraut, pigs' feet, and pickles.

Once he gave me a hint as to the reason for his friendliness. "Russell, you run about this post like a pea in a hot skillet. Why don't you come in here more often? You can have anything you want. My wife and I don't have children."

One noon I was enjoying a piece of his incomparable lemon pie and looking over *The Police Gazette*. Some of its scantily dressed girls looked like Follies beauties. Way down in the corner was something about a war in Europe. The company kitchen was alive, because in a few minutes 150 hungry soldiers would charge into the dining hall.

First Sergeant Wilson marched in for a look around. He spoke to me friendly enough, but that night my father said in his firm voice, "Russell, I want you to stay out of the company kitchen."

The next day I went to the 37th Company kitchen as soon as I could to tell my friend the awful news.

The chief wiped his heavy bronze face with his apron. "I tell you," he said, "'you have to throw the tub to the whale.' That is, give in some. What your dad means is don't be in here when he or the first sergeant inspects. Your father comes in here at eleven thirty sharp every morning except Sundays and holidays. Then it's eleven. The first sergeant's in at six in the morning, at noon, and at four thirty.

I tried his advice and it worked perfectly.

About a month later Chief Red Hawk was carried suddenly to the post hospital. Something was wrong with his stomach. And at noon that day they lowered the flag to half-mast. The bugler of the guard, about to blow "Officers' Call" through the big tin megaphone near post headquarters, told me. "The Chief is dead. Stomach too big, or something burst in it."

I was stunned. The day before we had walked to the company's garden—where a married officer or noncommissioned officer could share in the vegetables all summer by paying $2.50 to the company fund. Red Hawk had been concerned with the cucumber crop. "I'm going to make hundreds of delicious dill pickles for the company," he had said. It seemed incredible that this friend would die. Years later the famous sportswriter, Grantland Rice, wrote of the boatman at the River Styx. "Charon . . . why do you always look my way? . . . Why do you pick my pals?" Charon started to take my friends at an early age.

Red Hawk's death was a sledgehammer blow. My mother took Julia and me to the funeral. Again, it was in a little cemetery carved out of the pines. You could hear the procession approaching the cemetery before you could see it; a drummer was tapping out time. When the band entered the enclosure, it broke into the doleful "Dead March" from *Saul*. Behind the band came the Colors, and then my father marched, his sword drawn, at the head of the 37th Company, everyone in full dress blues. Strapped to a horse-drawn caisson was the coffin, the flag carefully draped over it. The company wheeled and lined up by the grave. The band stopped playing and the chaplain began to preach. I could not bear to look at Red Hawk's widow. I concentrated on Pete Dussen and the baseball team, standing behind my father. After they had lowered the coffin, three volleys of musketry crashed out and a bugler blew "Taps," the soldier's last salute. The notes echoing through the wood seemed to go on and on. If I pause to listen, I can still hear that bugle. Suddenly I felt better. My father marched the company about. It followed the band, which led the way out, playing "The Girl I Left Behind Me."

I stayed away from the kitchen after Red Hawk's death. It could never be the same. A week after his funeral his widow, dressed in black, came to our home. She lifted her veil and handed my mother a ring—a bloodstone in a plain gold mounting. "This was the Chief's ring," she said. "He prized it. He was taken so suddenly, I think he would have wanted it to go to Russell."

It was the first piece of jewelry I ever owned, but I could not wear it because it made me miss the Indian all the more. Julia took an interest in this ring. She said it was curious that Red Hawk had died and had left me a "bloodstone." The peculiar way she said this turned me against that stone.

One spring night my mother and father dressed up and went to a party. He wore his blue full-dress uniform with a red stripe for artillery down the side of the trousers. I forget what my mother had on, but it shimmered. She looked lighted up. They kissed us good night and told us to be good. "You are in charge, Russell," Mother said. "You're the oldest." Julia was really in charge; we all knew that.

It was a ghastly March night. A cold rain had washed away the last traces of snow. The wind was blowing hard and the rain thrashed against the storm windows, which were still up. Julia began talking about that bloodstone ring. She talked about bravery and how they were studying it in her class—the teacher was telling them about King Arthur and his friends, who killed dragons. Then she said a knight named King Richard the Lion Hearted was the bravest man the world had ever known outside of Jesus, and that we were related to one of King Richard's knights, the first man up the wall at a place called Acre.

Then Julia switched the subject to Red Hawk's funeral.

A limb of a tree crashed on the roof of the porch. I went out to see if the tree was damaged. It was our beech tree; we got good nuts from it. It had stopped raining, but the wind felt wet, and it was howling as if it were hurt.

Julia said what everyone liked best in a man is bravery. She said she would bet that I was not brave enough to go to the cemetery and touch Red Hawk's bloodstone ring to his tombstone and say, "Red Hawk, I wish you were here."

She did not say how much she bet, she just "bet."

I told her I didn't wish he were there. How could he be there?

Fred, playing train on the floor, knocked the engine off its track. He turned his big brown eyes on me. Julia said of course if I didn't think I could go to the cemetery and back that she would never tell anybody–Pete Dussen or anyone.

I put on my cap, Julia said she thought I ought to wear a raincoat, but I did not want to be bothered with a raincoat flapping around my legs on a night mission like this. Then Julia said it would be a good idea for me to leave a rock on the tombstone to prove that I had been there. She thought of everything.

When I tore through the woods toward the cemetery I was not afraid of a human getting me, I was afraid of the blackness and the trees. The big firs and balsams were moaning and groaning in the wind. They were waving their arms at me, and I remembered how the trees almost grabbed Dorothy in *The Wizard of Oz*. It was less than a half mile through the woods on the wet pine needles. It seemed like five.

I entered the cemetery, and in the dim light it looked only a few yards wide. My heart was pounding from running and from being in such an unhealthy place. The headstones appeared to be chalky stumps. I located Red Hawk's tombstone. There was something white moving along the fence. I stopped and was about to run back when I realized it was only Jerry Groh's cow. Jerry was a private whom my father had allowed to get married, and he lived in a small wooden house not far from the cemetery.

I went up to the grave. There was no grass around it, just dirt. My throat choked and it was hard to breathe. I wanted to take off my cap, because Mother had told us always to be respectful around the dead, but my arms wouldn't work. I said, as low as I could, "Red Hawk, I wish you were here." However, I did not want to see him at this time. I scurried around trying to find a rock. When I finally found one and placed it on the headstone, my hands were trembling.

I tore out of the cemetery. I swished through the woods far faster than I had run toward the grave. When I got to the house, I could not get in. Everything was locked up tight. I pounded on the door and rang the bell. All the downstairs lights went out. I slid into the cellar through the iron coal chute. Julia said she was telling Fred a story about a lady who lived in a lake and Fred got scared, and when I pounded on the door, he wanted to go to bed, so she just went with him. Julia said that on a nice day she would go to the cemetery and see the rock on Red Hawk's burial stone, and that if she had a chance she would tell Pete Dussen that I was very brave.

Julia was a kind of Boy Scout leader. Although the Scout organization had been invented, it had not yet spread to out-of-the-way places like Fort McKinley. My father spurred my interest in the Scouts by giving me a Boy Scout handbook with a brown linoleum cover. I studied that and Ernest Thompson Seton's *Rolfe in the Woods.*

Julia said we had to learn to march through Indian country. With us on our hikes was Ventura, a Filipino boy who had just come from the Philippines with William Wilson and his father, Colonel Wilson, the post surgeon. Julia let Ventura lead the way on the trails because of his experiences against the Igorots in the jungles of the Philippines, but she carried the book and tested all of us, deciding whether or not we could qualify in the different branches of scouting. It was on these hikes that I first discovered the joy of a campfire and drinking tea and coffee out of a canteen cup.

Julia was in charge of the hikes, but she was in my custody when we went to the Butler Grammar School in Portland. To get there we used a succession of vehicles. First a "glass wagon"—a carry-all with wide glass windows, drawn by two horses—called for us and other post children and hauled us to the Fort McKinley dock. In winter the glass wagon creaked along on runners.

Next we climbed aboard a thirty-foot gasoline launch that chugged out of the narrow horseshoe cove past the old bell buoy. That buoy seemed like a friend. It clanged out warm greetings, especially in a fog. On foggy days the launch cut the waves slowly over the five-mile course to Portland. I was so naive it took me fifty years to realize that in a heavy fog we were in danger. There was no warning system other than fog horns. When an ocean liner loomed out of the mist, I thought we children, huddled in the cabin, were lucky to be getting a close-up view. The biggest thrill of all, in a snowstorm, was to hear the Portland "no-school whistle." A great shout went up when the captain was finally convinced and made a U-turn and the launch chugged back to Fort McKinley.

On days when we made it to Portland, we landed near the entrancing Daggett's Fish Wharf, where men cleaned fish so expertly it was an art. There we caught a streetcar, transferred to another, and then, after a twenty-five minute ride, dismounted and walked two blocks to school.

I made friends in the Maine school. My special chum was Taites Morse, taffy-haired, quick-witted—a boy who saw the humorous side of everything. My mother let me invite him to the fort on weekends. Cow Island, across the race from Fort McKinley—a ten-minute pull for us in a rowboat—was our special haunt. Sometimes Taites and I would dig clams on the Cow Island beaches and steam them in seaweed on hot rocks, or catch flounders off the dock and fry them. Sometimes we would shoot yellowhammers with Taites' .22 and roast them on a stick. Yellowhammers are delicious. We *lived* over on Cow Island.

The special attraction was my father's six-inch disappearing battery. Its two guns were mounted on huge steel carriages and stood behind a concrete and dirt wall called a parapet. When coast artillerymen wanted to fire a disappearing gun, they rammed home the projectile, then a bag of powder, pressed a long lever, and the big gun rose up and poked his muzzle over the parapet wall. A yank on the lanyard ignited the primer in the breechblock and fired the powder. The shock of the explosion pushed the gun back behind the parapet, and when smokeless powder was used it would have been difficult for an enemy to pinpoint the gun's location, because it disappeared so quickly into its concrete nest.

One day Taites Morse and I were up on the hill on the center of the island. Below us lay a wood, Sergeant Snook's house, the disappearing battery, and a magnificent stretch of the bay. Sergeant Snook was the caretaker of Cow Island.

Taites said, "Russell, how do these disappearing guns operate?"

It was hard for me to describe their action, and I felt sorry for him. It was a pity. Here was a city boy who had no idea how a disappearing gun worked.

Taites said, "I'd sure like to go down there and take a look."

My father had cautioned me several times, "When you go over to Cow Island, stay away from those guns."

But to instruct Taites and show off my knowledge, I gave in. "Well," I said, "let's go down there, but we have to go way round Sergeant Snook's house. He's very particular."

The immense gun we approached had been put away for the winter. It had canvas tied over its breechblock and gears. Four big wooden boxes had been built to cover the trunion arms and these boxes were chained in place.

Taites asked again, "How does the gun work?"

I said, "Well, all they do when they want the gun to rise into position to fire is to yank on this lever."

"How?"

"Like this." I swung my weight on the lever and the big gun groaned. Suddenly it shook itself and all 118,000 pounds of it rose. The chains snapped. The boxes were smashed into a thousand bits. It rained splinters. The gun stopped with a great crash and thrust its long nose over the wall. All it needed was powder.

Taites and I took off at top speed for the woods two hundred yards away. We hid in there for a while, but when we found we were safe, we returned to the edge. Sergeant Snook had run out of his house at the crash and was walking around the gun wringing his hands. I wasn't afraid of Sergeant Snook, so we went back to the gun.

"I'm in great trouble," Snook said. "Boy, your father! It's my job to keep people away from these guns. Your father has just given me permission to get married and he gave me this caretaking job and this house. We want to live here. This gun was all buttoned up for the winter. Now look at it! Time your father gets through with me I won't know whether I'm afoot or ahossback." He pointed at the cannon with a shaky finger.

I was amazed that Sergeant Snook was not mad at me. He was just worried about one thing: *my father.*

"I just feel sick," Snook said. He pulled out a blue bandanna. He looked as if he were going to cry, but he blew his nose.

"How do they get these guns down when they don't fire them?" I asked.

"They wind 'em down with a crank. But, s'help me, look at all the canvas stuck in the gear teeth!"

"Don't you think we can worry it out?" I asked. "If you have some lumber we can build new boxes. Have you any extra canvas covers? Can't we fix this?"

"Maybe we can if we put our mind upon it," Snook said. "Thank you kindly."

Snook produced a crank, lumber and tools. We started to work as hard as we could. All of us were anxious to get that gun back behind the wall and to make things look the way they were. We even forgot to stop at noon to eat. We moved gears and took out canvas, bit by bit. We hammered together four new boxes to cover the trunion arms. Snook brought out canvas and sewed it to cover the breechblock, parts of the housing, and the gears. It was an all-day job.

Near the end, with things looking something like they had originally, I felt better. Snook went into his house and came out with a bucket of green paint and gave Taites and me each a brush. I enjoyed painting the boxes. I felt almost gay to think how well we had come out of the scrape.

When Taites and I left to row back to Fort McKinley Sergeant Snook said, "Please don't say anything about this to your father."

It was agreed by all hands that this was an excellent idea.

Four months later my father came home for lunch and I could tell by his expression that something was wrong. His face looked like a storm cloud.

"Russell," he said, "one day last fall did you trip a six-inch gun over at Cow Island?"

My gizzard turned over. Something told me this was a poor time to tell anything but the truth.

"Yes, sir," I said. Then I told him why I had done it. I expected his razor strop, but he did not whip me.

He shook his head. "I want you to know you cost me twenty dollars. Sergeant Snook forgot to take the sight off the gun when it was winterized, and the unusual smash ruined its cross hairs. When are you going to learn to carry out an order? You are not to go near the baseball field for a week."

I could not figure out how my father found out that I had tripped the gun. Obviously Sergeant Snook had not volunteered.

Almost a month passed before I could get away. When I could, I borrowed a rowboat and pulled for Cow Island.

I walked around the corner of Snook's house and surprised him spading his garden. "Holy Bejeebers!" he said. "You heading for those guns again?"

"No indeed," I said. "I want to know how my father found out."

Snook's weatherbeaten face took on even more lines. "Well, the cap'n come over here as soon as the snow was just left in the eaves to see how the guns and all stood the winter. It took him just ten minutes to figger out what happened."

"How did he find out?" I pressed.

"You painted your initials on them boxes."

My mind whirled back. "Yes, but I used green paint, the same color we painted the boxes.

"Didn't make no difference. When the winter faded the paint, your initials acted like a second coat. They stood out like Portland Head Light. Your initials are his, one'n the same. When he inspected the gun he never let on that he saw your dern initials. Then he found the broken sight and said, 'Who's been around this gun?'

"'No one, sir,' I said to him. 'I'm positive, and I'm on duty here twenty-four hours a day.' I tried to change the subject because a year ago I didn't carry out one of his orders. If there's been a hanging in the family you don't like to talk about rope. But he circled back on the course. 'Humph!' he said. 'I just can't believe it!' 'I wouldn't lie to the cap'n,' I said.

"Then he asked about the initials and held me to the burnin' cedar until I confessed. When he found that I shaded the truth he confined me to this island for three weeks. 'Telling the truth is the soldier's first duty,' he said. In those three weeks I couldn't even see my future missus."

Snook put his spade away and pulled his watch out of his watch pocket. "Mind you, Russell, stay away from here! I don't want you runnin' around trippin' guns. I have to go now and row over to McKinley. Want to get my blue uniform. I get married in three days. You're going to leave, I hope?"

"Yes," I said. "What can I give you for a wedding present?"

"Just two things. Stay away from me and stay away from those guns. Thank you kindly. That's all I want from you."

CHAPTER EIGHT

Latin by the Bucket

IN THE SPRING OF 1915 there was talk about the European War. The United States would not be involved. Many admired the Kaiser. My father said, "One thing about the Kaiser, he had his armies ready. *Hoch der Kaiser!* He's a friend of Teddy's."

President Theodore Roosevelt was my father's hero, and there was a faint facial resemblance. It became pronounced when my father wore his rimless glasses and snapped his jaw shut for emphasis. "Bully!" he would say, just like Teddy.

When a German submarine sank the steamship *Lusitania* in 1915, causing the deaths of over one hundred Americans, my father, like many other Americans, changed his thinking about the Kaiser and the Germans.

I was reading *The Police Gazette* in the company barber shop, and the war in Europe was overshadowed by troubles at home. The American League could not get Ty Cobb out. He stole base after base. The Fort McKinley football team had only a few excellent players, Pete Dussen, "Soldier" Adams, "Chick" Embleton and one or two others. This was a real worry. I was mascot and water boy and wore a football suit when I carried water to the players when time was out. The trick was to get there fast and not to spill water all over your stockings. My mother came to the games, and once she asked, "When you go out there with the water what do the players say?"

"They don't talk," I said. "They're too busy trying to get their breath."

When Assistant Coach Allen R. Edwards, my father's second lieutenant, heard of this remark, he said, "That's exactly the trouble. Yesterday I went to the Post Exchange after practice to get a beer and I couldn't get close to the bar because our football squad filled the room. They are training on long beers and short walks."

Mother took a dim view of football and asked Lieutenant Edwards to talk to me of the horrors of the game. He arrived on a Sunday afternoon and we went into my father's den and shut the door. He sat in the leather Morris chair, leaned back, and said, "Russell, football is a terrible game. I advise you strongly never to play it."

"Why?"

"Well, you really get racked up." Lieutenant Edwards pulled up his trouser leg. "You see the scar on this knee? I got it when I was a West Point plebe. Pot Graves, the famous line coach, was feeding us scrubs to the varsity when *crack*! I got clipped from behind and my knee went. They carried me to the cadet hospital and when water built up, they stuck needles in it, then operated. Stay away from football." He tracked a map of his troubles on his knee.

"It's grueling," he continued. "Almost every man who plays it gets marked up somehow. It soaks up your study time, too. Why, at West Point, while we players were out on the field getting mashed up, other cadets were in the library studying."

"What position did you play?"

He slid his trouser leg back into position. "Halfback. I always regret I did not make an A."

"Did you have some good teams at West Point?" I asked.

"Did we! Why, in 1908 Cadet Bob Hyatt shouted at a football practice, 'I'd rather be a plebe at West Point than admiral of the whole damned Navy!'" That set us afire. You've never seen such spirit. We upset the Navy six to four. Bill Dean rammed over a touchdown and Navy kicked a field goal. When our team returned to West Point, the Corps met it down at the railroad station and put them on a stagecoach, 'The Yellow Canary.' There was a rope a hundred yards long hitched to the front of the stagecoach and the whole darned Corps tugged the team up the big hill. When it got to the top there were speeches all around. You should have heard the cheering."

I could visualize the scene. "Tell me about West Point," I said.

"Well, it's our best military academy. At West Point they teach you how to be an officer, how to lead men, and they give you a fine education. The main sport of the cadets is football. Here, this soldier football is in-place wrestling. There, it is a sort of friendly war, much faster. Sissies shouldn't play. It's getting more popular all the time. Up at Yale they just built a bowl that'll seat eighty-thousand! Why, I'd give a farm to see it."

I made a mental note to learn more about West Point and to remember if I arrived there to be sure and be good enough in football so I wouldn't have to play on the scrubs and be fed to the varsity.

I was glad Mother had invited Lieutenant Edwards to warn me against football. He was nice to me and let me make the trips with the football team.

It was a big year. Over in Portland some of the windows exhibited an exciting picture. "September Morn." I enjoyed sneaking looks at it. She looked pretty chilly to me but very cute.

There was society at Fort McKinley when Mother and Father put on a series of dinners for grown-ups, with everyone in evening dress. For these affairs they hired Private "Yegg" Jones, a forty-year-old dog robber in the 37th Company, to play the part of butler. He had the face of a beaten-up prize fighter.

"Yegg's an old booze hound," Pete Dussen told me.

But at a formal dinner Yegg served as well as a waiter in the Parker House.

One night when Yegg was clearing the table, I was in the kitchen nibbling at the carcass of a turkey. He carried back a punch bowl of Fish House punch, one fourth full, and placed it carefully near the sink. You could smell the rum.

There was minor confusion in the kitchen. Dishes all over the place. Our maid labored to establish order as Yegg carried trays of dirty dishes.

After several trips Yegg asked anxiously, "Where's the punch?"

"Oh," said the maid, "I poured what was left down the drain."

Yegg sat down on a stool. It was the first time I ever saw a grown man cry.

The society days were broken up by orders for the coast artillerymen to practice as infantry. I went along on a hike in the foothills of the White Mountains west of Portland. It was fun. I carried a pack and a canteen of water like the soldiers, and especially enjoyed the advance guard problems (clearing the road of an enemy).

I marched at the head of the company with my father, while Lieutenants Strong and Edwards and First Sergeant Wilson brought up the rear. At night I slept on the ground in my father's wall tent, beside his cot.

"Funny thing about military life, Russell," my father said. "Sometimes you have to do things you don't believe in. As soon as we pitched this camp the colonel told us company commanders to order the men to stay out of an apple orchard over that hill. After twenty miles the men were too tired to go searching for apples. But I announced this to the company and sure enough, the farmer caught Private Dussen and a dozen others in the orchard. Now I have to discipline them."

I was worried, and found Private Dussen's pup tent. He laughed it off. "I'll just get a few extra tours on K.P., Red." he said. "K.P. doesn't bother me like it used to last summer. Have some son-of-a-bitch."

This was a dish made by mixing water, bacon fat, and hardtack, then boiling it over a camp fire. Son-of-a-bitch was delicious when Pete Dussen cooked it.

Sterner discipline was handed out when the soldiers returned to the fort. Four men had hidden their equipment in the supply wagons and carried fake packs that were lightweight. For punishment, the culprits walked for two days from daylight until dark around and around the big parade ground, a brick in each pack in addition to clothes and equipment. I felt sorry for these men, especially when they passed the barracks in the late afternoon, because the soldiers relaxing on the porches jeered them.

Just before the beginning of my freshman year in the Nathan Clifford High School, there was a track meet on the fort's parade ground that split the officers down the middle. The meet hinged on the last event, the mile relay. The anchor man for the 51st Company was wiry Private McHenry, and when he received the baton he put his head back, his long black hair falling almost to his neck, and ran like a gazelle.

"I can stand losing," my father fumed when he came home at noon, "but Captain Jiggs Del Rio has his track team up on his porch in their track suits and is giving them cocktails. What is this army coming to? Cocktails for enlisted men on an officer's porch! Next you know they'll be telling us what to do."

I went to the Del Rios' to congratulate McHenry and to take a look. I came back to my father's study and said to him, "They aren't drinking cocktails, they are drinking sherry." He slammed the red book down on his desk and I moved out of there.

The next big event was Lieutenant Edwards' return after his marriage. I went down to the dock with the officers and their wives and most of the 37th Company. The soldiers were not in formation, they were at ease. There was a wait, and during it I sat on a pier and watched the sea gulls and listened to the gentle clang of the bell buoy. Sometimes the simplest things are best. A sea gull riding an air current is beautiful.

When the boat churned around the bend and docked, everyone cheered. Lieutenant Allen Edwards and his bride were placed on an artillery caisson draped in red, white, and blue bunting and drawn by two white horses. Edwards made a speech and said it was the greatest time on record. Everyone clapped and called on the bride for a speech, but she just blew kisses. The crowd followed the caisson up the hill, where the band greeted the couple with "The Wedding March" and led the procession to Lieutenant Edwards' quarters. He carried her over the threshold, his bad knee and all, to more cheers. For friends who remained late he served champagne and Zu Zus all around. The enlisted men got nothing. I drank Moxie. His bride was lovely, and I got to shake her hand.

The new Mrs. Edwards was the daughter of a wealthy man. At the end of their first month of married life Edwards told my mother, "My wife has no more idea of prices than a robin has of the North Pole. She went to the phone all last month ordering beef—steaks and roasts—and legs of lamb, without pricing them. I've never lived better. Put on seven pounds. At the end of the month when I looked at my commissary bill it was five dollars more than my monthly pay. I sealed my check back in its envelope, gave it to her, and said, 'Honey, here's my pay check. Please pay all our bills and with what's left buy yourself a present.' This month she's on the phone saying, 'How much are pork chops?'"

In school I was up against a blank wall: the Latin language. I fell behind and the teacher was concentrating everything on me. It was Latin by the bucket. I saw no use in it and I did not study much. When I did study I could not understand it.

After several months of holding the Latin teacher on the one-yard line, I came home one day in 1916 and found my father in front of the fire looking pleased. That morning when the horses had pulled the glass wagon around on its runners to pick up us kids, he had been unhappy. "The news makes you ashamed of our government," he had said, "allowing that bandit Pancho Villa to come on United States soil and murder seventeen Americans at Columbus, New Mexico. Finally Wilson has his nerve up and has sent Pershing after him."

Now the birch logs were snapping out sparks. I placed my mackinaw on its hook in the vestibule and kicked off my arctics. My father beamed. "Russell, get ready for a seven-thousand-mile trip. I've been ordered to Fort Kamehameha, Hawaiian Territory, near Honolulu. We leave in ten days. It'll be Boston, New York, Savannah, Atlanta—to visit your uncle and aunt, the Willifords—New Orleans, San Antonio, Texas, and Los Angeles. We'll have a week in San Francisco and sail from there forty-five days from today."

I thought of the Latin teacher. My spirits soared.

"May I stop school now?" I asked.

"No, indeed. School's very important to you if you want to become a West Point cadet. You'll miss a lot of school on this trip." (Delightful news.) "And you may be out of phase with Hawaiian schools when we arrive out there."

Suddenly it was easy to swallow the insults of the Latin teacher, even though he became more fierce every day. "You are the most beef-witted pupil in this class," he told me once, "bar none."

The Latin teacher did not know I was leaving. On my last day he said, "Reeder, I've arranged for you to be dropped from the basketball team. Tomorrow, after the last class, you come in here at three-thirty—and every day until you improve. You can catch the half-past six boat home. I'm not going to let you be a dunce. *If* you apply yourself," he paused, "I *think* I can hammer this Latin language into your head. I want to help you. I will see you tomorrow."

The accused nodded his head silently. It was a delicious moment.

At ten the next morning we sailed for Boston aboard a commercial liner, on the first leg of our journey. I felt superb as the ship cut blue water past Portland Head Light. I enjoyed a deck chair in the lee of the funnel, out of the way of the breeze, while the steward served beef bouillion.

I could visualize the scene when Taites told the Latin teacher the reason why I was absent. "I'm sorry, sir, Russell Reeder could not come to class today. He had to go to Honolulu."

The ship was making twenty knots—too fast to be recalled.

CHAPTER NINE

Nardi

THE BIG DECISION of the trip, as far as I was concerned, was made as we steamed down the Atlantic coast on *The Yale*. My mother said to my father, "I think Russell's tall enough for long pants. It's better for him to get used to them on the trip rather than when we arrive in Honolulu." American boys near the turn of the century wore knickerbockers. Long pants were a looked-forward-to milestone. In New Orleans my father took me to a store and when we came out I felt grown up.

We spent a day in New Orleans, and the wide, muddy Mississippi made me think of Bocker, and I wished I could see Jackson's Island, where Huck Finn and Jim hid out. By then I had already read *Huckleberry Finn* five times.

When our train of Pullmans rattled westward, Fred and I sat long hours in the carpet-covered camp chairs on the observation platform. You could watch the train tracks form a V, miles back, as we flashed along at about thirty-five miles an hour. When we stopped, bronze cattlemen came aboard wearing wide-brimmed hats and fancy high-heeled boots, the kind Strawberry McKenna wore on Sundays. I was entranced with the ranchers. The seafaring men of New England and the Texas cattlemen have in common an air of determination.

When the train puffed into the dusty Rio Grande country, we saw National Guardsmen on duty at bridges and culverts. We flashed by lonely sentries in olive-drab shirts, sleeves rolled up, wearing wrapped leggings and campaign hats. Near each bridge stood a pyramidal tent or two. "Those men are on guard," my father explained, "to make sure a Mexican bandit doesn't come along and blow up this track and wreck a train." This idea made the trip more enjoyable than ever.

Mother thought of sending Fred and me through the cars to gather up newspapers. We tied them with string and tossed them to the soldiers as we rattled by their lonely outposts. You could see this made a hit by the way the National Guardsmen scrambled for the papers and waved their campaign hats.

The sun made the new steel car we were riding in almost unbearably hot; air conditioning had not been invented. Fred, the porter and I played a game of seeing who could hold their hand longest to a steel panel of the car. Four days out of New Orleans we finally reached Yuma, Arizona, and the temperature hit 110 degrees. "Always hot here," the porter said, "but this is an unusual warm spell."

My father said, "There's an Old Army story about a soldier who was stationed here who died, and when he got to hell, he sent back for his blankets."

We got off the train and stood in the shade of the water tank while the engine took on water.

"Can you buy me a watermelon?" my father asked the porter.

"Yes, suh. They cost thirty cents."

The porter placed the melon on ice and we thought of it for three hours while it cooled. I am often disappointed in watermelon, but this one tasted as good as it looked.

The desert at sundown fascinated me. Purple mountains in the distance with peaks rimmed in silver, bluish-purple sagebrush stretching toward them. Alongside the train the sage was almost gray. A yellow light, way out there. Who lived there? Fifty, sixty miles, then another light. A far cry from life on an island in Maine.

In San Francisco we enjoyed one of the world's most beautiful sights, a sight that changed its mood many times a day, the San Francisco Bay. I went exploring, with Mother's permission, while we waited for the transport that would take us to Honolulu, and found the zoo and acres of flowers in Golden Gate Park, the aquarium, and the seals on the rocks. This was real freedom. Loose in San Francisco by myself—I'll never forget the feeling.

When the transport *Thomas* docked, I was ready to leave for Hawaii, even if it meant facing another Latin teacher. I wanted to see the grass huts and hula girls that Taites Morse had talked about.

Whitecaps escorted us out of the Golden Gate, and by the time we steamed by the Farallones, thirty miles out, a gale was blowing. I took to my berth and did not get up until my father sighted Oahu. We had been at sea six and one-half miserable days.

My knees were shaky as I leaned over the rail, but the excitement of landing took my mind off my troubles. There was color everywhere. The country looked black, with streaks of green cane and pineapple fields and gashes of red dirt. Wraith-like clouds crowned a purple mountain range. The ocean the *Thomas* was slicing through looked painted. Surf pounded on jet-black rocks.

"Those rocks were thrown up by a volcano," my father said.

I wondered if it were safe to land.

The *Thomas* rounded a huge mound of desert sand and then steamed past a tremendous crested head of land. "Diamond Head," my father said. "An extinct volcano. We have a mortar battery in there."

Surf curled against a long ribbon of white sand. "That must be Waikiki Beach," he said. "Those palm trees. Mark Twain said they looked like feather dusters that had been struck by lightning."

I was amazed. I did not know he knew about Mark Twain.

"I thought Mark Twain was smarter," Julia said. "They look like stage scenery."

I was disappointed when the *Thomas* nosed into the tiny harbor because I saw a modern city of fifty thousand. (I had to wait twenty-six years to see grass huts—in Fiji—and they were hardly worth waiting for.)

But I was not disappointed long, because when the ship docked, Kanaka beach boys swam to the off-dock side and dived for nickels and dimes people tossed overboard—other people. The boys bobbed like corks, quickly upended themselves when they went below for a tip, popped up, and placed the captured money in their personal cash registers, their mouths.

An officer met us with men to handle our baggage. We went ashore, past fat Hawaiian women selling leis, up Nuuanu Street, toward a valley that looked down from between the heights above the city. A rainbow shimmered up there. The people on the street were more varied than those in Buffalo Bill's Wild West Show. Chinese women in black jackets and black skirts, hair drawn back from their foreheads. Japanese women in bright kimonos, clogging along in wooden sandals with doll-like babies tied to their backs. Hawaiian women in tents that reached to their ankles.

"I think those long kimonos are called muumuus," Mother said. "I read that when the missionaries arrived they taught the Hawaiians that running around naked was immoral." I know that missionaries are necessary, but they can ruin beauty. I felt I was arriving a hundred years late.

We rolled slowly past a fish market. The smells seemed to be a mixture of everything. Barefooted Chinese, trousers rolled to their knees, scrubbed the concrete sidewalk in front of the market. Chinese drugstores advertised dried devilfish and preserved snakes in their windows.

We waited for the little train of wooden cars, painted red, near the Honolulu station. Nearby stood a banyan tree that would have accommodated the Swiss Family Robinson, and across the street scarlet hibiscus and African daisies crowded a courtyard. We seemed to have landed in the Garden of Eden.

Fort Kamehameha, named for the ancient Hawaiian king, had the important military mission of guarding the narrow entrance of Pearl Harbor, but to me it was a disappointment. The flat coral land was dazzling white. You had to squint. The ball diamond had a low chicken-wire backstop, a few benches, and gunny sacks for bases. I learned later that the Fort Kam baseball team played like that diamond. Pete Dussen and crew would have swamped them fifteen to nothing. The residential part of Fort Kam had one or two streets bordered by low bungalows and scrubby algaroba trees. My father was given a bungalow slightly larger than the rest because in about a month he was going to be promoted to major.

We put our baggage on the wide-screen porch called a *lanai*. A giant flying cockroach struck my father in the forehead. "Damn it!" he said.

A Japanese maid walked out of a hallway. She seemed to come with the house.

"I kill mosquito," she said. "I fix papaya, fish cake, pineapple, blanket. Me twelve dolla a month." She laughed and ran to the kitchen.

After we had settled at Kamehameha, my father made arrangements for me to attend one of the world's best-known schools: Punahou. This was not easy to do, because Punahou was selective and because only two months of the school year remained. Going to Punahou meant daily travel by bus, train, and two streetcars, but it was worth it. If I could have attended school there longer, I might be a lot smarter. The school had a reputation for snobbishness, but this must have been before my time; I was welcomed.

The grounds were a lush garden. At noontime we dipped in and out of Punahou's outdoor pool and ate our lunch beneath palm trees near a pond covered with water lilies. There was even time for a few kicks at a football with barefooted Hawaiian and Chinese-American boys playing on the athletic field.

Two famous teachers, "Dock" Bergman and Frank Midkiff, labored one after the other to teach me algebra. "Didn't you even have arithmetic?" Mr. Bergman asked me.

"Yes, but I never understood it after we passed the nine-times table."

In the summer of 1917, when school was out, my father said, "There's a company of infantry from Schofield going over to the volcano on the island of Hawaii. It's a two-week trip. Do you want to go?"

On the little inter-island boat I was congratulating myself that its buck and roll did not bother me, when a flying fish flew aboard. It landed with a thud on the deck, and its winglike fins made a rainbow in the sun. An Hawaiian deckhand caught it, bit it as I would an apple, and wiped a trickle of blood from his chin with the back of his hand. I rushed for the rail.

The boat put supplies ashore at Molokai for the leper settlement. Across the thirty-mile channel two snow-covered peaks, Mauna Kea and Mauna Loa, reached into a Prussian-blue sky, looking as if they were on a huge Japanese print.

We took the railroad up the steep sides of Mauna Loa through a jungle of ferns twenty-five feet high, and chugged upward through a forest of Koa wood. When the train stopped on a plateau, we hiked toward the volcano's crater and camped near it in pyramidal tents that were already pitched for us, not far from the Volcano House. A cookshack with dining hall, and a smaller house for stores, were available for use of the soldiers at this rest camp.

The first sergeant led us over toward Kiluea's fire pit. Each of us had a canteen riding on his hip. We had hobnails on our shoes so the rough lava would not wear out the leather. It had begun to rain, and a cloud of steam shrouded the tremendous pit. Steam also ascended from cracks in the volcanic rock. There was a heavy smell of sulfur. At night the fire pit's red glow made the place look like Chaplain Easterbrook's hell.

On the second day we hiked down a narrow trail inside the volcano to the bottom of the pit. An old Hawaiian guide led the column. Fountains of molten lava spewed into the air from the molten lake and splashed back. The short time the lava was in the air was long enough for it to cool slightly, and when it fell back, it formed small islands on the fiery surface.

Our guide produced a stick about twelve feet long, shielded his face from the intense heat, and thrust the stick into the glue-like lava. The stick burst into flames. He shaved off the hunk of black lava from the end of the stick and, with two smaller sticks, fashioned ash trays and desk weights. I put a quarter into one of the desk weights, and an hour later it was brittle as glass. It broke and the quarter rolled down a crack. I don't like lava paper-weights.

The guide took off his coat and tossed it aside. "Want to see jump?" he said to the first sergeant.

"Where the heck are you going to jump to?"

"Island." The guide pointed to a small island whose edge lay about five feet out in the molten lake.

"That's the dumbest thing I ever heard of," the first sergeant said. "Don't do it. You slip and you've had it."

"No danger. Pele not at home."

I knew that Pele was an ancient Hawaiian goddess. I was afraid that when the man jumped over the fiery five-foot gap and landed on the island, it might turn over. Every fifteen minutes an island did this.

The Hawaiian guide backed off and got ready to run.

The first sergeant said, "Wait a minute, brother! You're nuts! Before you go, tell us how we get back up. What trail do we use?"

The Hawaiian laughed. He sprinted for the molten lake and sailed over the lava to the island, then jumped back.

When I got back to Fort Kamehameha, it seemed to me my mother was larger. I said, "Are you going to have a baby?"

She nodded. In 1917 you didn't talk to boys about babies who had not yet arrived. I was worried about her and noticed that she stayed indoors a lot.

I had a summer job as an electrician's helper at Pearl Harbor Navy Yard, and one June afternoon when I came home from work, my mother met me at our door. She had tears in her eyes.

"Stay away from the house a while," she said. "The baby is about to arrive."

"Where are Julia and Fred?"

"They've gone to the neighbors – the Meyers."

I was frightened and worried. I went down to the Post Exchange and hung around there. Then I sat beneath a thorny algaroba tree near the green shack that housed the telephone central. I imagined all sorts of things.

When my friend, Corporal Dan Timberline, switchboard operator, came on duty, he said, "What's the matter with you?"

I told him.

"Come in," he said. "I'll let you run the switchboard and you can listen in. You operated pretty well last time."

It was interesting. By flicking a switch you could hear the conversations. All you had to do was to keep quiet. Dan stretched on a bunk and read a magazine. Pretty soon I heard a woman telephone another and say, "Have your heard about the fine new baby girl at the Reeders? The baby weighs . . . "*

I jerked off the headset, told Dan the news , and tore for home. I was so relieved to see Mother and that baby.

"We are going to name her 'Narcissa Pillow Reeder,' your father says. Her nickname will be Nardi."

The Japanese maid served supper to my father and me. He was as happy and as relieved as I. Sitting there with him at the table on the lanai, under flickering candelight, was a treasured moment. I went to see Mother and the baby again. I never saw two people look more contented. Both of them were beautiful.

We had pineapple sherbet later. My father said, "The war in Europe is worse. The United States hasn't helped the Allies worth a darn since we declared war two months ago."

"Why?"

*This baby grew up and married Thomas B. Campion and lives with him in Hanover, NH. She is a popular public speaker and a skillful writer.

"Because we are not prepared. I sent a cablegram yesterday to the War Department asking that I be brought back to the mainland and transferred at once to the field artillery."

I knew he loved the coast artillery and work around salt water.

"I sent the cablegram," he said, "because the coast artilery will see little action. I've been preparing to help the country for nineteen years. Now I have to go."

The joy over Nardi's birth almost vanished. I could see my father in a dish-shaped steel helmet, directing fire over the heads of the infantry at the Germans, with enemy artillery bombarding him. I felt as if I were being pulled apart.

CHAPTER TEN

What the Colonel Said That General Sherman Said

BEFORE WE LEFT our home at the entrance to Pearl Harbor, my father opened a map. "I want to show you," he said to us three older children, "where you're going to live while I'm in France. Marbury, Alabama, is thirty miles north of Montgomery on the line to Birmingham. I think you children won't miss more than four weeks of school."

"How big is Marbury?" I asked.

"About two hundred and fifty to three hundred people. I'm leaving you and your mother there because it's near your Aunt Susie and her husband, Judge Mayfield, and their family. Your uncle, Forrest Williford, is sending his family to Marbury, too. He's going to France to run a trench mortar school."

I went to Punahou for the first day of school to tell friends good-by. I was always telling friends good-by. When I left this magnificent school, I was filled with misgiving. I tried to visualize a high school in a town of two hundred and fifty people.

There is a saying in Hawaii, "The islands never let go." I believe it. If you have lived for a length of time in that garden of Pacific, you will always expect to return. I felt the islands' grip when we sailed from Honolulu for the mainland in the late summer of 1917.

RR— Quarterback
Marion Institute, Marion, Ala., 1919

The army dock was crowded with people. A military band played the thrilling new song "Over There" as paper streamers did their best to hold the transport to the pier. Finally the whistle sounded, and with the band moaning "Aloha Oe," the ship backed slowly into the harbor. We tossed our leis into the water in the hope this would bring us back. The music, the leaving of friends for the unknown, and the thought of my father on the way to war made it difficult to see Diamond Head as we steamed past.

After we had docked in San Francisco and made the long train trip to Alabama, my father left us at the Mayfield home in Mountain Creek and departed for the Field Artillery School in Oklahoma. His orders would then carry him to North Carolina so he could train a regiment of field artillery in the Blue Ridge Division. I knew he would come back to see us before he left for France, so I was not too worried.

I cranked up my Aunt Susie's new Model "T" Ford and she drove my mother, Julia, Fred, and me to the district school in Marbury, two miles from the Mayfield home. The school was worse than I had feared. It had only five classrooms. The principal pointed out a half-completed building nearby. "We'll be in a better and larger building next year," he said.

It was fun to be at the Mayfield's home at the end of the day because my uncle, Judge J. J. Mayfield, arrived from work in Montgomery on the 4:30 L. & N. train. He was a huge man–a member of the Alabama Supreme "bench," as my aunt called the court.

In a law class at West Point, years later, an instructor said, "Alabama has the best law code of any state in the Union."

"Sir, may I make a statement?" I said.

"Yes, what is it?"

"My uncle, Judge Mayfield, wrote that code."

"Well, Mr. Reeder, you certainly don't take after him."

When a house became available in Marbury, the Reeders, Mother and we four children, moved into it–one family, one roof. This new home was small, almost crude, but we were as happy as a family can be with its father away. He visited us a few days after his course in Oklahoma, then departed for North Carolina. After he had gone, a boy named George Grant said to me, "Have you heard the story Cap'n Billy McCabe is telling everybody about your father?"

I knew that Billy McCabe was one of the old soldiers from the Confederate Soldiers' Home near Mountain Creek. He visited relatives in Marbury on weekends and was the unofficial greeter at trains pulling into the Marbury railroad station. He was the man who became overly excited when *The Birth of a Nation* was shown to the old Confederates in Montgomery. At a crucial point Billy stood up in the theater, opened his knife, and threw it at the screen in an effort to save the heroine.

When we arrived at the station, George, not telling Billy who I was, said, "Hey, Cap'n Billy, how about telling this fellow what Colonel Reeder said?"

Billy wore a wide-brimmed hat, a denim jacket always open, a white shirt buttoned at the throat , but no necktie. He carried a cane and wielded it like a scepter. I was then five feet ten, and Billy came up to my shoulder.

He said to George, "You're no relation to General Grant, are you?"

"I should say not. Tell about Colonel Reeder."

"Colonel Reeder? Why, I know him well. When he was here last time he come down to meet Number Four to pick up a copy of the *Advertiser*. 'Can't miss the war news,' he said to me. I was standing right where that mail sack is, and he was standing where this coal-oil can is." Billy rapped the can a belt with his scepter.

"Colonel Reeder spied this." The Confederate touched brass letters, three-fourths of an inch high, that he sported in his left lapel: C.S.A. "'Military man!' Colonel Reeder says to me. 'I kin also tell by the way you hold yourself.' 'Yes, sir,' I says. 'Thirty-third Alabama—Colonel Sam Adams. I was his favorite scout, a corporal. Wounded in the laig at Tunnel Hill in sixty-four defendin' Atlanta by retreatin' from Chattanooga.' 'Scouting's very dangerous,' Colonel Reeder says. Then I said to him, 'Colonel Reeder, what do you think about the war in France?'

"'Well,' he said, 'Billy, one of your enemy gen'ls, Sherman, put the whole thing in a nutshell. He said, "War is hell."' That's exactly what the colonel said the gen'l said. I have to agree, even if an enemy gen'l said it. I tell you, with officers like Colonel Reeder, we can't lose the war!" "Cap'n" Billy McCabe pounded his cane for emphasis.

I could have hugged the old fellow. I wanted to laugh and agree at the same time.

When we were out of earshot, heading for the football field, George Grant said, "I've heard Cap'n Billy say that four times, and he never varies a syllable."

George Grant was one of the first Baptists to recognize us Episcopalians. Here was a little town of 250 souls, faced with a problem. It had two large Baptist churches and plenty of pew space. Suddenly the Reeders and Willifords, seven in all, blew in and asked to be integrated, but said they still wanted to remain Episcopalians.

War news in Marbury took a back seat. We attended church and Sunday school the first Sunday, but mother was asked not to bring us back until this crisis was settled. People stared at us on the street. It was marvelous, being a celebrity. Mother and Aunt Honey talked a young Episcopalian minister, Reverend Coffin, into coming from Montgomery to Marbury every other Sunday so we wouldn't be shut out completely. We moved furniture around and made our home into a little church.

Finally the Baptist council decreed that we would be permitted to attend their church and Sunday school, provided we did not spread Episcopalian teachings. They were safe as far as I was concerned. I was more interested in football.

GEN George C. Marshall, Chief of Staff; RR Jr.'s father, COL Russell P. Reeder; and COL Dobie, toastmaster—VMI alumnae dinner, Norfolk, VA, 1939.

The football squad in the Marbury High School consisted of about sixteen boys. This was not enough, so when we practiced scrimmaging, we had to aim the attack at only half a line. Not a blade of grass marred the field that was near a few acres of shacks housing Negroes, our devoted spectators. Mother, a natural-born rooter, was too busy with the baby to come and root for us. It was cold, muddy, and bleak on that field, and Marbury High was usually defeated, though we had an excellent coach.

Baseball was a different story, because there were more players. We were helped by Mr. Rudder, cashier in the bank, who liked boys and baseball. Mr. Rudder looked like pictures I saw later of Warren G. Harding, except that Mr. Rudder smiled most of the time. He bought our balls, bats, and gloves from his own pocket.

So we could play faster ball, George Grant and I hiked about three miles every Saturday through the woods to a country diamond near Verbena. The trouble was to get George off from work. On Saturdays his father made him saw enough wood for their fireplaces to last the week, and the Grants burned wood by the cord. I was happy Mother bought our wood and coal.

To free George, I appeared in the Grant's back yard early on Saturdays and we labored at a crosscut saw. At noon I ate from a paper sack while the Grants ate in their house, then George and I hiked to the diamond. I was a pitcher, strictly fast ball, and George was a catcher.

In July 1918 my father made a brief trip home to tell us good-by before sailing for France. The hands tore around the clock that weekend. At the railroad station he shook hands with Cap'n Billy and kissed us all good-by. He said what soldiers have said since the days of Julius Caesar and before that, "I'll be back." When the train puffed down the track taking him away, I felt a terrible lonesomeness. Now I was head of the family, but there is no substitute for a father.

After he sailed to France, in command of a regiment in the Wildcat Division, I kept close watch on the casualty lists in the newspaper. The lists are frightening things to read when there are names you do not want to see.

Suddenly, on the morning of November 11, the whistle in Mr. Marbury's sawmill began to blow. It blew and blew. Church bells began to ring frantically. I ran over the hill to town.

Clerks and everybody ran out of the five stores into the street. There was great excitement. "The war's over!" everyone shouted. The drugstore gave away free Coca Cola. The people went to church. Reverend Coffin, who was in town, held a private Episcopalian session in our house, and we gave thanks. This was one of the happiest days of my life. In about two weeks two wonderful letters arrived: Colonels Reeder and Williford were not among the 81,000 United States citizens who had given their lives.

CHAPTER ELEVEN

Wit on the Staircase

THIS AUTOBIOGRAPHY almost ended in March 1919.

I was out in raw weather in the country west of Marbury with George Porter hunting quail. It had rained five previous days and great pools of water lay about. A breeze swept the broom sedge and whispered through the longleaf pine, the temperature stood at forty, and the quail were not stirring. I arrived home at suppertime with no birds, wet feet, and a pain in my chest.

When I woke up five days later in a Montgomery hospital, I heard Dr. Blue, the surgeon, say to Mother, "I am confident this operation for empyema will save him. We'll take out a section of a rib, get the fluid out of his lung, and then put in a couple of drains."

A nurse in the operating room clapped an ether mask over my nose, and when I woke up, I was shouting, "Kiss me, Miss Jones." Miss Jones was the blond nurse. This was at a time when influenza pneumonia, measles, and other diseases, stirred up by the war, were sweeping the world.

When I left the hospital at the end of April, Mother showed me a check for thirty-five dollars she had received from the Sunday editor of a Norfolk newspaper. "I'm going to send this to old Keenie," she said. For years on end Keenie had tended bar at the

Casemate Club in the old fort at Fort Monroe. He did more than that. Before the footbridge was built across the moat near the Club, Keenie helped officers home late at night by poling his boat, *The Maid of the Mist*, across the moat. This saved the officers a walk to the other bridge. Because he was polite and accommodating, Keenie was a tradition in the old Coast Artillery.

"Keenie's ill and needs medicine," Mother said, "so I wrote up his story and his mint-julep recipe, and they sent me this." She waved the check. "Keenie can use it to buy medicine."

As soon as she had mailed the check, our own troubles with medicine arrived. The postman brought her a bill for one thousand dollars for my operation and my fifty days in the hospital. Of course there was no surplus with which to pay this bill.

Mother had a theory that if you need money bad enough, you will receive a letter in the mail, and when you open it a check will fall out. The catch is you have to *really* need it, you can't just think it would be nice to have it. In this case the need was acute—and her theory worked. Mother was studying the matter when, during the following week, she received $995, her share of an inheritance. "This is the luckiest thing I ever heard of," she said. "It makes everything come out even."

Graduation came a month later, and I was eighth in my class. When we ten seniors were seated on the stage, behind the footlights, the boys wearing white carnations on their Sunday suits, the girls red roses pinned to white dresses, it was hard to see the common people because of the glare. Judge Mayfield, in a stiff-bosomed shirt and black bow tie, was the orator at the podium. He roared out a twenty-minute message in old-style thunder, yet with humor. He could easily have been elected to anything. It was hard to remember what he said because I was a senior and was graduating—and besides I was intimately acquainted with everything he talked about.

Judge Mayfield was a busy man, and the principal asked him to step in his office for a conference with us after everybody else had gone home.

The Judge said to me, "Your Aunt Susan says you want to go to West Point."

"Yes, sir."

"How are his marks?" he asked the principal.

"Well—he *has* been handicapped by his illness. His chemistry

. . ." The principal frowned like a bird dog who cannot locate a quail that has been knocked down. "Of course, he has been to some famous schools. I guess what he needs is a cram school–a good cramming all around."

"Then he'll have to go to one," Mother said, "whether we can afford it or not. Can you recommend one?"

I was Exhibit A, but I had no more control over the proceedings than a corpse.

"I think I can help land an appointment to West Point," Uncle Jay Jay said, "and if he has to be crammed, I am for it."

The panel discussion ended with Mother's making an application for my admittance to a military school.

This preparatory school was well established, accommodating about four hundred boys. On my first day I was interviewed by the dean. He was a kindly soul who taught English in addition to deaning.

"How's your vocabulary?" he asked.

"My er-ah what?" I said.

"Vocabulary. The collection of words you use."

"It's fine, thank you."

"How's your spelling? Do you misspell many words in your themes?"

"I only use words I can spell, sir."

This stopped him. Later I realized that the dean was just another average mortal–another slow thinker. I discovered that when I am pressed and have no time to let my brain clank over a problem, I am sunk unless there is a prolonged discussion. I am brilliant *after* leaving a conference. The French have a phrase for this: *l'esprit de l'escalier*–staircase wit.

The dean scratched his bald head. "I guess that's all right, just using words you can spell." He did not know what a small herd of words I *could* spell. "We use the West Point system. A tenth of a point deducted from your mark for every misspelled word." This system limited exploring the use of words.

All cadets at the school were issued olive-drab woolen uniforms, complete with wrap leggings. The food was good, and I liked the place.

"We are making you a corporal," my tactical officer (an officer who instructs in military tactics and who is especially charged with enforcement of discipline) said, "because your father is an army officer." Recognition of ability is one of the most rewarding things in life, and for me it started at an early age.

The next day, during study hour, when I was alone in my room, a splendid physical specimen wearing captain's insignia on the shoulder straps of a neatly pressed olive-drab shirt walked in and perched on my table. He swung his legs back and forth. He had a wide grin and an easy manner.

"Satterlee's my name," he said with a brush at his stand-up haircut, "Coach Davy Lee Satterlee. Sit down. I'm an assistant athletic coach and a Tac. Why weren't you out for football practice yesterday? Your high school coach wrote me that you are a good football and baseball player."

"Sir, I'm a poor student. I've missed schooling all over. I've been to so many schools since kindergarten I can't name 'em. I think I'd better not play football. I'm going to concentrte on my studies so I can get to West Point."

The coach was not bothered by *l'esprit de l'escalier*. He had his answer ready. "I'll tell you what we'll do with you, and keep this strictly under your hat. You make a letter here in both football and baseball and we'll get you into West Point on certificate."

"What's that?"

"This school is accredited with the government. All we have to do is certify that your grades are over 80% and West Point will accept you without examinations, just a physical. I have connections in our academic department here. You make a letter in both sports and I guarantee that you get into West Point."

This was the best news I had ever heard. I could just see myself in a cadet uniform walking about the West Point Plain. I would study after I got there. The thing to do was to concentrate on football and baseball. On the football field I could hit those pass receivers, and the only criticism that Pete Dussen had ever given me in baseball was that I did not slide soon enough. I would start my slide about where the second baseman plays.

"Where do I draw football equipment?" I asked.

After practice, the head coach told me to stay. "Mr. Reeder—Red," he said, "you're a good passer but you are about as slow a runner as I've seen. We'll make you our regular quarterback, but you won't carry the ball. It would waste too much time."

At the end of the first month of academics I received a blistering letter from Mother. My father was back from France, and they were now living at Fort Leavenworth, Kansas, where my father was on the faculty of the General Staff College.

"Your grades just arrived," Mother wrote. "Your father and I were astounded. You made a forty out of one hundred in mathematics. How in the world do you ever expect to get into West Point with such marks?" My mother was not all sentiment; she saw the facts of life.

I beat it for Captain Satterlee and showed him the letter. I was breathing hard. He bit his lip. "That hound in the damned math department crossed me up," he said. "I'll fix him."

The next month my math grade climbed to 88. "Congratulations," Mother wrote. "This is the fastest improvement I ever heard of."

In the baseball season I had far less pressure on me to make good, because of my background with the 37th Company. When I was thirteen at Fort McKinley, the post team sometimes let me pitch the ninth inning if we were ahead, when they were playing teams from Portland, even though it infuriated the opponents. This was before Public Relations had been invented.

At the military school it took the coach all of two afternoons to decide that I was not a pitcher. "You can't throw a curve as good as my Aunt Kate," he said. "But you'll make the team because you can hit. I'm shifting you to first base. You are too slow covering ground."

I was sunk and went to my room and stuck my lips out like Dussen when he had to do K.P. Few mortals know what is good for them. I discovered later that if I wanted to play baseball seriously, first base was my position.

That spring our baseball team was rapping out ten hits or more each game, but we were not winning. Suddenly a pitcher reported from the hilly regions of the state, and things changed on the diamond. His name was Billy-Joe Mabry, and he could throw every pitch in the book.

But the pitcher was unhappy. One day after a game he said to me as we walked into the barracks, "It seems to me we waste a powerful lot of time here. I'm always setting in my room waitin' for practice. Mr. Satterlee told me if I got restless to go over to the library, but all they have there is books. I did like lookin' at a refined magazine, *The National Geographical*, with pictures about a place called Syria. I used to read a lot when I was a tadpole, but the best hitter at the mill told me it's bad for your battin' eye. Don't know about that, but I do know if you try to read on a train the print gets all jumbled up. That *must* be bad for your eyes. You like it here?"

"Well, yes. The food is good."

"I have a powerful hankerin' for black-eyed peas and hog jowl. Here they pass out too much store-bought bread."

Coach Satterlee cornered me after a practice. "We are changing roommates around," he said. "I think you can make Billy-Joe feel at home. We want him to stay, so we're rooming you with him. Do your best."

I moved into Billy-Joe Mabry's room and Coach Satterlee helped by giving Billy-Joe a Victrola that we wound up by the hour. "This will keep your mind off your troubles," Coach Satterlee said to Billy-Joe.

We enjoyed "Oh, How I Hate to Get Up in the Morning," "I'm Always Chasing Rainbows," "The Rose of No-Man's Land." and "Missouri Waltz." I kept the pitcher company in our room for three days while classes were going on. It made me feel bad that I was not missed in class. No one even bawled me out. On the fourth day I became bored with "Smiles," and told Billy-Joe he ought to sleep more, and went back to class.

I realized—later—that in the preparatory school I had been trading my parents' dollars for a baseball and football suit. Wit on the staircase. The school has long since reformed and turns out students well equipped not only physically but academically.

Soon after leaving it, I was riding on the New York Central along the banks of the Hudson River. The train clattered to a stop at a river station and the conductor yelled, "Garrison! Change to the ferry for West Point."

Here was the start of a new life. I was determined to succeed. I picked up my handbag and camera. The camera made a lump rise in my throat. Mother's Sunday-school class back at Fort McKinley had presented that to her as a memento of four years' teaching. She gave it to me when I left. "You might use this at West Point," she said. "I wish I had something more valuable to give you." I never had anything more valuable than that camera.

A large group of boys walked to the ferry with me. Across the broad river stood the granite buildings of the United States Military Academy. They looked formidable. West Point was much bigger than I remembered it. It was an odd feeling, starting a career.

A boy who seemed to know said, "That large building over there is the riding hall. When we're first classmen, seniors, we'll bring the horses over here on the ferry for cavalry tactics, because the roads on this side are mostly dirt and better for riding. But we won't get instruction in horsemanship until we finish our plebe year."

Another boy said, "What's 'plebe'?"

"That's what we'll be in about half an hour. You'll soon see how an upperclassman treats a plebe. Rough, brother, rough."

The thought of upperclassmen did not bother me, but I was already wishing I had studied books in the year that I "crammed" for West Point.

CHAPTER TWELVE

"Close Enough! Rassle!"

AN OFFICER TROTTED eight of us over to the West Point Cadet Store, where we were issued uniforms. When I put on my cadet uniform for the first time, I felt like Marshal Foch—at least I knew how he must have felt when he was made generalissimo of the Allies. Then I came to earth with a crash. I had to lug a mattress across the area to my room.

"And hurry back," a captain barked. "Draw the rest of your equipment and put your room in order! You are to be at infantry drill in forty-five minutes."

I carried to my room blankets, sheets, shoes, overshoes (Two kinds), bedroom slippers, socks, gloves—white and gray—underwear, bathrobe, laundry bags, full field equipment, white belts, black cartridge box, rifle, bayonet, armloads of small items, and the full-dress hat called a tar bucket. I never owned so much stuff.

I felt sensational wearing the tall tar bucket, 1812 model. It fitted perfectly, and its pompom made me look seven feet tall. The chin strap, I fancied, made me appear as fierce as one of Winfield Scott's warriors. I brought my rifle to present arms and looked at myself in the mirror.

The captain stuck his head in the room. I executed right face and presented arms to him.

"You don't present arms indoors," he said. "What are you doing, anyhow, admiring yourself in that mirror?"

"Yes, sir."

"Didn't I tell you about twelve minutes ago to work on your room?"

"Yes, sir,"

"Then why aren't you doing it?"

"Sir, I was getting ready to. I thought—"

"The answer is, 'No excuse, sir.'"

"Yes, sir. No excuse, sir."

"That's better." The officer smiled pleasantly and I felt relieved. Then he said quietly, "I am reporting you for failure to carry out instructions. I'm sure you are the first one in your class to be awarded six demerits."

That shook me up and I felt shakier studying the puzzling room-arrangement card. The last thing my father told me when I left home was, "Carry out the orders." I had been at West Point two hours and had already been reported for going against them. "*Awarded,*" the Tac had said, as if I had won a prize.

In twenty minutes the captain was back. He frowned at the articles I had placed on the shelves of my tall wall locker. "You are not carrying out instructions yet," he said. "The room-arrangement card says, 'Underwear will be folded *neatly*.' Start over again."

"New cadets, outside!" a major bellowed at the bottom of the iron stairs.

We stood on the Plain in hollow square in our new cadet uniforms. A July haze shrouded Storm King Mountain. Over Garrison, across the Hudson, rain clouds were drifting our way. We held up our hands and were sworn in as part of the United States Army. A band played the national anthem. I have never been in higher spirits.

After the ceremony an officer announced, "You new cadets will cause all of your incoming mail to be addressed, '*New Cadet*.' You are not cadets yet. You become cadets when you join the Corps at the end of August."

This seemed to revoke part of the oath. I was in a sweat to get to my desk and write letters home and to my friends warning them to be sure to send my mail marked "New Cadet Reeder."

When we marched to supper, officers alongside us, I realized that I had been at West Point for eight hours and had seen only one real cadet – a sick one, swinging along on crutches toward the Cadet Hospital. After supper we new plebes got the word: we would not receive summer training from a detail of upperclassmen; we would have officers over us instead. This was General MacArthur's decision – a break with long tradition. When I entered the Military Academy, it was being run by Brigadier General Douglas MacArthur. We did not know he was going to become a national monument; he was simply the "Supe" and a famous combat leader.

It was quiet because the upperclassmen were away, on leave or undergoing field training at Camp Dix, New Jersey.

We learned quickly that being broken in by officers was thought to be a disgrace. Tailors in the cadet store, waiters in the dining hall, civilian clerks at headquarters, groundkeepers of the Army Athletic Association, and other army men fanatically loyal to West Point, all took pains to tell us. They explained carefully how the erratic, young Superintendent MacArthur was sending the place to hell in a hack.

We had been plebes a month. On a rainy Saturday afternoon a group of us assembled in the ground-floor tower room in the old barracks. A small brass plate ornamented the otherwise bare walls: *This room was occupied by Cadet John J. Pershing, Class of 1886*. It was now occupied by the three largest cadets in the Corps: Denis Mulligan, Sam Strohecker, and Sandy Goodman – a Catholic, Protestant, and Jew. Sandy Goodman, 240-pound tackle from California, wearing an Army Athletic Association T-shirt and cadet gray trousers, was barefooted, and swaying in front of the fireplace, he was singing "Come on, Nancy Lee, letty go your blouse!" About twenty-five of us seated on the floor were clapping and bellowing the chorus, "Yacka hula hickey dula. Yacka hula hickey dula . . ." This was almost as good as the Follies of 1912.

Sergeant Pop Swartwood stuck his head in the door, grimaced and handed a plebe a special delivery letter. Pop growled, "Took this from the bugler of the guard," and he made it sound as if he had captured the letter.

I walked downstairs with Pop to his office in the moat of barracks because I needed a shoe brush and Pop as head janitor could give me one. What I really wanted, of course, was a chance to talk to Pop, who reminded me of the old sergeants who had been the boon of my boyhood. Pop Swartwood had been the first sergeant of the infantry outflt that captured Geronimo and looked it. He was about Sandy Goodman's size, well over six feet, but fifty pounds heavier. He walked with sort of an elephant lumber. He looked best on Sundays when he wore his black suit with a boy's cap of dark blue, the kind they wore at Groton in 1885. He perched the cap just above his forehead, and when he gave his angular old-soldier salute to a Tac, the little cap seemed to be some kind of crushed halo.

"I don't know whether I can make it through this summer or not," Pop groaned. "Plebes singing in barracks! Why, if them upperclassmen were here, you plebes wouldn't be singing, you'd be shining your brass. Your class'll never amount to nothin'. I served forty years and a butt in this man's army. I fought the Indians and the goddam Boxers, and I know what I'm talking about. The first three days you fellows come in, the officers buzzed around and put on pretty fair imitations of upperclassmen. But the officers tire, and when four thirty comes, they go home. You're having it easy. what you fellows going to do when you're at posts way the heck out there, like Fort Huachuca, Arizona, and have to take care of your men?"

The first few weeks I had felt guilty over "You are no good because you don't have upperclassmen breaking you in," but now I was enjoying plebe life too much to worry about it.

The rain continued, and the officers found it a problem to keep us indoors and occupied. It was hot. The Hudson Valley was a gigantic steam bath.

About one hundred of us were marched to room 112, West Academic Building, and as many as possible were seated at the little desks. I sat on the floor. I knew this was a writ room where some day, not far off, we would take written exams in math. It was barren except for blackboards and desks.

An officer handed out gray pamphlets. "These are the guard orders," he said. "You already know your general orders. You will be detailed to walk guard as sentinels during the academic year, about one guard tour every month. On page twenty you will see 'Special Orders for Privates of the Guard.' You have to know the first fourteen verbatim. It *says* that the next fourteen need not be memorized, but I advise you to do it."

The cadet behind me whispered, "He means when the big bad wolves come back from Camp Dix, they'll ask us to spout off all twenty-eight."

"When you think you are ready to be tested, come in the next room," the officer said.

I got comfortable, my back against the wall.

The orders seemed pure jargon:

> 4(a) (If a member of the first relief) to inspect when assembly for call to quarters is sounded, except on Sunday evenings when Y.M.C.A. meetings are being held. On these evenings to make my inspection immediately after the sounding of the second assembly.
>
> (b) (If a member of the second relief) to inspect as soon as posted (except on evenings when visiting in barracks is allowed) and also at the completion of tattoo.
>
> ....
>
> 6. To enter no room unnecessarily when inspecting but to open the door of each room on my post, ask "All Right?" and demand a prompt reply. To inspect a room not more than once during any inspection.

I skipped to "Things a Sentinel Should Know":

> 13.07. If while talking to any person on his post, a senior who is entitled to the salute enters, the sentinel immediately stops conversation with the junior, salutes the senior and awaits the latter's orders. If while conversing with the senior, a junior entitled to the salute enters, the sentinel does not salute him, but continues his conversation with the senior until finished, whereupon he salutes the junior and awaits the latter's orders.

My head was spinning. I liked Special Order No. 3 best: "To see that the front doors of barracks are locked." It was the only simple declarative sentence I could find.

After about fifteen minutes a cadet from Alabama stood up. "I'm ready to be tested, sir," he said.

The room buzzed with excitement. I roomed down the hall from this cadet and had had no idea he was a genius. He passed the test. We expected great things of him, but he could not meet the physical demands of West Point life. Within a month he was gone—resigned.

After about an hour I rose to be tested and was sent back for more study. In another half hour first call for supper derricked me out of that room, with three dozen others who could not bring themselves to memorize canned language.

In the middle of the summer I caught my first glimpse of General Douglas MacArthur, and I was disappointed. I knew he had led soldiers "over the top" through fire, across no-man's-land in France in 1918, and I had seen pictures of him in the war in dashing pose: crushed cap, snappy mackinaw, riding crop tucked under an arm, riding breeches and shiny boots, but now he wore his hair long, down the back of his neck. Later, at football practice, I saw him in an overcoat, sizes too big, that brushed his ankles.

But when General MacArthur came out to football practice, I felt his uncommon magnetism and force. He was almost like a mystic. He even knew the names of us second-team players. He stood on the sidelines in a game the first team had placed beyond defeat. We were about to kick off. I was the end near the sideline. He said to me, "Reeder, I want to see you make this tackle." There was no choice. I *had* to make the tackle. When General MacArthur told you something, you did it.

Once after we lost a game when with better play we could have won, we learned from our coaches that the Supe had said, "To be second best is to be defeated in war or in athletics. Even a tie is a defeat."

The coaches were awed by General Douglas MacArthur, although he seldom interfered. However, one day at practice he paced an irregular course down the field and marked an X in the dirt with his toe. Then he said to our fiery coach Charley Daly, "Right here is where the pass should be caught."

"Yes sir," Daly said.

General MacArthur was often a spectator at "breaking-through" practice—unarmed combat in football suits, held three times a week just in front of Cullum Hall. Under the football rules, defensive linemen could hit with their hands as long as their palms were open. To get around this, the linemen wrapped their hands with tape until they produced a "fist." The tackles could not only smash the offensive end across the line of scrimmage in the face, they were encouraged to, and were bullied if they failed.

One of the most unusual line coaches in Army's football history conducted "breaking-through" practice. This was "Pot" Graves, a barrel of a man who looked as if he had stepped out of a "gay-nineties" picture book. At practice he wore a gray turtleneck sweater that crowded his ears, and a gray cloth hat that rose to a peak, and he filled a pair of football pants until the seams almost split. At his command, gladiators took position:

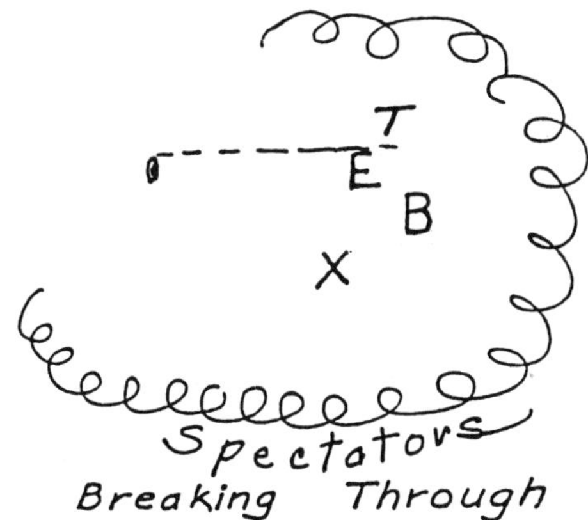

Breaking Through

When a cadet manager moved the football, the tackle charged and swung at the end's face. The tackle's job was to walk through the end and halfback to the spot marked X. The tackle's two opponents, who were dedicated toward moving him back, were handicapped because they could not use their hands.

"Blood! Blood! Blood!" Graves would howl at the tackles. "This practice has been going fifteen minutes and I don't see a single end with a bloody nose. This is a disgrace!"

When I crouched in the end's position, a tackle hit so hard he drove my own hand and forearm into my face. This was long before the day of the face mask. I staggered back into the spectators, my lip cut and tooth loose. Graves singled me out in a few minutes.

"Your face cut?"

"Yes, sir."

"Try to start faster, you're very slow. I'm sorry about your face. Let's see."

"My tooth is loose, sir."

"Well, see the trainer."

The trainer, Harry Tuthill, had prestige because in the summer he trained the Detroit Tigers baseball team.

"Tooth loose?" said Harry. "Tell you what to do, son. Tonight, take the handle of your toothbrush and push it back into place."

I did that and the tooth snapped off. Tuthill's prestige sank.

By November it was dark at practice, and there were no lights. Coach Daly mentioned this to General MacArthur. The next afternoon the general handed Major Daly a Very pistol. "When you want light, fire this," the general said. He made no explanation, and walked away.

At five o'clock it was so dark that the players looked like shadows. Daly fired the Very pistol. A star shell arched into the blackness and a white flare, supported by a tiny parachute, wobbled slowly to earth. Instantly the practice field was flooded by light from a battery of searchlights placed on old Fort Putnam, on a mountain high above the West Point Plain. It was so bright you felt as if you were looking into the headlights of the Twentieth Century's locomotive.

It was hard work in November. After practice, to ready us for the Navy, Coach Daly trotted us around Flirtation Walk, a rocky path bordering the Hudson River. I came into the gym after one of these mile-plus runs on a rainy day exhausted, and bumped into an upperclassman. I was puffing and covered with mud; his uniform was immaculate.

"Stand at attention, Mister! Why don't you look where you're going? Class of twenty-four?"

"Yes–sir."

He picked a gob of mud from his chest. "Gross! You people who never had a Beast Barracks!" He shook his head. "You'll never amount to anything."

The hundreds of disapprovers overlooked the fact that we had received training in discipline and in basic drills that plebe summer. In the long haul, over forty years, this class and the class after it, also deprived of the benevolent summer training by upperclassmen, produced one winner of the Medal of Honor, four generals, ten lieutenant generals, forty-four major generals, herds of brigadier generals, and swarms of colonels and lieutenant colonels. Maybe the officers in plebe summer did a better job than many realized.

I liked the Spartan life we were living. It did not bother me that there were no pictures on the walls of my room, no rug on the floor, that the bathroom was four flights below, and that we were restricted to parts of the reservation, and that no cadets got weekend leaves. Life at West Point in the twenties was especially rigorous, but I was making strong friends, and the time on the athletic field was a reward for a hard day.

Soon after plebe summer passed, stormy weather set in. Coach Davy Lee Satterlee's idea had placed me in the Academy; however, my plan for keeping up by intense study fizzled. I studied hard, or thought I did, but the galloping pace in math left me behind. We were covering college algebra and plane geometry in about forty-six lessons each. This was supposed to be a review, but you can't review something you are not acquainted with. The schedules showed that ahead lay advanced algebra, trigonometry and analytic geometry. Math was swamping me, and in addition I was playing football with a 1.9 average. (In grading, 3.0 was perfect; 2.0 was passing.)

Probably this was the only year in the Academy's history when deficient cadets were allowed to engage in intercollegiate athletics.

I hated to go to math, except when my instructor was the soft-voiced Captain Omar Bradley. He looked at you through steel rimmed glasses and smiled patiently. He was thoroughly interested in us. I once told him, years later, that I had a tremendous compliment for his leadership.

"What's that?" he asked. I think he expected me to say something about Africa or Sicily or Normandy.

"When you were teaching us math, I tried harder than I did for anyone else. I didn't want you to think I was a dunce."

The head of the math department, hard-working Colonel Charles P. Echols, inspired few, and if he did, it was through fear. He had been graduated from West Point twelve years before MacArthur. Colonel Echols was impatient. His rapid speech, high-pitched voice, fierce glare and superior knowledge made him seem like an angry wizard. He stood over six feet and was built like a top,

Colonel Echols marched into a large writ room one day when the lower part of the class was taking a written general review. The instructors were almost as much in awe of the angry man as the cadets. The captain at the desk near the blackboards shouted, "Section! Attention!"

The colonel returned the instructor's salute with a peculiar twist of his fingers. "Keep your seats, keep your seats!" he barked. "I came in here because I saw your grades in yesterday's work. Pathetic! I tell you, in this half of the class you are so stupid"—his voice rose almost to a shriek—"that you will fail in life unless you realize your limitations! Hard work is your only salvation. Go ahead with the examination."

I could hardly hold my pencil. This treatment, a holdover from bygone days, is a far cry from the relaxed attitudes of West Point classrooms of today. Later when he retired, Colonel Echols relaxed enough to be a good chess player. He was done to death by a hoodlum behind the New York Public Library one night in the thirties.

The pressure on the plebes increased. During the writs my marks, posted in the sallyport of barracks with those of other cadets, were frightening. Before a last writ I was detailed to walk guard in barracks at night. I needed time for study—about a month of it. Cadet Sandy Goodman went to see the Tac.

"Sir, I came to ask permission to walk guard tonight in place of Cadet Reeder, so he can study mathematics."

"No," the Tac said. "If you did, it might start an epidemic. Mr. Reeder will have to do his own duty."

When math class ended at nine thirty in the morning, we plebes were marched to the gymnasium. I liked best the classes where Tom Jenkins, former world's heavyweight champion, taught us wrestling in a large room covered with a soft mat. The mat was the only soft thing about his classes. His methods were as unique as those of his friend, Colonel Echols.

Jenkins was a paradox: the closest thing to a grizzly bear I ever saw, and as lovable as a bear looks. He even kind of sagged like a bear on his hind legs. If he could read this, he might say, "Lovable? Come here! I'm going to screw your head back on." This burly man, now far heavier than his prime weight of 198, had served a hard apprenticeship starting as a puddler in a Pennsylvania steel mill. In his day wrestling was violent. He had a glass eye that pointed askew, and he liked to make cadets think that he had lost it when his enemy, Frank Gotch, wrestled the world's title away from him. Tom would talk about Gotch, then say, "A gent that'll gouge out another gent's eye ain't no gent." He told this to generations of cadets. But he had lost his eye in childhood, when a toy cannon exploded one Fourth of July.

When our wrestling class stood at attention in front of Tom Jenkins, he snapped, "Fours, count off! Take distance, march! Odd numbers, about face. Shake hands." We were now in position to wrestle.

"I want you always to remember this: You don't have to be as big as the other fellow to win. Git that into your heads and keep it there even if you have to lock it up. What do you two cadets weigh?"

"One hundred and sixty, sir."

"One hundred and ninety-five, sir."

"Close enough! Rassle!"

It was always, "Close enough, rassle!" More than one cadet carried that lesson onto a battlefield.

One day Tom beckoned to me. "Git behind me and put your arms around my waist." This was quite an order for an average-sized mortal. He gripped my wrists and said, "I show you young gents what to do when your opponent has you like this." Then he threw his feet into the air and sat down. I was taken by surprise. My back felt as if it had been jerked in two, and I ended up in a position like a cartoon of an ostrich. A cadet laughed.

"Come here, you!" Tom released me and beckoned a finger at the offender. "You don't laugh at your classmates. The rest of you rassle at will. Mister, I am rasslin' you." This was the guillotine.

CHAPTER THIRTEEN

The Girl on the Piano Stool

THAT WINTER CADET Russell P. Reeder, Jr., failed to pass fourth class (plebe) mathematics.

After an incredible wait of twenty days following the examination, we cadets under suspicion of being extraordinarily poor students received our orders. The bad news arrived in mid-January, just before the noon meal. It was one of those days when the north wind sweeps the ice in the Hudson River, gathers up loose snow on the Plain, and blasts the barracks. My tactical officer sent for me.

"Mr. Reeder, you have been turned back without further examination to the next class. You are to proceed at once to your home at Fort Leavenworth, Kansas, and report back here on July 1, 1921, to join the next plebe class."

I reeled out of the orderly room. Old Sergeant Pop Swartwood greeted me. "Tough going, Red. Been waiting for you. The Tac give me the bad news ten minutes ago. I bet you feel like you're walking in a transom." (This made me feel slightly better.) "Oh, you'll be an army officer." Pop was more confident than I. "You cadets think West Point life is rough. Maybe it is at times, but when it's rugged it'll make things out in the service seem easy, except when you're fighting."

West Point had not been rugged for me. I liked the sweep of the Hudson with Storm King and old Fort Putnam standing guard, the friendships, the smell of the Plain in summer, the sound of tattoo played by the bugler of the guard a half hour before taps, my backbone getting straighter as well as stronger, and above all the way I felt when I stood in ranks with the rest of the Cadets, the world ahead of me and Battle Monument to the right of me. It seemed unbelievable that I was leaving a place I liked as much as West Point.

In the dining hall after the noon meal, the cadet adjutant called the Corps to attention. He held the official order at arm's length, as if he wanted to be as far from it as possible. "Attention to orders!" he shouted. ". . . The following named cadets, having been found deficient in one or more studies, will settle their accounts at once and will depart for their homes as soon as practicable: . . . Reeder . . ." The rest of the order sounded like a railroad engine grinding up a grade far in the distance.

I arose with other cadets whose names were on the order, put on my gray overcoat, and started for the door of the dining hall. It seemed a mile away. The Corps clapped—why I do not know.

By the time I reached the Grand Central Railroad Station in New York City, I felt even lower than I had when I left the Tac's orderly room. I thought of the hours I had wasted at the prep school. I could visualize my parents reading the telegram I had just sent from West Point: FAILED MATH. TURNED BACK TO THE NEXT CLASS. ON THE WAY HOME. LOVE . . .

In the gloomy railroad station a shabby man came up to me. "Buddy," he said, "I've just had uncommon bad luck. Can you spare me fifty cents?"

"Bad luck?"

"Yep. Everything I had planned on suddenly blew up in me face. Me whole life is changed. Here I am, down here in a railroad station, badly in need of a friend."

I calculated the money in my wallet. I had about twenty-five dollars more than I needed for the trip to Kansas. I knew how the man felt. Improbable as it sounds, I gave him ten dollars..

The bum took a step back. (That is, I realized about ten years later that he was a bum.) "Good heavens, sir! Let me give you a receipt! I want your name and address so I can return this."

We scribbled on scraps of paper which we exchanged.

"Your Honor, I live in Stamford, Connecticut. The very moment my luck changes, I'll mail you a check. God bless you!"

Either the mail is not dependable out of Stamford, or that fellow has had a most unusual run of bad luck.

My parents took my misfortune better than I had expected. Mother cried a little, then said, "I know you'll make good when you go back." My father said, "The thing for you to do is to study. I have made arrangements with a Mr. Bruce, in Leavenworth, to tutor you in math twice a week. Then there's a Colonel Thiers of the French Army on the faculty here who holds a French class three nights a week. You'd better go to that with your sister Julia."

My notes do not show what other subjects I studied. I must have at least read Shakespeare. I know I kept on with Mark Twain.

Colonel Thiers, tall and resplendent in his red-trimmed uniform, was efficient and humorless. He made French seem like Old Icelandic. The Kansas winter winds blowing against Julia and me after we left his classes at ten at night and trudged toward the bluff above the Missouri River where our house stood seemed almost a continuation of the classroom atmosphere.

I was the only male in the class. At the end of the spring term, the ladies proposed that we each donate ten dollars for a present for Colonel Thiers because of the long hours he had devoted to us and to the French language. I was happy to give him a farewell present. The money was collected, and on the hottest day in a hot May, a committee of three ladies traveled to Kansas City with the gaunt colonel to select his present. Julia was on the committee.

When the group left the interurban streetcar in Kansas City, the chairman of the committee said, "Colonel Thiers, tell us what you would like best. As you know, we have one hundred and forty dollars. We hope you'll select a present that will remind you, when you are back in France, of your days at Fort Leavenworth and of the sincere appreciation of our class."

Colonel Thiers bowed and touched the black visor of his red-and-gold cap. "*Mesdames et Mademoiselles,* I have been doing research considerable from ze *Kansas City Star.*" The colonel pulled a penciled list from his pocket. "It would be gratifying for me to have *les* presents in series. Notice my list is careful not to embarrass ze treasury of one hundred and forty dollars."

The committee stared at the list of fifteen items ranging from one suitcase at $27 to two neckties at fifty cents each.

"Colonel!" one of the ladies gasped. "Don't you want one present—say something in silver—something you can always keep?"

"Indeed not. I prefer *les* presents assorted." He tapped the list. "In all respects *très* substantial."

The committee and the colonel started out. By suppertime they dragged back to the car station laden with presents, the ladies exhausted. They waited beneath a "Coca-Cola" sign. Heat waves were rising from the street. The temperature stood at ninety.

"Everything is," the colonel said, "rewardableness. You recall, '*qualité de ce qui est digne de récompense*.' And now may I trouble you for the unexpended ninety-five cents?"

Math classes under Mr. Bruce, principal of the Leavenworth Colored Schools and semi-retired math genius, went smoother. However, I was more interested in playing first base for the Soldiers' Home Team than in a slew of analytic methods.

After my second game for the Soldiers' Home, the *Leavenworth Times* made a bad printing mistake. I had rapped out four hits in four trips to the plate, but the *Times* placed a string of zeros after my name. I was sick over this, especially when I thought of how newspapers are permanent records.

I used to ride out to the baseball park on the roomy interurban streetcars that whizzed along so fast they made the telephone poles seem like a picket fence. Once I sat beside an old soldier who wore a black hat and a blue uniform with a lead G.A.R. (Grand Army of the Republic) in each lapel. We became chummy. I was so cocky over the way I was playing ball that I said, "What do you think of the new first baseman out at the Home?"

"I think he's a louse."

"Why?" My mouth dropped open. I was sure my ears had tricked me.

"Last Sunday he could have caught a foul fly, but he quit because it was near the grandstand."

I stopped talking baseball with him. This was the last time I ever discussed myself with anyone unless I was absolutely certain they knew to whom they were talking, and I also started catching fouls.

One Sunday when I walked out of the dressing room and through the crowd of hangers-on after a game, a stocky gray-haired man wearing glasses and a neat blue suit with bow tie to match stopped me.

"I'm Dr. Darrah," he said. "I know your whole family. Come on, jump in my Chandler and I'll take you by my house for a little refreshment, then I'll run you home."

We sat in Dr. Darrah's den enjoying the spring breeze that was pushing aside the lace curtains at the window, drinking homemade root beer and eating cookies from Mrs. Darrah's oven. I felt important explaining the fine points of the game to one of the principal figures of Leavenworth. He had his own ideas and was a hard man to correct. We moved into the music room, where I met his two lovely little girls, Dort and Jane. Dort had black hair cut in a Dutch bob, and sat on the stool at the piano with her legs twisted around it. I did condescend to speak to them, and tried to talk more simply so they both would understand. If I could have looked into the future, I would have paid far more attention to them, especially to Dort, because she was the girl I married.

Finally, in midsummer, I headed again for West Point and the Hudson Valley. On my way I went to the Yankee Stadium to see Babe Ruth hit a homer against the St. Louis Browns. My seat was right behind the Brown's dugout. I was enjoying Babe Ruth, soda pop and peanuts. The Yankees filled the bases, and the Brown manager decided to try a new pitcher. The announcer, now at the plate, tilted his megaphone up toward the crowd and announced, "Ladies and gentlemen, attention please! Grant now pitching for St. Louis."

Grant? I paid little attention to Grant, because I was more interested in Ruth, his peculiar little mincing steps and his power swing.

When the inning was over and the Browns trotted into their dugout, I almost fell out of my seat. The pitcher, staring straight at me, was George Grant from Marbury, Alabama. I had not seen him since that summer when I worked with him at his father's woodpile on Saturday mornings so he could have time off to play. I could not understand the set look on his face as he ducked into the dugout.

After the game I waited for George Grant outside the dressing room, and then we headed for a steak. We brought each other up to date, and then I said, "George, why didn't you give me some sign of recognition when you saw me sitting behind your dugout?"

He smiled and drawled in his soft voice, "Well, I thought you might not like to associate with a ball player."

Back on the West Point Plain I felt a little out of sorts because I had to repeat the plebe summer training. But there was no time for post mortems, because the Commandant made me an acting company commander. "You help break in your new classmates," he said.

CHAPTER FOURTEEN

Beat the Navy!

AT THE END OF THE SUMMER on the day before classes started I staggered back from the cadet store to my room with a load of textbooks. "Mr. Reeder!" the cadet officer of the guard bellowed from the first floor of barracks, "Visitor at the guard room!"

I struggled hurriedly into my full-dress coat and ran across the area. It was Bocker. He looked frail and a bit stooped, but his eyes shone as they had at the Memphis track when Mr. Ben Peters came up a winner. He kissed me and I was almost stabbed by the whiskers in his neat gray mustache. "You look great in that Confederate gray uniform," he said.

I was certainly not going to tell *him* that it had been the West Point color since the War of 1812.

"How old are you now?"

"Nineteen."

"Are you going to win that gold watch—no smoking, drinking or chewing till you're twenty-one?"

"I sure am."

"By God, I knew you had it in you. Proud of you. If you have time I wish you'd take me to a place where I can buy some tobacco."

"That's easy," I said.

RR, "Turkey" Jones, Bill Wood, and Bob Owings gather for a night on the town, Baltimore, 1923.

I had only a few hours with him and I felt hurried because I wanted all my friends to meet the world's best grandfather. I did my best about that and did manage to talk to him a little.

When I walked with him to the top of the steps that lead down the hill to the railroad station, I felt sad. Something told me that I would never see Fred Martin again, and I never did.

A beautiful girl and a cadet in full dress passed. Bocker said "The most fascinating thing in the world, outside of a railroad train, is a woman."

He kissed me good-by, tipped his hat, and said, "Here's a little rhyme I made up on the train this morning. 'A smile and a kind word said are worth more'n a ton of roses given to the dead.' I hope you'll remember that."

I watched him go down the granite steps toward the power plant, then ran back to barracks. The drums and bugles were sounding first call for parade. The entire Corps of twelve hundred cadets, back together after the summer, was to be reviewed by General MacArthur. The general looked the same, hair reaching down the back of his neck.

When I saw General MacArthur a few weeks later, he looked as if he had just come out of a military Tiffany's. He sparkled; that's the only word for it. "Pink" cavalry breeches with just the right flare. Sam Browne belt, newer than new, matching his shiny Peal boots. You could almost see your reflection in them. He had a new cap and his hair was cut almost as short as a cadet's.

After supper, before the bugle sounded "Call to Quarters," summoning us to our books, I ran into Cadet Jerry Galloway near the French Monument. I had already discovered he was one of the smartest boys in the plebe class.

I just saw General MacArthur," I said. "Man, was he dressed up!'

"He's been that way for a week," Jerry said. "He's courting a widow from Philadelphia name of Mrs. Brooks."

Some months later each of the twelve hundred cadets in the Corps received a small white box, about three inches long, tied with a red, white and blue ribbon. Inside was a piece of wedding cake and a card: "Best wishes from Brigadier General and Mrs. Douglas MacArthur."

In July 1922 a new superintendent came to West Point, Brigadier General Fred Sladen, who, like General MacArthur, was a World War I hero. In comparison to MacArthur, Sladen seemed rigid and severe. "He's going to bring back summer camp and a lot of the old customs. He may even place the chain back across the Hudson River," the rumors ran. The two generals were opposites. MacArthur was brilliant and far-seeing, and no West Point graduate ever loved the Academy more than he. Sladen was able to get down to small things, and West Point became extremely military. On General Sladen's first Saturday he ordered an inspection of all post transportation. When his adjutant told him that the vehicles were assembled in the riding hall, the general said, "I will hold the inspection next Saturday. Without seeing the transportation I know it can be cleaned up better. Another week's work will probably make it sparkle."

When word of this reached cadet room No. 121, Cadets Garbisch, MacLaughlin and Reeder worked harder on their brass.

Both superintendents backed our athletic teams firmly, and that meant a lot to the players. The Army in 1922 had not beaten the

Part of the Army football team enroute to Yale Bowl, 1922. R. to L.: (1st row) R.R., Ralph Glasgow, Sandy Goodman, (2nd row R) Babe Bryan

Navy in their last three football games. Signs appeared about the post spurring on the football team. The one we cadets liked best—1200 MULE TEAM—seemed to personify the spirit of the Corps.

The first day of practice our dynamic coach, Major Charley Daly, said, "West Point has not won a major game since the war. We play some hard teams on this schedule. It's going to take intensive work on your part to defeat even one of them. We want to win as many as possible, but I tell you right now the mission is to beat the Navy."

We played on the field just north of Bartlett Hall, the old east academic building, where the Army Athletic Association had bleachers for fifteen thousand. On September 30 there was a doubleheader. The first team rolled over Springfield College 28 to 6. I got into that game for a minute or two near the finish as a substitute end because of an injury to a first-team player. At the end of the game, the first team went in and dressed and we second-team players went out to meet the team from Lebanon Valley. The game was about five minutes old when people began to realize that the coaches may have made a mistake, or that we second-teamers were below par. After a Lebanon player had run a punt back fifty yards, we could hear cheerleaders going through the crowd shouting, "First team return to the dressing room! First team return to the dressing room!" This was embarrssing. The half ended, Army 6, Lebanon Valley 0. The coaches blistered us in the dressing room. The cheerleaders trotted three first-stringers into the room: Ellinger a guard, and two halfbacks, Warren and Gillmore.

"These are all I can find," the head cheerleader said.

"Hurry up and get dressed," Major Daly said.

When these three stars entered the game, we scored again, but the coaches were not pleased. We eked out a victory, 12 to 0.

Three days before the game with Kansas University Major Daly caught a bad case of influenza. The doctors announced that he could not go to the game on Saturday. This was before radio broadcasting, so the Signal Corps erected temporary telephone poles across the Plain and stretched telephone wire to the Dalys' home, next to the Roman Catholic Chapel.

Captain Vernon Prichard, former star cadet quarterback and now an assistant coach, started relaying the game over the phone. The game went against Army. The K.U. rooters were moaning their singsong "Rock–Chalk–Jayhawk" yell.

"Our Charley Lawrence made a mow-you-down tackle," Prichard yelled into the mouthpiece. "Oh! Oh! Look at that! That K.U. back, McAdams, is dangerous. Sixteen yards around end."

Mrs. Daly cut in. "Vernon, this is Beatrice. I'll have to ask you to hang up. Charley's temperature just went up five degrees."

Army managed to win, 13 to 0.

One of the football players who was also one of the most interesting cadets in the Corps was John ("Honest John") Pitzer of West Virginia. He was rough-looking and popular. The cadets said he was "almost" human. He had a powerful build, a devil-may-care attitude where everything but football was concerned, and a

Team captain RR with Head Coach Moose McCormick, famous Giant pinch hitter, watching the Army baseball team in practice, 1926.

sense of humor. Once when the area of barracks was swarming with cadets who were forming into small groups so they could be marched to class, a cadet pinned a dead mouse, suspended by a string, to the back of Pitzer's gray dress coat.

A shout of laughter went up from the ranks. Pitzer, out in front of his section, knew something was wrong, but he didn't know what. He said to his section, "You fellows stop laughing. If you don't, Old Honest John will report you."

On reaching the classroom, Pitzer lined up his section of ten cadets at attention in front of their desks, saluted and reported to the instructor, "Sir, section 5-A present."

"Take seats," they were told.

When Pitzer about-faced to take his seat, the instuctor said, "Mr. Pitzer, what are you doing with a mouse on your back?"

"Mouse!" Pitzer sprang into the air and ripped off his dress coat. When the laughter had quieted, he said, "Sir, I dunno who did this, but if I find out I am going to be reported for murder."

Everyone was interested in Pitzer and everything he did. About two weeks before the Navy game he complained to an assistant football coach, "This is the fourth year I have been on this squad and you haven't played me against Navy yet. You keep moving me from guard to tackle, then from tackle to guard. As soon as I'm set in one position, it's 'Pitzer, you're transferred.' I want to play in the Navy game and I've earned it."

The next day Charley Daly said in his clipped Boston accents, "Pitzer! I am going to play you against the Navy—at end. That is if you'll lose some of that fat. How much do you weigh?"

"Two hundred and twelve, sir."

"A good weight but too much of it's fat. You bring yourself below two hundred, and if you learn the end assignments, you will be inserted in the Navy game."

Pitzer worked out as an end. He spent hours in a steam room in the gymnasium that was used to shrink wet football uniforms. I went over to see him on a Sunday afternoon. He was perched near the ceiling sitting on an asbestos-covered pipe. A blanket hooded his head, another was around his bulky shoulders. On an adjacent steam pipe, under an electric light, was an economics text book. Perspiration streamed down his dark-skinned face. He looked like a huge buzzard.

"Red, I'm down to two hundred two. I think by tonight I'll make the weight. Get me a tumbler of water, will you? Christ! I'm sweating all over this economics book—and I mean perspiration."

The post seethed with excitement as the Navy game approached. Midnight rallies were held, and the players got little sleep. Major Daly went over the characteristics of the fine Navy players with us: Conroy, Tom Hamilton, Norris, and Steve Barchet. "You let this Barchet loose," Major Daly said, "Then the best thing for you to do is to line up for a Navy point-after-touchdown."

Fifty-five thousand crowded the University of Pennsylvania's new stadium for the game.

The lead in this 1922 Army-Navy game changed sides five times. Just before the half ended, Ed Garbisch, one of the best players in West Point's history, sailed the ball across the bar by a place kick from the 48-yard line. But Navy led 7 to 3.

At the half, Daly was furious. "Only the first team and me in the dressing room!" he shouted.

"Who'll start the second half?" an assistant coach asked.

"The team that just came out will start." Daly slammed the door.

Pitzer said to me, "Well, I got inserted, but after me learning all about you damned ends they put me in as a tackle!"

In the last quarter, with three minutes to go, the West Point cause seemed hopeless. Shadows crept over the field. The Navy was in front 14 to 10. Colonel Herman Koehler, West Point's famous Master of the Sword, paced up and down the sideline. A policeman chased him back. Koehler sat down beside me on the bench and shook his finger at me. "There's nobody in heaven if we don't win this game. We are outplaying them." I agreed, but I did not want to be bothered by a colonel. I wanted to get in the game.

The clock was racing. The Navy punted and Cadet George Smythe caught the ball and ran all over the field. You could not hear yourself yell. After the Navy finally tackled him, the officials brought the stakes forward 50 yards. Then Smythe tossed a bullet pass to Timberlake and we were in front, 17 to 14.

Now the clock slowed down. Navy began to roll. Midshipman Norris sprinted eighteen yards. Colonel Koehler charged to the sideline and brushed the policeman back. Then the gun sounded.

Tim Cohane wrote in his *Gridiron Grenadiers*, "The crowd was limp and the coaches were ready for a sanitarium." Major Daly was so excited he remained in an upstairs dressing room and sent

Assistant Coach Bob Neyland to the squad's dressing room with a message, "Tell the players I am too wrought up. I don't think I can face them. Give them my hearty congratulations."

When Neyland delivered the message, the players, half undressed, stood at attention and gave Major Daly a Long Corps yell. I was disappointed that I had not played, but not for long. It was a great Army victory.

CHAPTER FIFTEEN

Baseball Bats and Brickbats

AFTER THE FOOTBALL SEASON I placed myself on the math rack. We yearlings were alternating analytic geometry with descriptive geometry—one subject one day, the other the next. The prize was Christmas leave, and to obtain it I had three star cadet coaches laboring over me: Thomas "Pop" Harrold, Frank Steer, and Bruce Clarke. *Analytic Geometry* by C. Smith was hard to understand. I was almost safe at home when I stumbled.

Bruce Clarke saw my marks before I did. "Bad news, Red. You blew that last analit writ." He produced a note with my written general review grades on it. "You have to make a 2.4 on the last descript writ on Monday, or . . ."

I sat down hard. "Whew!" I could see the class going on leave with Cadet Reeder staying behind to take the final exam.

"I'll help you all I can, Red. Are you willing to gamble?"

"How?"

"Knowing these instructors, I have a hunch that the last writ will be on the intersection of a cone with a cylinder. We might concentrate on that."

"You're my coach."

I did not now what a cone was doing intersecting a cylinder, but Clarke taught me how to draw and figure it, regardless of how it was shown, right or left, upside down or cock-eyed.

On the morning of the last writ we got up before reveille so Bruce could put me through descriptive geometry infield practice one more time. I went to the first math class right after breakfast carrying a fistful of sharpened pencils.

Bruce Clarke was scheduled to take the same writ during the second hour. He was standing in ranks with other cadets ready to go to class when I ran through the sally port giving a Siwash Indian war whoop. "It's the intersection of a cone and a cylinder," Bruce said to a friend. I like to think that it was this ability to look into the future and come to a decision which let General Bruce Clarke beat the Germans in the Battle of the Bulge in World War II.

It was a great feeling, floating down the hill in the snow to go on that Christmas leave.

When we returned, French and English made life enjoyable while I fought off Granville's *Differential and Integral Calculus*.

I kept an eye on Doubleday Field, the baseball field named after the Civil War general. About the time the snow melted and a confused robin flew into West Point on reconnaissance, the temperature dropped and it snowed again.

Spring really came for me on the first of March, for that was the date when John B. ("Hans") Lobert, former New York Giant baseball player, who was our coach, reported at West Point for duty. A dozen of us received permission to walk down to the river to the West Shore Railroad Station to meet him. He was a favorite, respected by almost everyone on the post, a harmless practical joker, and a wit. Ring Lardner obtained many of his baseball stories from Hans Lobert. Lobert influenced my life. My day began when I pulled on my baseball uniform and reported to him. Cares fell away. He looked on the bright side. In practice and during a game he barked his peculiar battle cry, "Yea Hah!" It was his signature, a cry adopted by his players. I liked his nose because it reminded me of a rudder in a rowboat.

Hans Lobert, as a young National League player, held the record for time around the bases and once before an exhibition game in Havana he sprinted around the bases against a race horse. The finish was close; the man and the horse were neck to neck. Then the announcer yelled, "Lobert wins by a nose."

At first I did not know what to make of Lobert. He was a master with a fungo stick, and one day at infield practice a ball he hit took a bad hop and banged me on the chin. I went down. In a moment

I staggered up, my chin cut. I expected sympathy, but Lobert, near the plate, was pumping his arm up and down and shouting in glee, counting me out as if I had been knocked down in a prize fight. "One–two–three–four–five . . . nine–ten. You're out!"

I threw the ball at him angrily as hard as I could, and missed.

"Go on in to the showers," he said. "You couldn't hit me with a handful of grapeshot."

That night at the training table I had my eyes on my beef soup when I heard Hans enter, talking to cadets at the other end of the table. When he walked down the table, he clapped me on the back and shouted, "Red, old dog, how are you?" I spilled soup all over myself. How can you be mad at a man like that?

Mother visited West Point and enjoyed Hans Lobert and our games. My parents had been ordered to Honolulu, and she charged him and almost everyone she met with keeping an eye on me. She seemed to smell trouble ahead. "Take care of my boy Russell," she must have said to fifty people.

The only one who took this seriously was Sergeant Neal Sullivan, Lobert's groundkeeper. Sullivan checked me often. "How are you doing in your studies?"

"I'm three tenths deficient in math."

"Who's the head of that department?"

"Colonel Echols."

"Why doesn't he wise up? What's the matter with that dodo?"

It was refreshing to be around Sergeant Sullivan.

In the middle of the baseball season I received a wire from Bocker and Lallie: DO YOU WIN THE GOLD WATCH?

I wrote back that I did. Three weeks later Brigadier General Merch B. Stewart, Commandant of Cadets, sent for me. His face was wreathed in a grin as he closed the door. I wondered what was up. He handed me a beautiful gold watch and chain engraved with my initials and *"Reward from Grandfather."*

"Your grandfather wanted me to present this to you at a parade before the Corps. I thought you would much rather receive it here in my office."

"Would I? Thank you, sir!"

I took that watch to show my friends Major and Mrs. O. J. Gatchell, whose home overlooked the Hudson. This instructor and his wife were genuinely interested in us. In the course of a year the Gatchells influenced and entertained scores of cadets.

When summer arrived, we yearlings (sophomores) were given a three month's furlough. What a feeling! I decided to visit my family in Honolulu, but I had twelve days to use up before the ship sailed from San Francisco. So I went with classmates to see the Ziegfeld Follies. I really enjoyed those girls, and I thought of staying in New York, hoping that I could meet some of them. But after a conference with myself, I decided I had just enough money for my trip, and that Follies girls were for millionaires.

An advertisement in the paper said you could choose any railroad route you wanted on a round trip across the country. I went to the Grand Central Railroad Station and said to the clerk, "I want to go to Chicago, St. Paul, Kansas City, Little Rock, Dallas, Fort Worth, Amarillo, Denver, Cheyenne, Salt Lake City, Reno, and San Francisco. I—"

"Hey! Write all that out for me, will you, bub?"

"I want a return trip on a beeline from San Francisco to West Point, New York."

"What are you, a salesman?"

"World traveler."

My ticket was eight feet long. The clerk timed my trip so that it took eleven days and I spent half a day and a night in San Francisco before I sailed. This trip cured me of train travel.

The voyage to Honolulu was more pleasant than my first one had been because the Pacific was like a blue lake. In Hawaii my parents were now living in style at Fort Shafter, for my father held an important position on General Summerall's staff. It was great to be home. Fred wore on his swim suit the hardest-to-win insignia in the islands, the paddle and O of the Outrigger Canoe Club, and we four Reeder kids spent days at the beach at Waikiki.

Mother was bent on seeing that I had the best furlough possible. She had five pretty girls lined up for me to take out. She gave a swimming party for me on the post, and we danced alongside the pool in the moonlight to accordion music and the soft strains from Hawaiian guitars. The tables held more fried chicken than I had seen since we were on the Northern Pacific heading for Memphis.

The next party Mother gave caused trouble. It was not her fault.

She said, "I want to give a swimming party on Haleiwa Beach, the other side of the island."

There was no place at Haleiwa for the men to undress, so a captain with a skeleton key solved the problem by unlocking the vestibule of an Hawaiian church.

After our swim, a Kanaka sheriff weighing three hundred pounds, who was sitting on the church steps, said, "Give your names and don't change 'em. I got your automobile numbers."

He reported us, and when we got back to Fort Shafter I thought it best not to mention the sheriff, even though this line of action had not worked when I tripped the gun at Cow Island.

Two days later my father came home to lunch and said, "Did you undress in an Hawaiian church?"

"Yes, sir," I said.

"So did some captains and lieutenants," Julia said.

My dad looked worried. He was not as used to trouble as I was. He handed me a typed letter headed, "Office of the Inspector General, Hawaiian Department." The letter told all about our mistake.

"You are in serious trouble," he said. "You have until tomorrow morning to answer this charge. There will be a formal investigation, and if you are thought to be guilty you will be court-martialed. I am very sorry."

Mother was upset. She took me to one side and said, "What will they do?"

"The worst thing that can happen," I said, "is that they can make me walk the area at the beach at Waikiki."

I took the letter upstairs and printed my reply with a pen:

Fort Shafter, T.H.
July 15, 1923.

Subject: Entering Church
To: The Commanding General, Hawaiian Dept.
(Through: The Inspector General.)
1. The report is correct.
2. The offense is unintentional.

R. P. Reeder, Jr.
Cadet Corporal
Co. "A," 3rd Class

"Whew!" my father said. "This is too brief. They will hang everything on you! I had a conference with the Inspector General. Some of the officers in this scrape have written reams."

"Well," I said, "this is how we make a written explanation at West Point, and I'll stand on it."

We evaded this storm because my sister Julia found the pastor and apologized. She explained that her brother, an ignorant cadet from West Point, and some very fine officers had made a mistake.

I was glad to sail for West Point, where the rules were written down. My Hawaiian interlude had been fascinating, although the only hula girls I saw were overweight and overdressed.

Back at West Point that fall, one of our major studies, "Natural and Experimental Philosophy," overwhelmed me. This was a short name for a course in technical mechanics, hydraulics, aerodynamics, graphical methods, wave motion, sound and light, astronomy, slide rule, and a few random subjects such as "Precision of Measurements."

At the end of the term I was pronounced deficient because my marks in the written general reviews were unsatisfactory, and carrying out the order of the times, I had to forfeit my Christmas leave so I could take the final examination.

It was a glum feeling, watching over a thousand cadets run across the area and streak downhill for the railroad station, going home or to friends' homes for Christmas. My division of barracks seemed as forsaken as a graveyard. I shut myself in my room with a slide rule and started at the beginning to cover Maurer and Roark's *Technical Mechanics*. It seemed an almost impossible assignment.

The next day was Sunday, and I climbed the steep hill in the snow to the Cadet Chapel. Two cadets on a bobsled whizzed by, almost running over me. I think these cadets must have been Roman Catholics who had been to early Mass. They seem to get more out of Sunday than Protestants do.

I sat in the pew that Bill Wood and I usually occupied on Sundays. The sermon concerned the various scenes depicted on the huge sanctuary window. A soft light filtered through the richly colored panes and bathed the altar, half of the choir pews and the west wall in every color of the spectrum. Tall Chaplain Wheat pointed upward as he described the heroes from the Old and New Testaments depicted in the windows: ". . . In the third panel the figures represent David and Jonathon. They symbolize the friendships you develop and forge here. . . ."

If I could not pass that four-hour exam, the friendships I had formed here might become a mere memory.

I felt lonely as I plowed through the snow downhill toward my room in barracks. Ice choked the river. To the west, blocked against the sky, Fort Putnam looked as if it had been cut from gray cardboard. A plebe at the console of the chapel chimes tinkled out "Good King Wenceslaus." Tomorrow would be Christmas Eve.

I got through Christmas somehow.

Early on the twenty-sixth the door opened and in walked Cadet Charles Saltzman, president of our class and distinguished cadet in his studies, who was destined to become a Rhodes scholar.

"Red, I was down in New York City, and I got to thinking about you up here. I came back to coach you. We have two days until the examination. Right?"

I could not answer.

CHAPTER SIXTEEN

Reveille

CHARLES SALTZMAN'S hard work on me and Mechanics failed to bear fruit. Not only was the four-hour exam hard, but I could not understand the language of two of the questions and I was too stupid to inquire. "Found deficient," the orders read.

Soon after the list of failures was published, Betty Gatchell met me on Diagonal Walk. "We just heard you were found in Mechanics! Jim and I are distressed. What in the world are you going to do? Your family is so far away."

"I am going to study for the reexamination. The law says I've ninety days to prepare." I felt bad but I was determined to pass the reexam.

To get ready for that test, I lived in the Gatchell's home, and Major Jimmy Crawford coached me in the late afternoons in his bachelor apartment. He was an instructor who embarrassed his students by being so nice. When I could not work a problem that he had explained the day before, he would stand up, grasp his head, and cry in anguish, "What a poor instructor I am!" This got me interested fast.

After three months of hard study under him, I took the four-hour examination in New York City. When I left that room to go to visit my aunt and uncle, the Willifords, and to study at Virginia

Polytechnic Institute in Blacksburg, Virginia, I was confldent that I had passed and would be able to return to West Point. But each day's wait became harder, and I grew shaky. After a week of anxiety a messenger boy delivered a telegram. It was signed "Crawford," and read: "YOU HIT A HOMER WITH THE BASES FULL." With a tall, joyous feeling of accomplishment, I ran to the telegraph office and wired Crawford and Honolulu.

Then Major Crawford wrote, "Congratulations! You made 96.7% on the reexam. It is the record." It is not a good idea to put yourself in a position where you can establish unusual records like that.

I asked my father now a colonel, "How will the army feel about me? Taking six years to graduate?" He said, "When you receive your diploma, you start off with a new slate. The army will be interested in how you do your duties, how you behave, and in your leadership.

Oddly enough, when I came back to West Point, I started enjoying school work for a change. Spanish was fun, and I could at last do the problems in Mechanics. The Professor of Chemistry and Electricity, Colonel Wirt Robinson–"P. Wirt," for professor, everyone called him–was delightful. He was tall, fat in the middle, and had a lightning sense of humor. He looked like a kindly chaplain because of his stiff white collar that rose an inch and a half above the stand-up collar of his uniform. When P. Wirt came in my classroom, I felt as though fresh air were blowing in through the door. He enjoyed teasing me.

Colonel Robinson had a rule he quoted occasionally to some confused cadet: "The Rule for Guess: Make up your mind and choose the opposite." Once when I was laboring to find out whether an electrical current had positive or negative charges, he listened to my recitation, and when I hestitated over the last step, he prodded me, "Rule for Guess, Mr. Reeder. Come on! Rule for Guess!"

I said, "Sir, the current is negative."

"I told you to apply the Rule for Guess."

"Sir, I did apply it."

He spread his hands across his chest, staggered back, and said with mock astonishment, "My! You're smarter than I thought you were!"

Leadership training in the mid-1920's was informal, and few officers talked to their cadets about it. My wonderful Tac, Major

O. W . Griswold, took time to talk to us about enlisted men and problems in leading them. We loved him. "Five and Ten" we called this salty character, because he did not report you for trifles; when he did write you up on a delinquency slip, he socked you and you usually received five demerits and ten confinements. (A confinement: one hour of free time spent in your room.)

I decided, when the football season rolled round, that if I were to graduate I had best not apply for a football suit, and that I would put in more study time. Lieutenant Eugene Vidal, assistant coach and one of Army's best halfbacks in his playing days, came to my room. He gave me his quizzical smile. "Coach McEwan wants to know why you're not out for football."

"Sir, I have too much trouble with my lessons."

"I agree you have to study, but you have to have exercise. Coach McEwan says he won't scrimmage you. You won't wear pads or headgear, you won't learn the signals. Just work out each day as a drop-kicker, and be available for games."

"We have the best drop-kicker in the country in Ed Garbisch."

"He won't last forever."

I seemed to be doing a pretty good job at lasting.

Ed Garbisch, captain of the team and All-American center, was, like McEwan, a leader, and he had his own ideas. Before the first game in Michie Stadium against St. Louis University, we were in the dressing room. It was always a tense, uncertain time. A trainer was checking bandages. You could hear the thump of a drum through the concrete wall.

Garbisch stood up. "Will the coaches and substitutes please leave the dressing room?" he asked. "I want to lead the team in prayer."

I was startled. How the coaches felt I do not know. We filed out into the runway under the stands and waited.

The sports writers were already hanging their columns on Garbisch, and when it became known that he was a prayer leader in football uniform, he received unusual publicity. He was sincere. People from many places came to see him; columns were written about him. One editorial ran, "Praying—not dwelling on victory but to 'acquit ourselves like men' . . . sounds like a knight of old."

Reporters gathered at our dressing-room door in the hope of gathering an interesting item about Garbisch. One reporter said to McEwan, "How do you feel about Ed Garbisch's praying?

"I have no objection. We're winning, aren't we?"

Being a drop-kick specialist was delightful. Breaking-through practice was still going on, but in a milder way; Coach Graves had left the coaching staff.

As 'Gene Vidal had explained to me, I did not need to know the signals. If I was sent into the game, I took my place ten yards behind the center, and if I received the ball I kicked it. Once McEwan sent me in on third down. The quarterback called a number. I got ready to kick. When the ball was passed to a close-up back instead of to me, I almost fell on my face reaching for it. It must have been the best fake on record.

Army-Navy games bring out all kinds of surprises. In 1924 Coach McEwan said to Will Rogers, famous cowboy star of the Ziegfeld Follies, "I bet you two hundred and fifty dollars that Army beats Navy. If Navy loses, you have to appear at West Point and talk before the Corps of Cadets." We won 12 to 0, and Rogers arrived at West Point in early December to pay his debt.

It was a dreary winter Sunday when the humorist climbed through the ropes of an elevated boxing ring in the old east gym. The cadets sat on camp stools and the people of the post sat in chairs on the balcony running track. When Rogers clasped his hands overhead in the fighter's signal of victory, then punched an imaginary opponent, the Corps went wild. When he finally made his audience quiet down, he said, "I've seen the day when I would jump off a ten-story building for that much applause."

He took a look at Major General Fred Sladen, sitting with his family on the running track. General Sladen, trim and Spartan, sat bolt upright straining to catch every word. Rogers tossed him a careless salute and said, "Boys, I hear you think that general is tough. Don't criticize him too much, 'cause he's trying to do for you in four years what it took him *five* years to do." Sladen turned red. The cadets howled and most of the officers tried not to. Then Rogers held up his hand. "Boys," he said "I learned this long ago, and I travel all over this world and use it: You can kid a big man, but don't you go kidding the little ones. Peewees can't take a joke. You got a big Superintendent, even if he's rough on you at times." The tension oozed out of the atmosphere.

Rogers talked two hours, and when he climbed out of the ring, he was exhausted. He ended up, "It's real fun to come up here to West Point and see you in your haunts. It's quite a surprise, because I only see you cadets in the Hotel Astor. Up here, you act like humans."

In my first-class year, as graduation approached, I began to view my departure with less enthusiasm than I had envisioned. It meant leaving good times on Doubleday Field, my cadet friends, and friends on the post such as the Gatchells. These were sobering thoughts. Then a month before graduation, tragedy struck. A promising cadet, Hamilton Hawkins, my roommate for one year, lighthearted and gay, author of the words to the football song "Slum and Gravy," was killed in a polo accident. The entire post grieved.

At five o'clock on the morning of graduation the door of my room rattled as if a cyclone were attacking it. When I jumped out of bed, Major "Three-oh" Spence (so nicknamed by his cadet math students because he gave so many 3.0's) and another Old Grad, back for June Week, walked in.

"Reveille!" the major said. "I've been in one hundred rooms looking for you. What are you waiting for? For the reveille gun to boom you out of bed?"

He lifted a grass hula skirt and some Hawaiian leis from a chair. "What's this for?

"I'm going to wear them to this last reveille, sir. We're all wearing costumes."

"Well, climb out of bed. The sun's coming up. It's shining at last on Graduation Day, a new day for you."

June 12, 1926, was one of those perfect early summer days you find in the Hudson River valley. It is a funny feeling stepping into ranks for your last formation. Over at Trophy Point our families, friends, and the rest of the Corps waited. We were wearing gray full-dress coats and starched white trousers.

In our march up Thayer Road to Battle Monument we followed the

Graduation Day Reveille
June 12, 1926
"Hank Flood talking to Miss Honolulu"

famous West Point band, playing "Stars and Stripes Forever," and the National and Corps Colors. My feet were not hitting the pavement. I winked at old Sergeant Sullivan, who had strolled over from Doubleday Field, and he presented arms with a garden rake.

As we filed to our seats in the bleachers, I spotted my parents and sisters. Mother looked weepy. I cupped my hands and called, "Mother, after all the trouble I've had getting through here, you wouldn't come up and cry about my graduating, would you?"

Acting Secretary of War Hanford McNider was the main speaker, but I heard only snatches of his excellent talk. When we formed in single line to receive our diplomas, there were twenty-five cadets behind me and the "goat"—the last man, and six times that many in front. Finally the adjutant called out, "Russell Potter Reeder, Jr.," and I stepped forward and saluted.

A great shout went up. Some cadets jumped to their feet. The noise sounded like the Sioux Indians at Little Big Horn. I know some of the cadets were yelling because the baseball team I captained had beaten Navy the previous week 6 to 5 in the tenth inning.

The Secretary of War shouted at General Stewart, Superintendent, "Why are they yelling?"

"Six-year man," the general yelled back.

When we had our diplomas, the Class of 1926 returned to barracks for the last time. Gus Farwick, All-American football player who had been graduated the year before, walked with my family and me. "Red," he said, "my graduation present to you is my coming back to see you graduate. Gad! You got more applause than the goat!"

Home for Christmas 1932. L. to R. (back row): 2nd LT C. P. Summerall, Jr.; his wife Julia Reeder Summerall; R.R.; Ensign Fred M. Reeder, USN. (Front row): Mrs. R. P. Reeder; Nardi Reeder; COL R. P. Reeder, Sr.

CHAPTER SEVENTEEN

President Coolidge's Remarks

AT MY FIRST POST the United States Army gave me a shock—a shock of disappointment.

I reported at Fort Eustis, Virginia, on a Saturday morning, full of enthusiasm and ready for work. I found the captain in his orderly room. After I had saluted and given him a copy of my orders, he settled back in his swivel chair and motioned me to a straight-back one.

"We have fifty-five men in this company," he said, "but not all of them are here."

Fifty-five men! I said to myself. I knew an infantry company was supposed to have 198 men. "Where are they all, sir?"

"On special duty. Hardly see them. They're on various jobs around the post. Commissary, fire department, landscaping, cutting grass, and so on. We have about twenty-three men for drill and training—the same twenty-three each day."

The first sergeant appeared in the doorway.

"Sir, the company's ready for inspection."

"Very well, we'll be right out." To me the captain said, "Take your place in the file closers."

The captain and I buckled on our swords, straightened our Sam Browne belts and went outside.

Twenty-one men were standing at rigid attention in their best olive-drab uniforms, shoes and visors shined. The first sergeant, another sergeant, and I stood in the file closers. There was no rear rank.

The captain inspected the twenty-one rifles, two pistols, and me. Then he and I inspected the barracks, and returned to his office. I expected him to talk about the training, but he told about duck blinds he was building on the James River and how cold it had been on the river at 6 A.M. last season when the birds were flying.

When he came up for air, I said, "Sir, what do you want me to do on Monday?"

The captain lit a cigarette and took several puffs. He turned in his swivel chair and waved his hand carelessly at a row of loose-leaf material bound in gray covers—about eight volumes.

"Why don't you start reading the army regulations? Tell you the truth, we begin marksmanship three weeks from Monday, and there's little to do until then, so why not put your nose in the regulations? Won't hurt you a bit."

I was feeling sorry for myself—sorry that I had asked for this post as my first station—when the first sergeant interrupted us to say, "Lieutenant, the colonel wants to see the lieutenant at post headquarters right away."

At headquarters I saluted Colonel Thomas Darrah, sparse, soldierly looking and gray. He smiled pleasantly. "Mr. Reeder"—he was using the Old Army form of address for lieutenants, and we new officers did not like it; a lieutenant wants to be called "lieutenant"—"did you have surveying at West Point?"

"Yes, sir." I expected the worst.

"The target range at this post is cattywampus and cock-eyed. The whole thing needs surveying and a good straightening up. The ordnance officer will issue you all the surveying instruments you need and the quartermaster can lend you mules, scoops, and teamsters. Any questions?"

To myself I said, *It's been over three years since I saw a surveying instrument. I wonder where those two little books on surveying are by Breed and Hosmer?* To the colonel I said, "No sir, no questions."

I went back to A Company and told the captain of my new job.

"I just got a note from the colonel," the captain said, "telling me all about it. See what I mean? Everybody's on special duty. That's why I am so interested in those duck blinds. Tell you what, I can assist you, or rather, Sergeant Dave Cass will."

"Is he a surveyor?" I asked hopefully.

"No indeed. Dave Cass is—How old are you?"

"Twenty-four, sir."

"Cass will have twenty-nine years service next month. Very dependable. He's a Texan. Probably didn't go beyond the fourth grade in school, but I'd say he could hold his own with a senior in college. I keep him here in reserve for myself in case Colonel Darrah dreams up a special duty job for me, but I'll lend you Dave Cass."

I did not see how Sergeant Cass could help me in surveying if he only went to the fourth grade.

I went to the infantry stables and talked the stable sergeant into lending me a horse, then rode though the woods to the target range. I saw what Colonel Darrah meant. The range *was* cattywampus, and it was dotted with ugly black stumps.

Sergeant Cass reported to me at eight o'clock on Monday morning. He had a face like leather, with deep crinkles and kindly eyes. "Sir, Lieutenant, the cap'n give me the job of helpin' the lieutenant with the range. I went down to the Audience Sat'day noon and drawed a stadium rod, chains, steel tape, and everything they said we'd need. I got a Liberty truck out back and a hundred stakes, a mile of twine, a hatchet, and our lunches. I hope the lieutenant don't mind me bringing my bird dog, Mike, along. I noticed a fine-looking pointer in the lieutenant's Chevrolet coupe."

I spent the first morning setting up the transit and working those four contrary thumb screws to level it while Sergeant Cass and the dog roamed the range after quail. In the afternoon I studied Breed and Hosmer and figured my Surveyor's Notebook.

The next morning I arrived with my dog Jerry at the range. Sergeant Cass was watching nine teamsters handle their mules. They formed an endless chain and were scooping up dirt near the butts and dropping it to fill in a hole.

Cass saluted me. "Fine mornin', Lieutenant. Sir, I don't want to set a precedent, but I thought we ought to get the job under way, so I started 'em off."

"How did you know that was a high point down there?" I asked. The level was in my Chevrolet.

"I lay down on my face and squinted. At least four feet got to come off."

I set up the transit and level and finally got them and their plumb bobs over some stakes at the 200-yard firing point. I asked Sergeant Cass to help me with the surveyor's chain, as I wanted to get the exact distance from the butts to the firing point. Meanwhile our two pointers pointed quail, and the birds had to be flushed.

"Mike'll stand there all day, if we don't get up those birds," Cass said. I wasn't so confident of Jerry.

"In the afternoon I missed the dogs. "Where are they?" I asked Cass.

"They went to have lunch at the barracks."

The project was going great guns. Cass had the teamsters and their scoops attacking high points near the butts. Suddenly, out of the woods galloped the colonel. He dismounted and tossed his reins to an orderly.

I hurried up, stopped at attention six paces away, saluted and reported in the customary manner. "Sir, Lieutenant Reeder reports to the colonel. I am surveying this target range. My job is to–"

"Yes, yes, I know. Russell, how are you getting along?"

I liked this man, Dr. Darrah's brother, but I was not fooled by his friendly tone. I knew he could be as tough as steel. I hoped the two bird dogs would remain out to lunch.

"Fine, sir, thank you."

"Who do you have holding that rod up there on top of the butts like the Statue of Liberty?"

"Sergeant Cass, sir."

"Good man. Now, what's your method of attack?"

I whipped out the notebook I had found when I liberated Breed and Hosmer. The little book was marked in bold print: "SURVEYOR'S NOTEBOOK". I flashed a sketch I had drawn on the notebook's faint-blue cross-section paper.

"Sir," I said, "I am establishing a mean datum plane."

"Er-What?"

"A mean datum plane. See this sketch, sir?"

Colonel Darrah started for his horse.

"Sir," I said, "when I have this mean datum plane established I will–"

"Very good," he shouted from the saddle. "Keep going."

When he had gone, I waved Sergeant Cass in with my campaign hat.

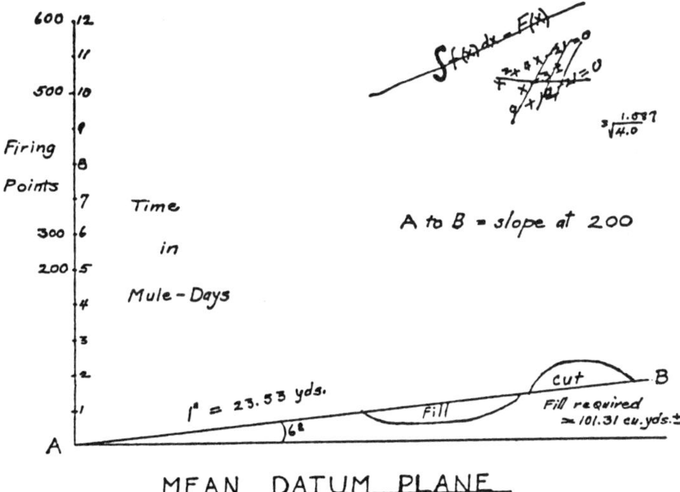

"Sir, Lieutenant, sir," he said, "we don't need these damn' crinkling chains. Last night after quittin' time I took a teamster and checked the distance of the butts from both ends of this firing point. We have to shave off five yards down there and place that dirt at this end so it won't slope. Course, we have to fill up that hollow. Then we can move back to the next firin' point. Is it OK for me to go ahead?"

I put the mean datum plane away. "Go right ahead," I said.

After that fall at Fort Eustis, probably because I made a touchdown for its team, I was ordered to report to the All-Army Football Squad assembling at Fort Benning, Georgia. "Second Lieutenant Reeder will report to Major James A. Van Fleet as a player-coach," the orders read.

Before I left I received a telephone call from the adjutant. "You have been selected to be aide de camp to General MacArthur when he comes here to inspect next week. Please come over for instructions."

I felt great. Maybe the general had put in a special request for me.

"The general will be here only a few hours," the adjutant said. "When he comes you ride in his car and show him the regiment, which will be on a practice march on the Yorktown Road. Colonel Darrah will meet the general on the march. Do you want to know why you were selected?"

"Yes, sir."

"Because you have the newest uniforms. The other new second lieutenants are commanding companies."

I was glad to leave Fort Eustis for Fort Benning, even though it meant leaving my parents at nearby Fort Monroe – happy because after the football season I would be assigned to the 29th Infantry, the only full-strength infantry regiment in the United States. I was sick of playing soldier in a company of fifty-five men, most of whom were on special duty.

The 29th was the demonstration regiment for The Infantry School, and we second lieutenants worked hard long hours, especially on the target range.

My new battalion commander turned out to be my wonderful Tac from West Point, Major Oscar ("Old Five and Ten") Griswold. He wore his campaign hat on a slant over one eye and surveyed his second lieutenants with a distrust coated with amusement.

It was so hot on the range the rifles had to be kept in the shade of an awning so we could handle them. Ammunition would have exploded if it had been exposed to the Georgia sun.

Down the firing point, looking at the shooters and talking to them, walked a tall, military figure, Lt. Col. George C. Marshall, assistant commandant of the Infantry School. The word among the second lieutenants was that George Marshall was "OK." He would have been happy had he known he had the lieutenants' approval.

He stopped behind me. I was lying on my stomach firing at the target a light-year away.

"What was it, Reeder?" he asked.

"A center five."

When the target was marked with a low 3, he laughed. "Pretty poor for an All-American football player," he said.

I was ranks removed from the All-American selections. Later, at a party, he said about me, "Gad! How that redhead could run." It dawned on me that he had me confused with Army's Red Cagle, one of the great college halfbacks of all time. I let George Marshall remain in a happy state. I enjoyed being Red Cagle around him, and reveled in my long runs against Notre Dame, Stanford, and Navy.

When the football season rolled around and the All-Army "All-Americas" reported to Head Coach James Van Fleet, he was disappointed. No doubt he compared us with players at the University of Florida, where he had coached five years.

After he had seen us work out for several days on a beach at Fort Screvens, near Savannah, he said to me. "This is the greatest gang of palookas ever assembled. We have only four months to get ready to beat the Quantico Marines for the President's Cup. That's not time enough. But there's one good thing about this squad and that's its trainer, Mabbutt."

Charles J. Mabbutt, World War I officer, was physically one of the biggest men in the Army, six feet two and 270 pounds– and one of the most unusual. He had a red scrubbing brush for a moustache and an honest look. On the inside of his lengthy Sam Browne belt was a silver plate engraved:

To My Friend
Captain Charles J. Mabbutt
from
Douglas MacArthur
MAJOR GENERAL, UNITED STATES ARMY

There were scores of stories about the fabulous Mabbutt. I liked best the one in which he said, "After the Armistice I had the job of helping Herbert Hoover in the food relief of the Balkans. People starving all over the place. Mr. Hoover told me to sail out of Trieste, Italy, and go to Alexandria, Egypt, to hurry up a cargo of grain. To get up the gangplank I threw the general's aide overboard. I marched up the plank, found the general, salutes him and says, 'Sir, I reports as your new aide.'"

The players on the All-Army football squad laughed at this tale behind Mabbutt's back. But when we played in Baltimore, several of us were with Mabbutt when he ran into a pal of his World War days. After much laughter and backslapping, his friend said "I'll never forget the day in Trieste when you threw the aide overboard."

When our squad arrived in Washington to play the Marines, I went to Fort Meyer and called on General Summerall, now Chief of Staff of the Army. My sister Julia had married his son, Charles.

"What kind of defense is Major Van Fleet going to use in the game?" the general boomed. His voice had the resonance of an organ.

I drew a diagram.

"Same defense I used on the Marne River. Defense in depth. Who is captain of the team?"

"We have a different captain for each game, sir. I am the captain of this game."

"Good!" he said, "Officers should be the leaders. We should take every advantage to practice leadership."

I had little opportunity to practice leadership in this game, because in its early part a herd of Marines crashed into me and I hurt my leg. Mabbutt and the team doctor rushed out and removed me to the dressing room.

Both of them examined me, and the doctor wrapped my leg up with yards of adhesive tap, as you might wrap a baseball bat.

When the team came in at the half, Coach Van Fleet said, "Red, how's your leg? We're behind a touchdown. Can you go back in there?"

"No, sir. I can hardly stand on it."

"I think he may have a broken bone," Mabbutt said.

"I don't," the team doctor said. "He's all right. I think he can play."

I felt embarrassed.

"You start," Van Fleet said.

I limped out with the team to receive the kickoff. Sergeant Clarence Umberger, fine fullback, and I stood near the goal line.

I said, "Umberger, my leg is hurt. If they kick to me, I won't touch it. You catch it."

The Marine observation post was not alert. They kicked to Umberger and I hobbled up to the line of scrimmage. I connected with two passes and we gained thirty yards, but in a few minutes, when time came for me to punt, I had to lie down on the ground. Mabbutt, at the coach's orders, took me out.

After the game I stood with President Coolidge while he presented the cup to First Lieutenant Allan Shapley, U.S. Marine Corps. A newsreel cameraman, who seemed to be running things, readied his equipment and said, "All right, Mr. President. If you will present the Marine with the cup, we're all ready. Please speak loudly."

Mr. Coolidge gave Shapley the cup, smiled like a satisfied cat, and said exactly nothing. Then the President climbed into his limousine and departed.

President Coolidge presents cup to Allan Shapley, Captain of the USMC football team. RR, captain of the All-Army team is standing up very well with a broken leg, 1927.

At the ambulance our team doctor said to me, "I think X rays at Walter Reed Hospital may show a broken fibula. I had fifty dollars riding on our team and hoped that by your playing in the second half you could complete some more passes and pull it out of the fire."

I was aghast.

Mabbutt expressed my feelings. "And ruin his goddam leg for life," he snapped.

The ambulance chugged out of the stadium, Mabbutt riding with me. I am not putting down Mabbutt's and my idea of the team doctor; this paper wouldn't stand it.

CHAPTER EIGHTEEN

Cup of Coffee

AN EARLY SPRING DAY in 1928 found me on a dirty day coach on a rocky roadbed, bumping across Georgia. The crack in my fibula had healed, and I hoped it would stand up on a new adventure. I was studying a dog-eared book, *The Science of Baseball,* by Byrd Douglas, which Ed Garbisch had given to me when we were cadets. If my other texts had been worn like this one, I might have been on General Groves's staff of near-geniuses who developed the A bomb.

Because I had had a good season on a Fort Benning baseball team, I had been invited to try out for Connie Mack's Philadelphia Athletics. When I wrote to Hans Lobert, now a coach on the Giants, that I was going to take a leave from the army to try out with the "A's," he sent me a wire: WHICH WOULD YOU RATHER DO: PLAY FOR THE ELEPHANTS OR GO WITH THE NEW YORK GIANTS, JOHN J. MCGRAW, AND ME?

When I arrived at the Giants' training camp at Augusta, Hans met me and said, "How's your leg?"

"All right. The muscles are a little sore."

"Don't mention it to McGraw. He'll find out soon enough. Remember to call him 'Mister.' Everyone does except those of us who have been around him a long time. And out at the park, don't expect to go to the bat every five minutes. You are a rookie, and the rookies – well, they'll get *some* hitting. Now John McGraw may bawl you out, but he's a great man and that's his way."

"I've been bawled out by experts."

We found Mr. McGraw at his desk in his hotel suite. He was short, about five foot seven, but seemed shorter yet because he was fat. He had a round red face, gray hair at his temples that made him look distinguished, and quick blue eyes. In a minute he yelled, "Blanche, come in here. We have a West Point cadet." To me he said, "Or should I say 'officer'?"

"That's better," I said.

After we exchanged a few niceties, Mrs. McGraw excused herself and McGraw said to me, "What are we going to tell the newspapermen about you?"

"What do you mean, sir?"

"About what you're doing here."

This stopped me. I always thought you told a newspaperman exactly what was going on. That's how much I knew.

"They'll want to write about you. I'm going to have a press conference, and they'll all be in here in a few minutes. Suppose we don't say you might resign from the army, but that you are here to study baseball under me – the principles of the game – and that you will pass on what you learn to the soldiers?"

This was all right with me. I was not certain I wanted to resign my commission, and if I stayed in the army I would indeed teach soldier teams what I had learned. In 1928 they were glad to let a lieutenant resign. I had talked to my father a little about the idea of leaving the army to play big-league ball and all he said was, "First you'll have to find out how good you are." I *knew* I was good.

Mr. McGraw was interested. "How much leave have you got, Red?"

"A month and a half, sir."

"Good. We can find out about you in that time. Can you hit?"

"Yes, sir."

"Against any pitcher in the game?"

"Yes, sir."

McGraw laughed. "That's the way you have to feel. We'll see."

Eighteen newsmen, about a third of them from New York, trooped in. Many of them are still my friends. McGraw got off his little spiel about me and then began to talk about his pitching staff and about how Rogers Hornsby, the hard-hitting second baseman who had been traded to the Boston National League team, would not be missed, even though he had batted .361 last year. "We'll adjust," Mr. McGraw said.

On the way down in the elevator, Hans said, "You certainly gave the boss the right answers. I hope you look as good in the ball park."

The month at Augusta was the hardest physical work I ever did. We rookies were at the park from nine until five, and those are long hours in a baseball suit. We gobbled a sandwich in the clubhouse at noon and rushed out to the diamond so we could bat while the regulars rested.

One morning I was fifteen minutes late and McGraw an hour early. "You're late," he snapped. "Why?"

"Yes, sir," I said. "I was having my leg baked."

"I don't like alibis. What do you say up at West Point when they ask a late why he's late?"

"You say, 'No excuse, sir.'"

"Well, you say that to me from now on."

There was an indefinable something about John J. McGraw that I liked. He had a sense of humor. I saw him umpire an intersquad game, calling balls and strikes while he sat in the dugout about a hundred feet from the plate – and he did a good job. When I began to hit he shouted, "Get that Navy!" I was in a streak and he kept this up until I cooled off. "I think yelling 'Get that Navy!' peps you up, Reeder," he said.

The physical strain began to tell. At the end of two weeks I was so tired I could hardly move. One noon McGraw called the sixty Giants players to him and said, "This afternoon the first team has off. The second and third squads will play an extra-inning game here against Macon. I say 'extra innings' because the game will start at one o'clock and go to five. Everyone on the second and third squad will play. I'll be away, so Lobert, you and Bresnahan run things."

Just before game time I dragged myself to first base, determined to take things as easy as possible. Lobert came by and whispered, "Red, if you ever played hard, I want you to play hard this afternoon." That was all he said. I was surprised, but I knew he had a reason.

The "reason" walked out of the left-field stands at the end of the game. It was a warm day, but McGraw wore an overcoat, dark glasses, and a felt hat. "Get a shower, everybody and report to me in the hotel at eight."

That night he cut the squad from sixty to thirty-five. I survived, thanks to Lobert's warning. I expected the departing players would receive a fond farewell. After McGraw had discussed some of the glaring errors of the afternoon, he snapped, "You people who are leaving! Most of you lay down in this game like a pack of hounds. I know you're tired. I was a player once and I've been a manager twenty-nine years. I am looking for players who can produce when they're all in.

"Unless you're a pitcher, catcher, or shortstop, if you can't hit at least .280 you don't belong in baseball. You'd better hunt a new profession. Think it over. That's all. See Mr. Tierney to get your train fare home or wherever you've been sent." Then he stalked out of the room.

I was delighted I had survived, but I had the wrong idea about a professional baseball squad. I thought we were all teammates. The regular first baseman, "Memphis Bill" Terry, had been in various kinds of professional baseball for fourteen years—a Giant regular for the last three. He was a splendid fielder who had batted .326 the year before. It was obvious that if I were to play big-league ball, the Giants would probably sell me.

I walked up to Terry, who was sitting in front of his locker. About a half dozen of his bats leaned against its wall.

"Say, Bill, I'm using a 'Terry model' bat and I broke the one I have. I have more coming. Will you loan me one until they arrive?"

Terry scowled. "No," he said.

The year 1928 was Ty Cobb's last year in baseball, and Augusta was his home town. He received permission to work out with the Giants; he would join the Philadelphia Athletics later. McGraw invited him to work out with the first team.

"No, thanks," Cobb said. "That would rob players of time at bat. I'll work from five until about six thirty. If any of your men will stay and pitch to me, I'd appreciate it. I'll hire boys to chase balls in the outfield."

We found the famous Cobb delightful. Myriads of sportswriters have painted him as an ogre, even a sadist. However, he laughed, joked and relaxed. But of course we were not his competitors. When he talked to me about life in the major leagues, he drawled, "Now, you have to go to the picture show with somebody, but don't pal around with a pitcher. Learn to hate 'em. I think they have a fraternity and pass secrets to each other from club to club."

The daily attendance at the park stood at about 250. When the papers announced that Ty Cobb was working out, it zoomed to 4,000. I was surprised at how big the star was. Because he was one of the best base runners of all time, I had visualized him as smaller. He was powerful, slightly over six feet, weight 185, as dynamic as McGraw and as smart.

The first day he came, about fifteen Giants volunteered to stay after the long day's practice to pitch to Cobb. The novelty wore off quickly. After the second day just "Lefty" O'Doul, Mel Ott, Leslie Mann, "Buck" Lai and I remained. In appreciation, Cobb began to coach us in hitting. My batting average started to climb.

Ty Cobb gave an exhibition in place hitting one day. He asked me to stand near the plate and *after* the ball had left the pitcher's hand, I was to shout either "Left," "Center," or "Right."

"I'll line the ball wherever you yell."

Only a superstar could adjust in such a brief time. Average players seem fortunate to hit at all. Good batters can hit to two fields. Only a handful in either major league can pull an inside pitch, hit one over the middle of the plate to center field, and smash a pitch over the outside edge of the plate to the opposite field. Cobb's reflexes let him wait until the last fraction of a second to swing, and he would hit the ball on a line in any direction he chose.

Cobb's batting was the talk of the baseball world. That is, except in my room. I was rooming with a player who talked in laconic phrases—when he *did* talk. He could have made the Sphinx seem chatty. In the Atlanta Biltmore Hotel he sent for the chef and said, "I have a food invention. Can you make anything?"

"*Oui, monsieur.*" The chef readied his notebook and pencil.

"Make me a lemon pie à la mode."

I complained about this player as a roommate and Mr. Tierney, the secretary, moved me to the room of an Hawaiian-Chinese, "Buck" Lai. "He's alert a guy as we've got," Tierney said. "I just wish he were bigger and stronger."

When the two squads started north on different routes, Buck Lai and I, on the second team, thought up a game we called "King of the Room." The "king" was the man who made the most hits in a game, and he remained king until the "goat" deposed him. The goat had to take care of the king's luggage, do all the tipping, answer the telephone, buy newspapers, and arrange for the king's shoes to be shined. I fell into a hitting streak and was king for five straight games. Lai was wild.

In Raleigh, North Carolina, it looked as if Lai would dethrone me, because in the first two trips to the plate he made two hits and I made one. In the last inning the Giants were leading by ten runs; Lai still had only two hits and I only one. He had had his last time at bat when I walked to the plate for my last time. I hit the ball over the center fielder's head. I visualized Lai's face as I ran the bases, and I ran slower and slower. When you laugh you can hardly run. I tripped over third and lay there in the dirt. A Raleigh player tagged me out.

"Come here!" Lobert said to Lai and me after the game. "There will be no more of this king of the room. They are charging admission to these games. Lai, what's the matter with you? You're a good hitter. You let Red be king of the room for about eight days."

RR, 2nd team—NY Giants, catches ball, but has foot off the base. Augusta, GA, 1928.

Whenever the second team faced strong opposition, McGraw bolstered it with first-team players. Sometimes they arrived just a few hours before game time. We never knew who would come. Just before an exhibition game in New Jersey, several players joined us. My diary reads:

> April 8.
> . . . I was fined five cents yesterday by Dick Kinsella, who is acting as secretary for the second team, because I usually eat more than the $3.50-a-day allowance. Barnes told Mr. McGraw about it, and the manager became angry at Kinsella. But he laughed when I told him it was a joke, that I get all the food I want . . *Problem coming up:* Am I to be a ball player or not? Man, I hate to give up this soft life . . .

Just before Jersey City trotted out on the field, Lobert showed me the lineup. "I'm moving you from third in the batting order to eighth!"

"Eighth! I didn't know there was such a place!" I threw my bat down. "I'm no eighth-place hitter. That's a disgrace."

"Well, we have all these first-team guys." He shrugged.

McGraw revised the order and I batted third and felt better.

"Sergeant" Jim Bagby, former Cleveland star, was on the mound for Jersey City, and we lost 2 to 0.

McGraw was furious. In the clubhouse he said, "Giants beaten by Jersey City! That'll look good in the papers. Reese, your dumb base running was the worst I've seen in five years. Cost us the game. I've a notion to send you to the wilds of Arkansas. Reeder, you're a natural pull hitter. Just because I told you once when there's a man on first I'd like to see you hit to right field so the runner can move to third doesn't give you license to stop using your head. There was a man on first every time you came up, and you hit four line drives to the second baseman. And a strong wind was blowing in from right." He shook his head and crawled up and down the backs of the other culprits.

When we rode into New York City, Lobert said, "When McGraw gave you hell, you played it right."

"How was that?"

"You kept quiet."

We played an exhibition game at West Point and I was delighted when Terry hurt his thumb and I entered the game to play against many former teammates. The cadet pitchers looked as if they were pitching slow ball and the West Point team lacked intensive training. The Giants won 16 to 4.

I sat in my old seat at the training table and it made me miss boys who had been graduated.

The next day at the Polo Grounds, Mr. McGraw sent for Hans Lobert and me. "We've come to the point in the road where a decision must be made. Red, you hit .413 in thirteen exhibition games. I recommended to Mr. Stoneham, our president, that you be signed, paid five thousand dollars a year, and carried as a pinch hitter. He approved the money."

"Five thousand a year!" I exclaimed. I was astonished that a pinch hitter would be paid that much. My army pay was $1,716 a year, and the government helped by lending me two rooms with beaver board walls in one of the Fort Benning bachelor buildings.

Mr. McGraw took my statement for a protest. "Maybe we can get Mr. Stoneham to make it $5,500. But he's the boss. He overruled me about your staying and said to send you to Milwaukee for a year's seasoning. There'll be a string on you so we can recall you in twenty-four hours if we desire. Think it over. Talk to Hans, or you can talk to me, but it's your move. Tell me your answer in the morning."

I went to my hotel room and sat down. It did not take me long to make up my mind. I had worked too hard to toss my commission aside. Milwaukee seemed a long way off. Besides, I wanted to wear "New York Giants" on my shirt.

When I told Mr. McGraw my decision, he said, "You made the right choice. You forget to duck a fast ball coming at your head and you'd be lucky to tend cigars back of a counter." He shook hands. "See Tierney. He'll give you a check."

Lobert rode in a taxi with me to Penn Station. We didn't talk much. I hated to tell him good-by. He said, "Red, you made the right decision to stay in the army. But I think you enjoyed your cup of coffee with the New York Giants."

CHAPTER NINETEEN

Tin Goose

A MONTH AFTER I returned to Fort Benning, I was ordered to the Presidio of San Francisco for duty. I went to see a captain who had just made the trip by automobile and asked his advice. He gave it liberally.

"Yes indeed," he said. "Buy yourself one of those canvas waterbags and hang it on your radiator, because when you get out west some of the filling stations are a hundred miles apart. And another thing: Pay no attention to 'detour' signs. Out west they don't mean a thing. If you hit construction, they will always let you through."

I drove to Fort Leavenworth and my father lent me his copy of *Routings for Motor Car Tourists—Central United States.* "Many of the roads aren't marked," he said. "This will help you." I looked at Chapter XI. It told how to leave Kansas:

Miles

Finney County 0.0 At Sage head due west. Keep Arkansas River on left.

1.7 Jog left, then .4 mi. of new construction. Just beyond crossroad bend right and continue west.

4.5 Through Grant. Joe Haggerty's Famous Sandwiches Restaurant on left side of Main Street. (Suggest gasoline check.)

65.4 in Andrew, left over *single track.*

79.3 At Nunda, *don't cross* railroad, turn right with main wires. Eagle Hotel is on right at turn. Cross trolley tracks to huge oak, jog right .1 mi. past Ed Ehlen's Blacksmith Shop and proceed. *See Chapter XX for Colorado.*

I knew this book. Our family had used it on cross-country trips. My mother, sitting on the seat next to my father, held the book on her lap and would announce, "Horseshoe curve. Now go straight until we have mileage 50.7. Descend hill." Then she would become interested in something we four children in the back were talking about and in a little while the directions would not match the scenery. My father would grab the book. "You forgot to say, 'jog left,' back at Evansville." Then he would turn the car around, attacking the wheel with angry motions.

I was buzzing along at forty miles an hour, west of Rock Springs, Wyoming, when a large "detour" sign blocked the road. I eased around it and sped on. Forty miles later I came upon a road gang rebuilding a bridge that had been swept away. The foreman came up.

"Isn't that detour sign up back there?"

"Yes," I said, "but I thought I could get through."

The foreman waved his hand at the one-hundred-foot gap. "If you think you can make it, go ahead."

It's about time I quit trusting captains, I thought.

I had been sent to the beautiful Presidio of San Francisco so I could help Lieutenant Frank Fraser coach his West Coast Army football team. It was a better team than the All-Army team that had slumped to defeat in front of President Coolidge.

In the spring I received a wire from Harry ("Fats") Ellinger, husky West Point teammate who had not been commissioned because of his heart: COMING TO VISIT YOU FOR WEEKEND.

He stayed a memorable sixty-seven days. Ellinger was sort of a junior Falstaff, only more lovable. His favorite resort in San Francisco was a tiny speakeasy named "Rummy Joe's." Rummy Joe, former Greek wrestler, loved Harry Ellinger's laugh as much as I did. The Greek would shout with happiness when he appeared, lock the door to keep out others, then they would wrestle. After a five-minute no-decision go, Ellinger became the barkeeper, and Rummy Joe played the parts of various customers who frequented his speakeasy, and all drinks were free. It was splendid to have a visit from a friend like Ellinger, but he recuperated while I was at work, and when I came home at five, he was ready to go to town again. When the sixty-eighth day of his "weekend" arrived, I was happy to see him depart.

Before he left, Major Ralph Sasse, Ellinger and I were invited to attend "Pop" Warner's spring football practice for two weeks at Stanford University. It was fun watching Pop, colorful and smart—one of the first coaches elected to the Football Hall of Fame. He contributed to the relaxed atmosphere at practice by wearing an old sports jacket and golf knickers. At other times he wore a business suit, vest, and a beat-up soft-brimmed hat.

When Pop Warner had a new play he wanted to try, he would assemble his players and would fish through his pockets for a scrap of paper. Once he discovered the play scratched in pencil on the back of a sealed envelope. "Have to do something about this," he said. "Mrs. Warner gave me this letter to mail last week." He looked like a foxy old grandpa; his players thought he was marvelous, and so did I. Sometimes, when nothing suited him, he could be grumpy.

I asked Warner how he coached his kickers, what fundamentals he stressed. "I just tell 'em to kick 'em further." he said. And that was what he was doing. Many of the halfbacks he received from high school were already expert punters.

Pop was getting old, and although at Stanford in 1929 he had some of the best players in the game, his mind often went back to the days when he was coach of the Carlisle Indians. "They were the greatest," he said, at a dinner with Ellinger, Sasse and me. "Thorpe and his crew. Those Indians taught me a lesson: never swear at a player. Once during a sloppy practice I cursed them. They picked up the football and walked to the goal post, forty yards away, and held a powwow. Then they walked off the field. One of 'em, I think it was Little Boy, came back and said, 'If coach swear at us, no more practice.' I haven't so much as said 'darn' at a player since."

West Point head coaches "Biff" Jones, Ralph Sasse, and Gar Davidson brought me back to West Point for seven football seasons as an assistant coach with the Army team. Each was effective and had his own brand of leadership. Biff was experienced and was great fun to work for. "Your special instructions," he said when I reported, "are to stick your ugly head in my office first thing each morning and give me a laugh. You will scout Stanford University."

"I suppose you're assigning that team to me because you can spare me the longest of anyone on your staff. I'll never get back."

"You can fly."

"Fly! Why, it takes military planes three days to make the trip to the West Coast. I'll be in the air all fall."

"The TAT is starting up—Transcontinental Air Transport, a civilian airline. Try them."

"How much shall I draw from the treasurer?"

"I don't know what the fare is. Take a thousand dollars. Oh, yes, among other things bring me the weights of the Stanford players. I hear this is one of the heaviest teams Pop Warner ever coached. Pay some attention to that. Get the weights as nearly accurate as possible."

When I reported to the TAT office in the Pennsylvania Station in New York City, I was treated with respect.

Army Football Coaching Staff, 1934

L. to r.: Moe Daly, died Japanese POW; RR, lost leg in Normandy; "Babe" Bryan, future Supe USMA; Gar Davidson, head coach and future Supe; Bill Wood, future head coach; Blondy Saunders, lost leg in China; E. J. Doyle, KIA No. Africa.

"You are a pioneer passenger," the agent said. "Here's a souvenir desk set. There will be no charge because we want the reactions of you guinea pigs when you finish the round trip. Going west you climb on the Pullman sleeping car here at six tonight. You'll be met at seven tomorrow morning in Columbus, Ohio, and we'll put you on a Tin Goose – newest transport plane in the air. Cruises at eighty-five miles an hour. You'll fly all day to Waynoka, Oklahoma, just south of Wichita. There you catch the Atchison, Topeka and Santa Fe Railroad and ride all night to Clovis, New Mexico. Then another Tin Goose will lift you the following day to L. A. This is fast transportation, sir. Think of it! Less than two days from New York to the Pacific Coast. At L.A. you can catch the Owl to Palo Alto."

The Tin Goose was a Ford trimotor plane that had corrugated sides, aluminum seats that vibrated, and a sign screwed to the front wall that read: "No Smoking. Overhead Gas Tanks." A man wearing a sweatshirt escorted me to the steps. When I went up into the aluminum tube, he handed me a paper bag. "Your lunch," he said.

This plane rocked its way across the country, its motors imitating a regiment of riveters. Late in the afternoon blue flames spurted from the left engine. I brought the copilot back to look. "I don't think it'll catch fire,"he said. "If it goes out, we can limp in on two motors."

When we put down at dusk at Oklahoma I had a splitting head ache from the foul air, and the riveters were still drilling. I spent an hour watching ranchers and cowboys play in the domino parlors. A man was out of uniform in Waynoka unless he wore a black hat.

When I returned from the trip, I told Biff Jones so much about the teamwork of the splendid Stanford eleven he was alarmed. He said, "On your last scouting trip out west I'll send Gar Davidson along with you as sort of a check."

"Here's a list of weights of the Stanford squad, Biff. Look at 'em."

"What are you, a novice genius? You've estimated the weights down to the pound. You could get a job in a circus guessing weights. How did you arrive at this, Red?"

"I took them off the bulletin board in the Stanford varsity dressing room."

When Davidson and I flew west in a Tin Goose, the TAT people shifted the times and the schedule. Over western Oklahoma we ran into a bad snowstorm. You could hardly see the wing tips. The pilot said, "We are putting down at Clovis, New Mexico."

When we landed, the pilot said, "No more flying today. We're grounded." It was almost 1 P.M.

Gar Davidson and I were concerned. A blizzard was blowing snow parallel to the ground. We explained to the young passenger agent in the hangar that we were en route to Stanford to scout a football game. It was Wednesday noon. "We miss this game," I said, "and we'll all never hear the end of it. It'll probably even be in the newspapers."

"Wow!" he said. "You miss it and it'll reflect on the whole aviation industry." He consulted a timetable. "To make that game you have to catch a train out of Albuquerque at seven tonight. It's 207 miles to Albuquerque. The only transportation here is my new Ford automobile. It's gone only fifty miles, but I don't mind running it at top speed. We want people to think TAT is dependable. Come on, let's get out of here before the snow's too deep."

If this man had known how little I saw when I scouted a game he would not have stirred a foot.

We had gone only a mile when the snow plastering the windshield overcame the wiper. There was no such thing as a defroster. The driver stuck his head out of the left window and tried to steer, but the cold drove him back. He stopped at a country store and bought candles. We lit them and placed them against the windshield, and they cracked the glass.

"I'll buy a blowtorch at a garage up the road thirty miles," said the agent, a man not to be daunted by anything.

I held the torch to the windshield while the car skidded on. In the foothills east of Albuquerque the snow slowed us to ten miles an hour. Just as it looked as if we could not get through, we rolled out of the storm area and eased down into the town. My suit was coated with tallow and gasoline. We relaxed the next day in warm sunshine on a Santa Fe observation car headed west. Our remarkable scouting was a great aid to Biff Jones. It let him hold the Stanford team to thirty-four points while we scored thirteen.

During football practice sessions on the West Point Plain, the coaches had a rule, "No visiting with spectators." This was necessary because the cadets were on the field for only an hour and forty minutes. But one day Biff Jones said, "Red, there's a deer slayer over near Doubleday backstop. Looks like an unusual visitor. Run over and see him a few minutes.

I was surprised. It was Pete Dussen, looking almost as husky as he had at Fort McKinley, but much older. It hurt me to see the heavy lines in his face; he was far from the brash athlete I had known in Maine. On top of his car he and his partner had a buck. "We've been hunting up in the Adirondacks," he said. "I live down in New Jersey now."

It is hard to bridge a thirteen-year gap in thirteen minutes. He took me aside and barged to the real purpose of the visit. "How are your parents? Your father still living?"

"Yes. They are both fine."

He shifted awkwardly. "Give your father a message from me. I was a real pain to him back in those days, and I thank him for growing me up."

At his car Pete said, "How's the team? Any good players?"

"Only one as good as you: Red Cagle."

He laughed, stepped into his station wagon, and rolled away. I tried later to locate Pete but I never saw him again.

The next fall Head Coach Ralph Sasse sent my friend Lieutenant "Moe" Daly and me to scout the University of North Dakota's team at Fargo the week before they came to West Point to play us. Daly, an aviator, had to get flying time in and the idea also floated around that an Air Corps plane would make the trip easier. "It'll be completely at our disposal," Moe explained.

We flew out in an O-1 G, Moe at the controls. We buzzed over the landscape at about 130 miles an hour, and on the evening of the second day reached Fargo. There was no hangar. Moe said, "We'll just stake the plane to the prairie."

We left it here and taxied into Fargo. I have seldom seen prettier girls. The weather gave them peaches-and-cream complexions. We saw the university play a night game, and on Sunday morning early taxied back to our plane.

During the night the temperature had dropped from thirty-five to about five above. We pulled up the stakes and got in. Moe turned on the starter. The engine groaned a few times, the propeller whirled halfheartedly, then the battery quit. Moe got out a hand crank. "Turn the motor over, will you, Red?"

I stood on the wing and cranked and cranked. After a while my side hurt and I was exhausted. "Listen, Moe, you are a flying instructor. You crank, and let me sit in the cockpit. You can tell me what to do if the thing starts up."

The engine did not like Moe's cranking any better than it liked mine. When Moe tired, he hailed a farmer and rode into Fargo. They came back with several empty five-gallon oil cans, drained the plane's oil, and took it into a garage in Fargo to be heated. On their return Moe placed the hot oil in the engine, and after I had cranked a while the propeller grabbed hold. It was a little after three o'clock Sunday afternoon when we finally took off for Chicago. There was no way to send a message that we were coming, and consequently no one expected us.

I fell asleep in the rear cockpit and about ten thirty at night Moe wobbled the stick and woke me. We were flying just above the tops of the Chicago skyscrapers. The roar of the motor made talking impossible. Moe scribbled a note, "Can't find airport, No radio in this plane."

After almost an hour of intense anxiety we saw the lights of an airfield and came down. The airport janitor said, "I heard your motor, so I ran in and turned on the lights."

"Where can we eat?" I asked.

"Everything's shut up, but I have the keys to the soda jerk's place. You like some free Coca-Cola?"

Moe was exhausted. "I need a Scotch," he said, "but I'll settle for a dozen Cokes."

The next morning Moe and I peered out of our windows in the Edgewater Beach Hotel. It was pouring rain. The airport weatherman said, "Zero zero visibility, but flying conditions tomorrow will be excellent."

"Moe, do you think I'd better get on a train? They'll want our scouting report."

"No. With good weather tomorrow I'd beat you to West Point."

On Tuesday morning it was pouring even harder. The weatherman promised fine weather for Wednesday. "Red," said Moe, "you've got to gamble. No use getting on a train now."

On Wednesday the same low-pressure area gripped Chicago. We went out to the airport and sat there. "When I see a hole in the clouds we are going up through it," Moe said.

A few hours later we landed at Selfridge Field, Michigan, and while we were taxiing for the visiting-plane hangar, a motorcycle messenger rode alongside us. Moe stopped the plane. The telegram read:

> BASE COMMANDER, SELFRIDGE FIELD. IF A LT. REEDER ARRIVES YOUR FIELD WITH LT. M. F. DALY, AIR CORPS, TELL REEDER TO DISMOUNT AND PROCEED BY TRAIN.–R. I. SASSE

I walked into the football office at West Point on Thursday, just before practice, with the scouting report on the team we were to play on Saturday. "The Big Three," as we lowly assistants called Ralph Sasse, Red Blaik and Harry Ellinger, looked daggers at me. Sasse was furious. When he came up for air, I said, "We will beat North Dakota by three touchdowns. Fine backs, weak line. Here are our notes."

This pacified Major Sasse. Red Blaik, of more inquisitive mind, followed me to the dressing room, and I gave him details that supported our optimistic estimate.

Daly walked into the football office at noon Saturday. No one was angry at him; he *had* to stay with the plane.

I was not nervous at game time. I had confidence that Cadets Price, Trice, Stecker, Summerfelt, Molloy, Messinger, and others would save me from being classified as a tin goose.

And we won: Army 33; North Dakota 6.

It was not all athletics in the army in the twenties and thirties. I also put in hard work in barracks, on parade grounds, and on maneuvers. At some posts I performed two jobs: company officer and athletic coach. This happened to me one year at the Presidio of San Francisco. The colonel of my regiment, the 30th Infantry, sent for me.

"I want you to coach our baseball team," he said.

"Sir, I said, "my company commander, Captain Fountain, has played professional ball. He'd make a far better coach."

"I don't think you understand me. I said: 'I want *you* to coach our team.'"

"Oh," I said, "Yes, sir."

This team became one of the best I ever played on because it developed team play and spirit. The players were like a band of brothers, as Lord Nelson called his ship captains. I do not know how this spirit started. It just grew. Maybe a fine pitching staff helped get it off the ground.*

The games were well attended, but many of the soldiers in the bleachers rooted hard against me. "Strike the bum out!" one fan would always shout whenever I stepped into the batter's box.

I was bolstered by a thought of Hans Lobert's: "Fans are part of the game. What they say should go in one ear, out the other." I also realized this was a soldier's chance to yell at an officer.

The leather-lunged fan could be heard a quarter of a mile away. He even taunted me between innings. I asked a catcher, "Alibi" Deming, to point this heckler out to me.

"That's him, that big guy sitting next to the drinking fountain. You want me to go fight him?"

"No," I said, "I want you to get a hit when you go to the plate."

The next morning the San Francisco Bay was a misty blue wash and the breeze that swept the Golden Gate automatically filled your chest with salt air. I was headed across the parade ground on my way to work when I saw ahead the fan who had been taunting me. Our paths were about to cross when he saw me and veered away.

"Hey! Wait a minute!"

The giant saluted and stood at rigid attention.

"We play the battleship *Texas* on Saturday," I said. "I know you like baseball. Just thought you'd like to know about it."

On Saturday this foghorn switched from me to the sailors. For nine innings he bathed them in abuse, and for the rest of the season he taunted the opponents. This was a good lesson for me; I learned that the lower people are on the totem pole, the more they crave recognition!

*Our young third baseman, Pvt. Theodore J. Conway, went all the way to four star general.

CHAPTER TWENTY

War on the Horizon

IN 1934 I FINALLY persuaded Dr. Darrah's daughter, Dort, to marry me. For the wedding, Fred came to Leavenworth from his navy ship on the West Coast, and Moe Daly came from the East Coast. Aunt Susie Mayfield rode buses all the way from Alabama, holding a silver tray in her lap. The Kansas summer broke all records for heat; the golf course was so dry that when you hit a drive the ball kicked up dirt like the splash of a bullet. At night in the bachelor building at Fort Leavenworth, where Fred, Moe and I were staying, we tried to cool off by taking showers while wearing our pajamas, then lying down wet, but in fifteen minutes we were perfectly dry.

At a celebration in Dort's home the night before the wedding, Dr. Darrah recited an Irish story: "Jimmy Butler and the Owl" (he was a wonderful owl) and sang "Tim Murphy Was a Sober Man." Mrs. Darrah served beer. We were married in Leavenworth's St. Paul's Episcopal Church, having rehearsed the ceremony several times the day before—although I had been ready six months.

Dort made the transition from civilian to army life easily. In the Canal Zone she overhauled my apartment in an effort to make the quartermaster furniture look as though an interior decorator might have selected it. At Fort McClellan, Alabama, she helped make

Dort Darrah Reeder
Wedding Day, Leavenworth, KA, August 11, 1934

friends in nearby Anniston and took care of eleven bird dogs I accumulated and our four children as they came along.

The mess sergeant in Company L at Fort McClellan was worth the price of admission. An Italian, Anthony El Rezo, he took fierce pride in his kitchen. I say *his,* and it was his. I was just his boss who helped him occasionally with problems. The soldiers in the company were his customers—the men who ate the food that the cooks prepared under his direction.

About every two weeks he was in my office. "Sir, Sergeant El Rezo reports to the captain that the men in this company don't appreciate nothing."

"What's the matter?"

"Last night at dinner—we had cream of potato soup, cold cuts, lettuce-and-tomato salad, whole wheat bread, butter, milk, puddin', and coffee. When Private Jones was eating his puddin' he yelled, 'This food's lousy!' I asked him, 'What's the matter?' He said nothing. I have him outside the door."

"Bring him in."

I lectured Jones. A few days later a parallel incident occurred. It was obvious this was a game the privates in the company played. They, too, knew that the kitchen was Sergeant El Rezo's life.

Food was also a keen interest of Lieutenant Colonel Paul Franson, battalion commander. One day he blew into my office. "Red, an astounding thing. You, as an army boy, know baked beans are traditional. I was over at Harry Kirby's company and what are they serving? *Canned* beans!" (Sergeant El Rezo had served canned beans a week before. I was thankful the colonel had not inspected us then.) "I have ordered a baked-bean contest for next Saturday noon. I want each company to put beans on the menu for Saturday, if you please, and to send me a sample. The recipe to be used will be the one in the Army Cookbook. I've appointed a committee of three ladies as judges. We'll see who can bake the best beans."

Sergeant El Rezo flew into a tizzy. He had baked beans at once, just to practice the cooks on the army recipe. Saturday noon I saw him depart for headquarters, a K.P. wearing a starched white jacket and carrying a deep tray of beans at his side. I was busy and could not attend. In half an hour El Rezo was back in my office.

"Sir, I want you to know about the dirty work. I want you to know it right from me. We baked our beans strickly from the army recipe. Over in Captain Rees' Company, that cheat Sergeant

Blairickson says to himself, 'Ladies on the committee.' So Sergeant Blairickson sugars the beans. There's no sugar in the army recipe, sir. The ladies smacks their lips—they like sweets—and vote him unanimous the best beans. We come in"—he shook his head over the disgrace—"second."

We had hardly lived this calamity down when more trouble hit. Captain Adamson, post quartermaster, telephoned. "Red, the officer who was quartermaster ahead of me loaded up on artichokes. Soldiers don't like artichokes, so they're not moving off the shelves of the commissary. The cans are getting soft. We had to throw out a case this morning. I'm asking all the captains to please have their mess sergeants help me out by buying artichokes."

"I explained this to Sergeant El Rezo. A few mornings later he was back in my office.

"Sir, I have to ask the captain not to buy no more artichokes."

"Why?"

"Last night we served 'em for supper. Private Jones howled, 'How the hell do you eat these things?' So I gave a demonstration. I stood on a stool in the center of the mess hall and had a K.P. hold up a saucer of melted butter. I peeled off the leaf, dipped it in the butter, and ate it." El Rezo bared his teeth and jerked his head back as if he were cleaning the meat off a leaf. "Private Hailey—I have him just outside the door—yelled, 'Don't serve us no more of these damned pinecones!'"

If I could have taken Sergeant El Rezo along on my return to Panama, life would have been happier. I served a total of five years in the Canal Zone, and it was not the most pleasant service. I felt shut in there, and the tropical sun is hard on redheads.

During my first tour, the commanding general devoted himself to the little things: brass doorknobs in the barracks must be shined. We spent hours practicing close-order drill; and parades in the merciless sun, wearing steel helmets, do not endear you to the man who ordered them. Once he assembled about five thousand of the soldiers on the Pacific side at Albrook Field so we could pitch shelter tents and display field equipment. Where the airplanes landed while we spent the morning trying to line up a square composed of 2,500 pup tents I do not know.

The next commanding general, Harold B. Fiske, who had been the training officer on General Pershing's staff in France, believed in maneuvers, and we learned from him. However, General Fiske could be petulant. Once when he inspected our barracks he ordered that "everything" should be open so he could see into it. All wall lockers were open, all footlockers, every drawer, all shoe boxes, match boxes, packing boxes, everything. After the inspection he said, "Captain Reeder, your barracks look fine." Then, in the next breath, he said, "Why isn't that switch box open?" He pointed to a black iron box cut into the wall behind me.

It was the first time anyone had noticed that box since Goethals built the Canal.

"Sir, I do not know."

"Well, get it open! I am timing you." He pulled out his gold watch.

I ran to the supply room to get the supply sergeant, who had keys to everything, while General Fiske, my colonel, my major, two senior officers on Fiske's staff, and an aide waited. The sergeant, having been inspected, had gone to the Ordnance Department.

I returned and told the general.

"Go get him! I am timing you." General Fiske glared at the switch box.

I sent six corporals in all directions to bring back the sergeant. Time to open that switch box: fifteen minutes. I thought my colonel and major would be mad at me, but they were angry with General Fiske. So was I.

But I liked him. When the rainy season quit, he put us in the jungle and on the pampas far to the south of the Canal, three weeks at a time, while we practiced fighting.

On one maneuver my company and I were part of six thousand troops who were "attacking" the Canal. General Fiske placed us about fifty miles south of it, told us we had just landed, and that we were to fight our way to it. Opposing us were about four thousand men. He even derricked the clerks out of headquarters, and I liked that. Umpires ruled instead of bullets. On the seventeenth day of the maneuver the colonel who was the supply officer for the attacking force screwed up his courage and approached General Fiske. The general was about six feet two inches tall, and when he was angry looked about seventeen feet. The colonel was frightened.

"Sir, I made a bad mistake. Misplaced a decimal. As a result, sir, for the last four days the attackers will not have enough food. Maybe you want to stop the maneuver for two or three days while I send trucks into the Zone to bring out food, sir."

"Stop the maneuver! Do you stop a war?" The general walloped his leg with a riding crop.

"No, sir."

"What will they have to eat? I want to run this maneuver three and a fraction days longer. That would be ten more meals."

The colonel looked at his notes. "Sir, they won't have anything but tuna fish, coffee, and bread for 8.2 meals. That is, the bread will give out after 8.2 meals, sir."

General Fiske laughed. "Let the maneuver proceed. I am eating chicken at the umpire camp."

Tuna fish, coffee—and bread for 8.2 meals—is not conducive to good work when you are on a sixteen-hour day. I took my best sergeant, Aurechio, who could speak Spanish, removed him from the maneuver, gave him five men and money from the company fund and told him, "You're on food patrol, Aurechio. Bring us anything but fish."

Aurechio brought in chickens, sweet potatoes, papayas, mangoes, bananas, pineapples, limes, sugar, and bread. L Company, 33rd Infantry, never performed better. We starred.

When one officer dragged wearily home at the end of the maneuver, his wife had prepared as his welcome-home luncheon—tuna fish salad.

It was a hard maneuver, but as long as General Fiske was in command, his ten thousand soldiers felt they could defend the Canal until help arrived from the States.

When we were in the jungle, many of the shoes worn by the soldiers disintegrated. My supply sergeant said, "It's just the rot. No shoes are going to stand up in this heat, mud and water."

"How about my shoes? I bought these in the States."

The supply sergeant shrugged.

I gathered up twenty specimens of the worst field shoes, put them into a barracks bag, and took them to the office of the quartermaster. I knew the lieutenant colonel, J. J. Muggins. I dumped the smelly shoes on his office floor.

"What you got there, Red?"

I picked up one covered with green slime. Its sole was about to depart. "These are shoes L. Company wore on the last maneuver. They were new when we started."

"No shoes are going to stand up under this heat, the muck of the jungle and General Fiske."

I showed him mine. Then Muggins' tack changed. "Did you bring these to me through channels? What does your supply officer think?"

"I don't know."

"Take 'em out of here and bring 'em back with the proper paperwork."

I gathered up the disgraceful shoes and returned to my regiment. I drew up a letter of recommendation, took it and the shoes to my regimental supply officer, who endorsed the letter, and returned to Lieutenant Colonel Muggins' office with my bagful of Exhibit A.

"You back?" Muggins wrinkled his nose at the awful-looking shoes. "Listen! If the government wanted you to have a better field shoe, you would have a better field shoe. That's all. Now get these shoes out of here."

I did. My game around the greens was in need of repair, so I went to the Fort Amador golf course and concentrated on it.

But about this time I read an article by Major General Hanson Ely, World War I leader, that influenced me. One sentence was particularly striking: "A man will do more for Company 'A' than he will for General So-and-So." I decided to try this out by building an *esprit de corps* in the company. This took work, not just talking to the soldiers but improving their existence, bettering the efficiency of the unit, and relating everything possible to the company. I enlisted the help of the noncommissioned officers. Gradually I could see the truth in General Ely's thought.

After nine months of intense effort along this line we were ordered to make an eighteen-mile test march. I warned the two hundred men before we started, "This is going to be hard. Each of the companies that have made this march so far has had four men or more fail to go the distance, and the company that marched in this heat yesterday lost 8 per cent of its men. I do not want a single man in L Company to fall out."

The route was an old, flaky macadam road cut through dense jungle. At midday, the reflected heat from the macadam struck you in the face and seemed to bake the air away. The sun was merciless, and the weight of the full packs ground into the men's shoulders. Even our canvas leggings were dyed brown with sweat. At the sixteenth mile not a canteen in the company held water. When we began the last hard mile, I decided to walk at the end of the company, and what I saw astounded me. Two men in the last platoon had fainted. These two unconscious soldiers were being transported on the shoulders of the weary men. They were passing them from one to the other. The entire company seemed to be staggering. We crossed the finish line exhausted physically but with everyone present and happy in mind. From then on General Ely's observation became my belief.

For relaxation in the Canal Zone I played golf with a major general who had a wonderful sense of humor, only you had to locate it. This was Ben Lear, who had been in the army since 1898. He was six feet three and glared at people as if he were peering through fog. I decided he had poor vision, but he could always detect an unshined belt buckle, especially on a fat lieutenant colonel. That made the general yell.

General Lear had been in two wars and was heading for another. Even the Panama newspapers were recognizing the war in Europe. The United States began to be involved. When we gave fifty over-age destroyers to Great Britain in 1940 in exchange for leases on naval and air bases in Newfoundland and the West Indies, war seemed just around the corner. Troops were sent from the United States to Panama to bolster the Canal's defenses, and housing them was a problem.

I was at Fort Clayton, Canal Zone, and our three thousand infantrymen were taken from us and "given" to the engineers to help reclaim from the jungle old Camp Paraiso, one of the posts when the Canal was built. This was almost a disgrace: infantry under control of engineers! We infantry officers went to school while our soldiers worked as laborers under the engineer specialists to build an army post for the reinforcements from the States.

My colonel, "Shorty" Keeley, a hero at the Marne River in 1918, sent for me. "Red, I'm taking you out of school and am giving you a job under General Lear at Camp Paraiso. They're having some trouble out there with lumber."

"I don't know anything about lumber, sir."

"That's all right. Ben Lear said that common sense and force are the main requisites. He said to send my best captain and I am selecting you." Keeley beamed.

I left his office feeling confused–salved by a compliment.

I found Ben Lear standing beneath a mango tree at Camp Paraiso. It was pouring rain. "Sir," I said, giving him my best salute, "Captain Reeder reports as ordered."

He turned his glare on me. "What are you reporting to me for?"

The angry way he said this made me mad. "I don't know, sir." Then my West Point conscience got the upper hand and I said, "It's something to do with a lumber pile, sir."

"Oh, my God! I told Keeley to send me his best captain!"

This made me laugh; it was the beginning of a firm friendship.

The place was a beehive of confusion. One of the things that made the lumber business frantic was the Lear system of competition. At the end of each day's work he and his engineer, Captain Oxrieder, published a percentage of completion: "A Company's barracks, 76.21 per cent complete; B Company, 76.24 per cent; C Company, 76.22 per cent," and so on.

The engineer sergeant who helped me parcel out the lumber said. "This per cent of completion is working backward. It doesn't speed up the work. Some of the barracks are behind because the companies who are quick on their feet steal lumber to keep others from getting it." In spite of this mathematical jumble Camp Paraiso was built in time.

However, I knew General Lear best when I was transferred to the Zone commander's staff at Quarry Heights. My job was to direct athletics for the army, manage a motion-picture circuit of fourteen theaters, build two more, operate a "jungle circuit"–movies for men at remote antiaircraft positions, and run two rest camps. Because I was not under Lear, I could be–I think the word is "informal" with him. We became staunch friends. He got mad at me at times; he got mad at everybody: not really mad, just angry for the moment.

He called me up one morning. "Reeder, let's play golf."

"Sir, as you know, I'm the chairman of the greens committee at the Fort Amador Golf Course. I've planned to work there this afternoon."

"That's where I want to play."

"Yes, but I've scheduled a meeting with Corporal McCalley, my greenskeeper."

"Bring him along."

When we were on the first tee, Corporal McCalley, who was dressed in his best khaki because I had told him General Lear would be present, was sitting on a bench under a lime tree. The general was getting ready to tee off. I wanted to speak to the corporal, but pressed him back down onto the bench because I did not want to bother Lear's golf swing.

RR with Reeder Brothers' Golf Cup
Canal Zone, July 1934

The general stopped his swing and roared at the corporal, "When an officer speaks to you, *you stand up!*"

"It's my fault," I said.

"That goes for you, too," he shouted.

It was not pleasant walking down the first fairway after such a blast. I had intended to talk to Corporal McCalley as we walked along, but he was hanging back fifty, sixty yards. There was no noise except for a few wild parrots that squawked at us. After about two hundred yards, General Lear pulled a new golf ball out of his pocket. "Want this?" he said.

We were friends again, but I never could get McCalley up where we could confer.

Some of the movie theaters I was responsible for were on the Atlantic side, and once when I told General Lear I was going there to inspect, he said, "I can save you time. I'll get a plane and we can fly over. You inspect your theater in the morning while I look at the colonel over there, then we'll play the Fort Davis golf course in the afternoon."

We had a good game. I liked him for my partner because he drove such outrageous bargains on Tee Number One.

On the way back we walked into the Gatun railway station. A "transit guard" (details of soldiers who ride ships through the Canal to prevent sabotage while the ships are in transit) was standing under a shed by the tracks, also waiting for the train. An old sergeant saluted promptly, a new second lieutenant looked the other way.

Lear and I walked down the platform carrying our golf bags. The train was rumbling toward us. "Say, Red, why didn't that lieutenant salute me?"

I did not like this. I was a captain. Why didn't Lear say, "Why didn't that lieutenant salute *us*?"

"Well," I said, "that sergeant's been in the army since Richard the Lion Hearted and he salutes automatically. I know that lieutenant. He's a fine one. Lieutenant Wilson, 5th Infantry. He's only been in the army five months. *We* surprised him."

At nine that night the general called me up. He seemed in high spirits. "Reeder," he said, "this is General Lear's aide."

I recognized his voice. "Hello, General," I said.

He roared, "I said this is General Lear's aide!"

"How is the general?"

"I am sore—he's sore because that lieutenant didn't salute him at the railroad station this afternoon. He wants you to get ahold of that lieutenant and tell him to report at nine in the morning. The general's going to straighten him out!"

I was irritated. It was Saturday night and I did not want to go looking for a second lieutenant. Fortunately I located him on the first telephone call.

"Wilson," I said, "General Lear is upset because you didn't salute him in the Gatun railroad station this afternoon. He wants you to report to him at nine in the morning."

I could hear Wilson breathing.

"Put on your best white uniform," I said. "Tell him you're sorry, and don't offer an alibi. He explodes at alibis."

At five minutes before nine Sunday morning Wilson telephoned me. "The general's not in his office," he said anxiously.

"I don't care where he is, find him. He's at home, I think. Get down there fast."

Later Wilson said that he rang the doorbell and the general came to the door in golf shorts and sport shirt, carrying the Sunday paper. He peered over his silver-rimmed specs at Wilson.

"Come in, come in," the general said. "Nice of you to call. Let's sit out on the porch where it's cooler."

The lieutenant sat on the edge of his chair. The general read a headline and said, "That madman Hitler will drag us into a war." Then he changed the subject. "How are things out at the 5th Infantry?"

"Fine, sir."

"What state you from?"

"Arizona, sir."

"Why, I've ridden all over Arizona in the horse cavalry." The general yelled, "Grace! Please bring me and the lieutenant a Coca-Cola, will you, dear?" The general chatted on. At the end of a quarter hour he stood up and said, "It's splendid of you to come in."

Wilson grabbed his hat, "Sir, I am the lieutenant who did not salute you in the Gatun railroad station yesterday."

The general glared. "Don't let it happen again."

When I saw General Lear in a day or two, I said, "You're the toughest fellow on the beach. The way you straighten out lieutenants makes the whole Canal Zone tremble."

"Do you want to play golf?" he said.

War was coming over our horizon. David Low, the British cartoonist, said, "I never met anyone who wasn't against war. Even Hitler and Mussolini, according to themselves."

I subscribed to Low's statement, but I had been trained to defend my country and felt that if the United States was going to fight, it was my duty to get in it—not to serve in the Canal Zone. Most of my friends in the Zone felt the same way.

This was not a happy decision for me, because we had four fine children: Ann, six, Dodie, four, Julia, three, and Russell, one. It takes two to raise a family, and sometimes you need a committee.

Finally, orders sent me back to the Infantry School in Georgia for a battalion commanders' course. One evening at sunset, while the ship was plowing the Caribbean, the band played "God Bless America." The sun, the waves and the music created a somber mood. I knew how my father must have felt in 1917.

At the Infantry School, for the first time in my life, I studied effectively. I guess I was what they call "motivated."

After the course, in November 1941, I drove my car west for duty at Fort Ord, California. When I passed through New Orleans, I met my brother, Fred, a graduate of the United States Naval Academy, now a lieutenant commander wearing wings.

"Things look black in Europe," I said, "and they're having a rough time in Washington negotiating with the Japanese."

Fred said, "We're going to have to fight the Germans and the Rising Sun, too."

"Let's agree to die fighting rather than to be taken prisoner by the Japanese."

We shook hands, kissed good-by and parted. I drove on to locate a home for my family in Carmel, California, near my new station.

CHAPTER TWENTY-ONE

Japanese Periscope

SUNDAY, DECEMBER 7, 1941, was a beautiful day. I rose early. Carmel was sleeping. At the foot of the town small breakers pounded the sand with monotonous rhythm, as they had done since the beginning of time. I drove southward out of town through fields of artichokes, past the peaceful Mission of San Carlos Borromeo where mellow bells summoned a few people to early Mass. Turning back to the Seventeen Mile Drive, I stopped under windblown cypress trees. Not even a fishing boat rode the broad blue Pacific. From Midway Point misty clouds almost screened Point Lobos and the faint headlands to the south. Carmel Bay lay before me like an exquisite jewel.

The Pebble Beach golf course was like a park. Deer browsed in pine groves guarding some of the greens. I played eighteen holes with the assistant pro, relieving him of five dollars and planning golf dates with this new source of wealth for the remaining two weeks of my leave. I invested six dollars in a wedge and practiced in a sand trap for a half hour, then walked into the house where the golf professional had his shop.

The radio was blaring awful news: "Tons of Japanese bombs are raining on Pearl Harbor. Our fleet is damaged. How badly, how many Americans are dead, no one knows. Clouds of smoke are rising from Pearl Harbor.. . ." I left the shop feeling as if I had been punched in the stomach. The bottom had dropped out of everything.

I drove back to Carmel as if in a trance. Dort was lying on the bed with Ann, reading to her. "Keep quiet," Dort said softly, "the rest of the children are asleep."

"The Japs are bombing Pearl Harbor," I said. "The radio–"

I can still see the horror on Dort's face. Ann looked from one of us to the other, trying to fathom our talk.

Dort said, "You have fourteen more days of leave before you report to Fort Ord. What are you going to do?"

"I'm going to report right away. We are at war. Please help me pack my bedding roll."

A lump came to my throat when Ann tried to put one of her dolls in my blankets.

In the car with our four small children, heading for the army post, Dort and I tried to make plans for the future. It was impossible. When they left me at Ord, I shouldered my bedding roll and walked up a short path to the headquarters of the 32nd Infantry.

There was turmoil on the Fort Ord streets. People were running in all directions. Inside the frame building a sergeant major said, "Sir, the colonel is up the coast on reconnaissance at Half Moon Bay, looking over defensive positions. I'm packing up the records. What do you think will happen to us?"

"I haven't the faintest idea."

In about two hours a broad-shouldered man with a suntanned bald head barged in–colonel's eagles on the epaulets of his field jacket.

"Culin!" he introduced himself.

I saluted and reported.

"Well, this beats all!" Colonel Culin said. "I was up the coast seventy miles when the car radio gave us the goddam awful news about Pearl Harbor. I said, 'Driver, turn this car around and hightail it back to Ord.' I told Captain Finn–do you know 'Mickey' Finn?"

"Yes, sir. He was an end at West Point when I was an assistant football coach."

"Right! I told Finn, 'I wish I could get ahold of that Major Reeder. He's somewhere around here on leave. We're as shorthanded as the devil at a baptism.' Finn said, 'He'll be waiting in your office when we get back.' And here you are."

The sergeant major stuck his head in. "Colonel, two things. What am I to do with these old filing records? Shall I keep them?"

"Yes. Keep 'em. Then when no one is looking throw 'em away. We poor mortals on this damned green footstool try harder if some ink-slinger is making marks about us on scraps of paper. What else?"

"Orders from corps headquarters say we are to evacuate the post by seven tonight. Enemy planes may sweep the coast and Ord is likely target. About 85 per cent of the officers are present for duty.

Culin's nose seemed sharper. "There'll be no enemy planes! I understand we can eat at four thirty. Get the orders out for the regiment to be ready to march at six thirty. Phone those officers who are absent and tell 'em to get in here at once."

The temporary building serving as a dining hall was filled with officers and their wives. Culin introduced me. I wished that Dort could have been there to meet some of the ladies of the regiment. The only person either of us knew in Carmel was the man from whom we rented our home across the street from the La Playa Hotel.

In the middle of the meal a lieutenant ran into the dining hall and yelled, "Lights out!" A flight of Japanese planes just flew over the Golden Gate Bridge!"

The lights went out, plunging the room into gloom.

Colonel Culin stood up. "Turn those damned lights on!" he howled. "Excuse me, ladies. Absolutely no bombers flew over the Golden Gate Bridge! Let's quiet down here and pay no attention to rumors."

I knew I was in the hands of a pro.

"Come here," Culin said to the lieutenant. When the young man was at his side, Frank Culin said quietly, "Where'd you get your information?"

"It just came in on the radio, sir. San Francisco station."

"You better learn to believe *half* of what you hear, young fellow."

Colonel Culin led his regiment, the 32nd Infantry of the 7th Division, out of Fort Ord at precisely six thirty. I marched at the tail of the long column of companies. It was a strange feeling to be with a regiment of three thousand and to know only two men: the colonel and Captain Finn.

A private walking just ahead said, "Where we going, Sarge?"

"I don't know," the sergeant said. No one seemed to know.

LTC RR ready for combat, Jan. 1942

As we climbed a dirt road I looked back. In the afterglow of the sunset Monterey Bay was a sheet of dull silver. Dark clouds shrouded the Presidio of Monterey. I tried not to think of what was happening to my loved ones. I felt numb. The 32nd Infantry was, like the United States, on an uncertain road.

There was a halt. The soldiers cleared the road, took off their packs, and relaxed in the ditch on the right.

"Officers to the head of the column," came the word.

Colonel Culin stood in the center of a ring of 140 officers. "When this rest is over," he said, "we'll bivouac in the sage brush the other side of that hill. Now there may be days when Jap planes will bother us, but it won't be tonight. Nevertheless, no lights. It'll be good training to pitch camp in the dark."

When we moved out, he asked me to walk alongside him. He carried a long stick he used as sort of a shepherd's crook. A huge white bulldog trotted at his side. I enjoyed hearing this tough colonel talk baby talk to his dog with the unbelievable name "Let's Go."

"Let's Go, old boy, is 'e old feddow tired? You can't quit now, 'ou has to walk another twenty minoots."

I liked this colonel and felt at home with him. He was ten years older than I, graduate of the University of Arizona.

"Now, Red, here's the situation. We had a show regiment here—absolutely—wish you could have seen it. Now," he shrugged his powerful shoulders, "they keep cadreing and cadreing us."

"What's that?"

"About every two weeks a levy will come in from higher headquarters telling me to send a dozen of our top officers and maybe thirty NCO's somewhere, to help form a new outfit. This keeps up and keeps up. It's poison. I can see the regiment falling apart, but I'm not going to let it.

"Fine policy we got, Red. We're unprepared in this grand United States. We let the sweet-scented sons of the Emperor wallop our fleet and now we have to twist their tail." He let loose a string of oaths that were almost poetic.

"I'm a miner from Arizona. Came in the army in 1916. Tell me about your family. I knew your dad. *Mucho hombre.*"

I told him that Dad was retired and he and Mother lived in Phoebus, Virginia, and I told him about Dort and our four children.

"I'll have Ella get hold of her. Red, this is the second world war I've been in. I swear to you and"—he touched the bulldog with his stick—"and old Let's Go, here, that if they have a third one I'm going to it as a private soldier so I won't have to worry about a damned thing except my own pack and rifle. I'm tired of fretting over the equipment, food, ammunition, a thousand kinds of problems, sweethearts and other troubles of three thousand bozos."

"What job are you going to give me, sir?"

"Tomorrow at reveille you take over the second battalion. Those 900 buckos you'll command are good, but with us losing key people every two weeks. I'm worried about the whole outfit."

I lifted my sleeping bag out of a truck, spread it under a big sage bush, and crawled in. The stars were peeping out. Maybe the men were as tired as I was; they made surprisingly little noise as they pitched camp. There was a sage root under the small of my back and I shifted the sleeping bag. I prayed that God would take care of Dort and our children and help them. You needed every friend you had.

In the morning Colonel Culin spead out a map of the coast on his tiny field desk. "Red, here's your orders. If the enemy comes, fight! You are responsible for observation and defense along the coast from Point Lobos Reserve"—he moved his finger down the map—"to Pismo Beach, inclusive." He snapped off that word with a chop of his jaw, like my father. "Move out with the second battalion. Trucks will be here for you in fifty minutes. Make your headquarters at Camp San Luis Obispo. Any questions?"

I gulped. "How many miles between those two places, Colonel?"

"One hundred and forty-eight—make it one fifty."

At the Infantry School our instructors had preached that an infantry battalion in defense should never be extended beyond 2,700 yards.

"Red, you'll have three G.P.F.'s. You know what they are?"

"Big guns."

"Right. Monsters. The French call them '*Grande Puissance filloux*.' These cannons fire a 95-pound projectile ten miles. They're towed by tractors. A battalion of redlegs—artillerymen—comes with 'em. You also have an observation plane with two pilots, complete. I met them. They're fresh out of Chicago. I'm giving you twenty-four of these new-fangled jeeps for patrol. Remember, don't run 'em to death. Maintain them."

"Yes, sir." I felt like a general.

"Have you any questions, Red?"

"Tell me about the officers in the second battalion."

"A lot of 'em are green but they're learning. Some of 'em will be tops."

When the battalion moved down California Route 1, my spirits rose—after we passed Carmel. Colonel Culin was fine, but I would be on my own, a long-distance call over a shaky telephone system from his headquarters. Almost any headquarters can irritate you.

The first thing I did was to make the G.P.F. artillerymen unhappy. I placed the three tremendous guns about ten to fifteen miles apart so they could protect oil-tank farms.

"We have to be close together," the artillerymen said. "We have only one kitchen."

"Sorry. You will have to reorganize."

When I placed my headquarters in the desolate-looking Camp San Luis Obispo, I asked Captain Don Sendly, my adjutant, about the battalion.

RR's brother, CPT Fred M. Reeder, USN, CO-US Naval Air Station, New Orleans, chats with his exec Comdr. Jenkins, about 1944.

Sendly said, "Fine group. Good officers." He hesitated. "All except one."

"Who's that?"

"Second Lieutenant 'Catfish' Casmir."

"What the hell's the matter with him?"

"Well, he has a Master's degree in ichthyology."

I was going to say, "You shouldn't hold that against him," only I did not know what ichthyology was.

"That's a branch of zoology, sir. Something about fish."

"Is he a fisherman?"

"No, sir. He only studies them. Goes around looking in creeks and in the bays. Sloppy uniform, always needs a haircut. He talks well but his brain isn't hooked up with his common sense. Excitable."

"What's his job?"

"He commands the Intelligence Platoon."

I knew it was a peacetime infantry dodge to hide an incompetent officer who could not be discharged in the Intelligence Platoon. Now, suddenly, the Intelligence Platoon, with its mission of gathering information about the enemy in front of a regiment, was important.

I went forty miles up the beach to inspect an outpost at the Hearst Ranch. The fabulous castle rose from a ridge above San Simeon, maybe a mile back from the ocean.

Colonel Culin, coming to see me, hailed me, and we stood looking at the magnificent stretch of beach—miles of it. Let's Go, his bulldog, sat in his car.

The colonel said, "I just found out that a year ago Japanese civilians came in here and spent a day looking over this beach. At the same time fishing boats manned by Japanese appeared offshore. They probably were making a reconnaissance."

The colonel looked over his shoulder and lowered his voice. "Don't tell anybody, Red, but the Japanese fleet left Pearl Harbor and is heading this way." (This was correct information. The Japanese lost their nerve and made a U-turn between Hawaii and California.)

I took a step back. Suddenly the beautiful beach looked like a treacherous trap.

"If they land here," he said, "you hang onto them. Fight 'em. Give 'em everything you've got and keep me informed."

After the colonel had gone, I said to the Mexican who was driving my jeep, "Rodriguez, take me up to the Hearst Ranch."

"I drive you anywhere," he said, "but can't you skip that?"

"I have to go."

"I hate that lousy he-camel." Rodriguez buckled on his steel helmet.

We drove uphill through pens of kangaroos, elk, zebra, deer, and came to the camel's domain. Rodriguez opened the gate by yanking on a rope suspended from a yardarm. We chugged in and stopped. The boss camel spread his legs in the center of the road about sixty feet away, his head lowered and his mouth driveling saliva.

"Oh," moaned the Mexican, "I don't want that he-camel to drool on me." He blew the horn. The camel did not move.

We started up the steep grade at about ten miles an hour. The camel loped alongside and stuck its suitcase of a head into the jeep. It tried to bite Rodriguez with yellow teeth as long as your finger. Rodriguez drove the jeep with his head almost in my lap.

When we were out of the camel's area, I located the six men at the observation post. They were lonely, marooned with a magnificent view.

We talked to them, then ran the camel gauntlet and came home by moonlight just in time to witness a drama. A Japanese submarine, hugging the coast, had sunk an American freighter. Infantrymen of the 32nd were helping two lifeboats of badly shaken-up sailors ashore. Our soldiers were aghast. A sergeant said to me, as we worked in the moonlight to carry some of the sailors to our trucks, "I can't get over it. What kind of war is this? Think of a submarine machine-gunning helpless men in open boats."

Later another submarine, or the same one, shelled an oil-tank farm near Los Angeles. The two aviators attached to our battalion flew long hours in an effort to locate the sub, but without luck.

Fog rolled in, making it hard to see over two hundred yards, and it remained this way for the better part of a week. On Sunday afternoon Lieutenant Casmir knocked on my office door.

I had been so busy I had not had time to become acquainted with him. I could see why they called him "Catfish." He had a long nose, hair too long, and a silky brown moustache that drooped about the corners of his mouth. With a little encouragement he could have raised a goatee. He was about five feet six and his shoulders sloped so they wouldn't hold rainwater. When he talked he gesticulated with his glasses. After he saluted, he eased into a chair without invitation and made himself at home.

"This fog makes me feel as if I were in a bathysphere. Sir, I came in to see you on behalf of our two aviators from Chicago."

I felt like saying, "When was the last time you got a haircut?" But I held on to myself.

"They have not had a flight for seven days. Four days of fog and three days of plane maintenance prior to that. They are as sedentary as a pair of aqueous rocks."

I remained silent. I was an infantryman.

"I have a request, Major Reeder. Would you be kind enough, sir, to permit me to borrow your command car for the afternoon? I'd like to take these aviators on an excursion of the San Simeon lighthouse. I am acquainted with the lighthouse keeper and I am certain he will not object but will welcome an informal call." Casmir put on his glasses and peered at me as though the fog was in the office.

I made a mistake. I said, "OK, take the car."

I saw the truck-like vehicle pull away into the fog. Casmir, on the front seat, had his rifle upright between his knees, ready for a Japanese landing.

I learned later that as they crept up the coast, Casmir slowed the car suddenly and shouted at the driver, "Stop! Pull to the right behind that sand dune! I see the periscope of a submarine."

When the car was hidden behind the dune, Casmir, the two aviators and the driver clambered up its slope. "Don't expose yourselves," Casmir warned. "We are on a skyline. Lie down."

He focused his field glasses in hopes of seeing through the mist. "Yes," he said, his hands trembling, "Japanese periscope."

He passed his field glasses and rifle to one of the aviators.

"I'm going to get the G.P.F.," Casmir shouted. "We will blow that submarine right out of the water. I want one of you to fire the rifle until your bullets splash right at it. One act as observer. Then read the sight setting on the rifle. The results will be the correct range."

Casmir and the driver sped south through the fog. When they drove into the camouflaged artillery position where the monster gun lay under a covering of nets, Casmir jumped out of the automobile. The artillerymen were being served stew and salad from five-gallon milk cans.

"Japanese submarine!" Lieutenant Casmir yelled. "Three miles up the coast. Bring that gun! Bring that searchlight! Bring armor-piercing ammunition! Come on!"

The gun commander yelled, "March order!"

The startled soldiers dropped their mess kits and ran to prepare the heavy gun so it could move. A truck backed up to the tremendous searchlight. Another truck hitched to a large portable generator.

Then the captain in command of the big gun remembered his mission. "Wait!" he said. "By whose authority are we moving?"

All the soldiers stopped trying to move the twelve-ton gun.

"Do you want to win the war or don't you?" screamed the Catfish. "I am Lieutenant Casmir of the Intelligence Platoon, 32nd Infantry, 7th Division."

This is too much for the captain. He yelled, "March order!"

After thirty minutes of frantic work the procession barged up Route 1. First came Casmir in the command car, unarmed, next a tractor towing the gigantic gun, then an ammunition truck, the searchlight and its generator, and a range-finding section in jeeps.

While the artillerymen were laboring to emplace the gun and ready the searchlight, Casmir crawled to the top of the dune. "Is she still there?" he panted.

"Hasn't moved an inch," one of the aviators said.

"What's the range?"

"Two hundred twenty-five yards."

Casmir called to the artillery commander, "Range, two-two-five. Armor-piercing shell. Direct fire. There it is—that periscope right there!"

The G.P.F., ready to fire, had its long barrel out over the black-topped road. The muzzle of the gun cleared the road by about nine feet.

"Are you ready?" asked the artillery commander.

Casmir waved his hand right and left at his waist, palm down—the infantry signal for "Commence firing." The searchlight cut through the fog and made the periscope seem closer.

At this moment an automobile drove underneath the muzzle.

The tremendous roar of the gun sounded like an explosion in a canyon. The car wobbled into the ditch, all its glass bursting outward.

"Cease firing!" shouted Lieutenant Casmir.

A man in a blue suit reeled out of the automobile. He was shaking. When he could talk, he said to Casmir and the group clustered about him, "What happened?"

"We are firing at the periscope of that Japanese submarine," Casmir said.

"What did you say?" the man asked. "Louder! I can't hear a thing."

Casmir cupped his hand at the man's ear and shouted.

"Submarine?" the man said. "Why, that's a spar buoy and it's been there twenty years."

Captain Sendly got wind of the incident and reported it to me at breakfast. I sent for the Catfish. He looked different. I had tipped off our headquarters company barber and the Catfish had just had a haircut.

"It is just a regrettable, unfortunate incident," he said, "and, sir, I strongly suggest you say nothing about it."

I investigated and in two hours I telephoned Colonel Culin at Fort Ord and reported the affair.

"You understand now what I mean, don't you, Red? Damn it! I'm going to the next war as—" His voice faded. When he came in again, he shouted, "You got that lieutenant still in your Intelligence Platoon?"

"No, sir. He's been transferred to E Company."

I was happy later that I had reported the "regrettable incident," because the paper work on the complaint became thicker and thicker. By May Lieutenant Casmir was en route to a unit where his peculiar talents would be more helpful to the war effort, and we began to train for desert warfare.

CHAPTER TWENTY-TWO

O.P.D.

I WAS PROMOTED to lieutenant colonel—not as a result of the incident with the G.P.F.'s—and when our regiment was pulled inland, Colonel Culin made me his executive officer.

The regiment was equipped with half-track armored vehicles and was ordered to train in wastelands near Lost Hills, California. I never saw a town more appropriately named. June temperatures soared above 105 degrees. The regiment was preparing to fight in the deserts of Africa, but its first battleground turned out to be Attu, in the Aleutians. Abrupt changes are the hallmark of a national emergency.

After a scorching day near Lost Hills I walked into Colonel Culin's tent. He handed me a tin dipper of cool water and an official telegram. "Red, you've been ordered to O.P.D., on the general staff in Washington."

I could scarcely believe him or the telegram. "What's O.P.D.?" I faltered.

"Operations Division, General Marshall's command post. I lost Colonel Ed McDaniel on an order like this. He's there in charge of an ocean."

"An ocean? Which ocean?"

"Did you know anything about this order coming, Red?"

"No, sir. My family is right this minute packing up to move tomorrow from Carmel to San Luis Obispo. I can't figure why they would place me on the general staff. I have never had staff training above that of a regimental headquarters."

"You'll be on a big-league staff now," Colonel Culin said.

I phoned Dort to hold up on the packing and made a hurried trip to Carmel to the home I had barely seen. Dort, like Mrs. Whistler, was to pay, pack and follow me eastward.

"Better stay in Leavenworth," I said before I departed. "I'm sure my stay on the War Department General Staff will be temporary. They must be sending me to some unusual place."

When I arrived in Washington, Colonel Bill Ritchie broke me in. His salty air braced me and helped me overcome the feeling of depression I received from the gloomy halls of the Munitions Building. I knew Bill Ritchie. When we were cadets he had been the baseball manager for Hans Lobert. Ritchie gave me a close-up of the situation.

"You're here for some time, Red. You might as well send for your family. You know how you got here? General Marshall is sick of what he calls 'the staff type.' He said, 'Bring in some officers who know how to get soldiers out of the rain.' General Eisenhower selected you from records before he left for London."

Ritchie answered a scrambler telephone, then turned to me, "General Marshall, as Chief of Staff, is under tremendous pressure. He has on his neck the army's war effort, President FDR, the 'Prime,' Congress, and you can add in the Navy. We all admire him, but he can blow like a geyser. Recently, he blew and a half-dozen officers left. He shouted, 'Bring in new staff officers who know what a soldier smells like.' You're in that category."

It seemed a dubious compliment.

"This gloomy Munitions Building!" I moaned. I felt half ill.

"It'll be better over in the Pentagon. We're moving there."

"What's my job, Bill?"

"We're in a hot spot. Read yourself into the situation by going over the 'Top Secret' radios between Marshall and MacArthur and study Australia and New Guinea. Then get the 'Eyes Only' radios out of the safe and read them."

"What's 'Eyes Only'?"

"Private little billets-doux between Marshall and MacArthur. Here we represent both generals. We're General Marshall's command post for the Southwest Pacific Area, and we represent General MacArthur in the War Department. O.P.D. works with the Joint and Combined Chiefs of Staff. Our section keeps an observer or two in the theater so we"ll be informed. We just lost a splendid officer, Colonel Francis Stevens. He was killed on an air mission out of Port Moresby, New Guinea. You're his replacement. You have to learn how this War Department works, and it's moving in high gear."

My head was whirling.

In about two weeks Ritchie started giving me papers to work on, and I was lost. I could solve problems involving infantry, but if a radio request from General MacArthur's headquarters involved other parts of the army I had to ask scores of questions before I had a solution. I was slow.

Colonel Ritchie would read my work and say, "Well, Red, your idea is acceptable, but I wish you would clear it with General Somervell's executive officer, then . . ." (take it to twenty other places).

I sat up most of one night composing a draft of a radio to General MacArthur for Brigadier General Hull, in O.P.D., who had to present the finished product to General Marshall. The only part of my work that was around at the finish was the opening phrase. "Your situation is appreciated . . ."

The work was frustrating. After O.P.D. moved into the newly constructed Pentagon, I ate lunch in the cafeterias with other lieutenant colonels, many of whom I had known at West Point. But when noon hour was over and I was marooned at my desk, a messenger would plop secret radio messages to my "in basket" marked "*Action*: Reeder. *Suspense date*: Two days."

My family moved to Warren Street, in Washington, to the section of the city a janitor in O.P.D. called "the great northwest."

The frustrating work continued. When our daughter Dodie said, "Daddy, will you buy us some goldfish?" her mother cut in, "Your father's too busy. Don't ask him that."

Here is one problem I can do, I thought. I went to the dime store and bought four goldfish and a bowl and carried them home on a crowded streetcar during the rush hour. A lady on the car said, "It seems funny, seeing a lieutenant colonel carrying goldfish."

I said, "Lady, this is a funny lieutenant colonel. Will you hold the fish while I get my fare out?"

The radios pouring into O.P.D. from every front made the work interesting, even if my lack of ability frustrated me. One night while I was the duty officer, a Top Secret radio came in from the Solomon Islands telling of an aerial ambush. Because the Japanese secret code had been broken, our Army and Navy leaders had discovered that the Emperor's foremost military mind, Admiral Yamamoto, would fly on a certain date to Bougainville Island in the Solomons. The radio to General Marshall predicted the date and hour of Yamamoto's death. When our army, navy, and air force sent P-38's crashing through the flight of Zeros guarding the Japanese admiral and killed him on schedule, the hallways of the Pentagon seemed more eerie than ever.

With fighting going on everywhere, I felt as if I were being shelved. I was sure I could be more useful elsewhere. Bill Ritchie knew that I felt this way and said, "Red, here's a trip that will get you some fresh air. You ever hear of Cat Island?"

"No, what's that?"

"Well, the Quartermaster Corps has a secret project on Cat Island, in the Gulf of Mexico, involving the training of dogs for war, and somebody has to go evaluate it for General Marshall. He often sends people to do work of this kind as a sort of check on official reports. I think I'll send you. We'll talk about it first thing in the morning."

"Combat dogs?"

"Right."

I wrote my "report" that night and Dort stayed up late typing it. In the morning I handed it to Colonel Ritchie.

The report described my flight to Cat Island. It had seventeen paragraphs in this vein:

"*At Cat Island* the question of rank was discussed. The highest rank authorized for dogs at the present time is lieutenant colonel, and this is hardly considered fair. Numbers of these dogs have been to the two-week summer encampment each year and should have more credit. Then, you take the Old Army dogs. They think the present expansion has not given them the rank they deserve. Many of the dogs wanted to be brigadier generals and were writing their friends on the mainland to see if this could be accomplished. There was one old gray, cranky, rheumatic, nasty dog, age thirteen, who it was said would make a fine major general if and when this rank is authorized. This dog bit his best friend the morning I saw him.

Some dogs are in special towers, so high in the air they only know what is going on through rumors."

Colonel Ritchie sent the report, with a note, to General Handy. "Thought you might be interested in Red Reeder's report on the assault dog project. Red is afraid that I will send him to the demonstration scheduled there next week."

General Handy, the marvelous chief of O.P.D., forwarded the paper to General Marshall. Fortunately it struck the top on a good day. The word came down, "Don't send Reeder."

The next day General Handy called for me. He was a lot like Will Rogers, even to the lock of hair that fell down across his forehead, and with just as keen a sense of humor. "Red," he said, in his Tennessee drawl, "the fine officer who does the liaison work between the War and Navy Departments is going away on a top-secret trip. You take his place until he returns in about a month."

This was a high-sounding job. I left the Pentagon in style with a chauffeur every day at 9 A.M., made the rounds of top offices in the Navy Department, and brought back the word.

One morning after I had returned from the Navy's establishment, General Handy sent for me. "Red," he said, "did you bring the news on that U.S. ship being sunk by a Japanese sub?"

"Yes, sir."

'The intercom on Handy's desk roared. "HANDY! Come up here at once! When are you coming? Hurry up."

"Everything OK, General," Handy said. "Don't worry. I'll be there in a few minutes."

When the box had shut itself off, Tom Handy said, "General Marshall has lots of pressure on him. Give me the news about that ship in a hurry."

I said, "Sir, its most important cargo was 275 caliber-thirty machine guns. The rest of the manifest was blankets, cots, tentage, C rations, and mimeograph supplies."

"Where was it sunk?" Handy was at the door.

"Longitude 170 degrees, 30 minutes east; latitude 5 degrees, 0 minutes south."

"My Gad! Don't tell me that. Tell me where it was sunk *at*."

"About one hundred and fifty miles off Guadalcanal."

"Thank you very much," he said.

After I had been liaison officer about two weeks. General Handy said, "What do you think of your job?"

"Well, I go over to the Navy every day and visit all those admirals—that is, their assistants—and I guarantee to you that if they don't want to give me the news, a team of horses couldn't drag it out of them. If we had a sergeant who couldn't do this job, we ought to bust him."

Jack Francis, colonel from Army Ground Force Headquarters, had a somewhat similar job between his home base and O.P.D., and he was skilled. People *wanted* to give him information. One day he said, "What are you doing at 4 P.M. tomorrow afternoon, Red?"

"Nothing."

He grinned. "I'm getting a Legion of Merit for laying out airfields in China before Pearl Harbor, and General Marshall is hanging it on me at four." Jack showed me a pen-written note from a secretary to General Marshall's office: ". . . You will bring twelve friends, no more, no less, and at 1600 hours tomorrow General Marshall will present you with the medal in his office."

"You are subpoenaed," Jack said. "Get your shoes shined."

We filed into the big office and stood in line. Francis was out in front with the general. An aide read the citation with his arms outstretched as if he had astigmatism. When he had finished, the general pinned on the medal and flashlight bulbs popped.

This was a big moment, not only for Jack Francis and his friends, but for General Marshall. He commanded 11,600,000 men in the name of the President, but he did not see them. Here were twelve soldiers lined up in his office.

"Right face!" he snapped. "Come by and congratulate Colonel Francis."

This placed me at the end of the line. I carried out the order, and as we were leaving the room. General Marshall said, "Reeder, come back here! Sit down." He waved at a chair at his elbow. "Just a minute, until I read this paper, then I'll tend to you."

I sat on the edge of my chair, ready for anything. When he had signed the paper, he said, "How are you getting along in O.P.D.?"

"Fine, sir."

"Well, one day we will be sending you out of here. That is, when the right time comes."

"Sir, we're extremely well organized in our section. I could go now."

"No," he said. "Not now."

A real crisis came when Bill Ritchie himself decided to go to Australia and New Guinea for two months. This left me in supreme command of the section.

The first day I was in authority a major came in and handed me a sheaf of papers about engineer soldiers and airmen who would be sent by ship to General MacArthur. He said, "This paper has been concurred in by Generals Marshall, Handy, Wedemeyer, Edwards, Somervell, Arnold, Stratemeyer, and McNarney, and by Colonel Esposito. Will you concur?"

"I think I will. Where's my pen?"

A few hours later, on the "hot line," the secretary of the General Staff said, "General Marshall wants to see right away the secret map showing the next island General MacArthur is going to take."

I took the map out of the safe. I stood quietly while the great man inspected it. The drawing was in color; a sweeping blue arrow pointed at a yellow island dominated by a Rising Sun flag. At the top of the map was the Kamchatka Peninsula and the polar regions; below them Japan. In the center lay the Philippines, then New Guinea, off its coast the island in question, and at the bottom Australia poked its head up.

General Marshall put his nose in the air and howled, "There's no north arrow on this map!"

I understood perfectly. It was his infantry training.

When I was back in the Southwest Pacific Section, I called a meeting of our eleven officers, a warrant officer, a master sergeant, two staff sergeants, two WAC sergeants, and four civilian secretaries. "I want north arrows put on everything. I want them on the globe, on the safe, on the doors, and on the chairs. From now on, if anybody around here turns out a map without a north arrow, he will be sent to Cat Island."

When Bill Ritchie returned from the far Southwest Pacific and relieved me of my responsibility as section chief, he said, "Red, get ready. I am going to send you to Australia in a week."

I made my will and tended to other matters.

General Marshall summoned Ritchie and me the day I was to depart.

"Go in his office and sit down," Colonel Bob Young, secretary to the General Staff, told us. "Don't salute. Just sit there until General Marshall speaks."

Ritchie and I sat in front of his desk. You could feel the pressure on the general. I am positive that George Marshall is one of the principal reasons the Allies won World War II. In a few minutes he said to a lady stenographer. "Have Somervell draw me up a memorandum no bigger than that—" He held up his thumb and forefinger about four inches apart. "I want it to show the status of the armament of all our divisions in this country. Weapons are being shipped out too fast. I want to show the memorandum to Mr. Donald Nelson, head of the War Production Board."

He turned to Colonel Ritchie and me. "Reeder, I hear you are going to the theater."

"Yes, sir."

"Now here is what I want you to do. First, I want you to go to Hawaii and see General Emmons. Tell him . . ." Then General Marshall launched into a long harangue involving joint army and navy staff work in Hawaii. Emmons was not to go to Admiral Nimitz with the idea but was to radio General Marshall personally. I got that much.

"Now," the general said, "repeat that back." Here was his infantry training again. You always have a runner repeat back orders.

I faltered. I did the best I could but I had never heard of this scheme, nor did I know of the army and navy politics involved. I made a poor job of repeating his message.

"REEDER!" he roared. "I am going to tell you *one more time!* You had better repeat this perfectly."

Ritchie's pointed chin looked sharper. "General," he said, "the things you are telling Colonel Reeder belong to the Central Pacific Theater. We are in the Southwest Pacific Section and we don't know anything about them."

"Listen, Ritchie!" The general leveled a finger at him. "This goes for you, too. *You* pay attention! Reeder, I want you to go to headquarters at Fort Shafter, Honolulu, and deliver this message personally to General Emmons. I'll give the message one more time, and when I get through I want you to repeat it back correctly. Understand?"

I surprised myself by repeating the paragraph perfectly. This shows what you can do under stress.

"That's better," the general said. He calmed down. "So Colonel Ritchie is sending you as an observer to Australia and New Guinea?" He was being pleasant now.

"Yes, sir," Bill and I both said. I was ready to depart immediately.

"When you are in New Guinea I want you to explain to small gatherings from six to sixty why the United States is making the Germans the main enemy at this time. After we beat the Germans, we will all return to and defeat the Japanese. I will have Lieutenant General Richardson en route shortly to Australia to explain this important matter to senior leaders.

"Also I want you to go to Guadalcanal. Give my respects and congratulations to General Vandegrift of the Marines. Check in there with our General Patch and tell him I want his idea of how staff work on naval task forces can be improved. I want you to bring back the lessons our Marines and soldiers are learning on Guadalcanal."

He stood up, smiled, shook hands and said, "Good luck, Reeder. I look forward to seeing you on your return."

Down the hallway I thought about explaining to gatherings from "six to sixty" that the enemy shooting at them was not the main enemy. This part of the mission was doomed, and I knew it.

Bill Ritchie said, "General Marshall has plenty of heat on him. That was a nice send-off he gave you at the end."

Ritchie was right, but the headache General Marshall gave me over repeating that message back lasted clear to Chicago.

CHAPTER TWENTY-THREE

General MacArthur

THE C-47A BUZZING SOUTH over the Pacific from Honolulu carried precious cargo: me, Major Lou Walsh, a colonel, and four thousand pounds of mail. There was one seat aboard, and the colonel plopped himself into it and sat there all the way across the Pacific. Dynamite couldn't have dislodged him. He said solemnly, "R.H.I.P." (Rank hath its privileges).

At the end of the first day the plane circled horeshoe-shaped Canton Island, an atoll of dazzling-white coral set in a turquoise ocean. When we had landed, I inched about in the shade of the wing practicing walking and trying to get the gas fumes out of my lungs.

A white jeep rolled up and Colonel Bob Ellsworth, whom I had know as a cadet, jumped out. "Splendid!" he said. "You're just in time for graduation parade."

"Who are the graduates?" I asked.

He pointed toward a long line of artillerymen standing on the edge of the white landing strip. "Those twelve buckos in front of the colors. They've been here seven months and tomorrow they escape."

"Where will they go?"

"Hawaii."

I thought the artillerymen were wearing white tennis shoes until I glanced at my own shoes. They were coated with white coral dust that covered, and filtered into, everything.

Colonel Ellsworth took his place as reviewing officer and I stood on his left. He shouted, "Graduating class, front and center, march!" The band at the far left blared an unrecognizable march. It reminded me of the West Point cadet rally band at the beginning of an off year. "We have to order people to be musicians," Ellsworth explained, "because we don't have enough. But they can play one song well, 'The Canton Island Song,' and they practice it all day long.

When the graduates were behind him, Colonel Ellsworth yelled, "Pass in review!"

Here they came, the band tooting the spirited "Canton Island Song" to the tune of "The Marine Hymn." Bob Ellsworth sang it for us late that night in his suite of rooms dug out of a coral bank. It started something like this, "We're going to leave this goddamned eye-a-land and get the dust right off our shoes . . ."

Before the sun sank rapidly into the Pacific, Ellsworth placed me in his jeep and we toured the island. It did not take long. He showed me the artillery positions and talked about the Japanese submarine that had hidden in the sunrise a month before and had shelled the landing strip. "We don't have near enough artillery," he explained. I agreed and sent a radio to General Handy the next morning advising that Canton Island be reinforced. When I saw things later in Australia and New Guinea, I hoped that radio had been lost in transit, or wherever radios get lost. We were shorthanded everywhere.

The jeep rolled up a slight grade. "Here's the highest point," Bob said. There stood a palm, the only tree on the island, tightly enclosed with a blue picket fence. Nailed to the fence were two signs: "Elevation 14.01 feet," and "TREE—Keep Away." Things like that help make Americans unique. They can laugh under almost any circumstances.

On the flight to Brisbane the load on my mind was the mission to Guadalcanal. How was I to bring back lessons? The motors of the plane seemed to say. "Lessons! Lessons! Lessons!" Lessons had always been difficult for me. How could I make them easy for others? It seemed impossible.

In Brisbane I checked in at Lennons Hotel, where the quality stayed, and walked to the headquarters of the Southwest Pacific Area to report to General MacArthur.

Major General Sutherland, his chief of staff, barred the way. "You can't see General MacArthur. He's too busy."

I was very disappointed. This was mid-October 1942. Almost everyone in the world was interested in MacArthur's dramatic escape from the Philippines. I knew that when I returned to Washington a logical question would be, "How does General MacArthur look?" In addition, I liked him.

"I know the general," I said.

"I will tell him you're in the area," Sutherland said. "You can't get in at all. He's tremendously busy."

I went back to the hotel and felt better when I saw Lieutenant Colonel "Vald" Heiberg, one of the smartest men in my class."When you get back to California," he said, "please call my wife, Evelyn. She has no idea where I am, and I'm not allowed to tell her in a letter."

I asked about his job.

"I'm General Hugh Casey's executive officer. He's MacArthur's engineer. I handle everything from mapping, to engineer supply, to purchasing. The big job is building airfields. You can't win without them."

After talking with staff officers in General MacArthur's headquarters for three days, I made arrangements to fly north in Australia and to New Guinea. Before leaving Lennons I tipped a bellhop and handed him a recent copy of *Look* magazine. I had marked an article by Major George Fielding Eliot, "The War's Greatest Generals." Eliot described General MacArthur, Field Marshal Rommel, Marshal Timoshenko, General Yamashita, Field Marshall von Rundstedt, and General Sir Archibald Wavell. I scribbled across the title, "To General MacArthur from Red Reeder, one of your old cadets." "Take this up to the general," I said to the bellboy and departed.

The plane flew north above sheep and cattle country and landed at Rockhampton, the headquarters of Lieutenant General Robert Eichelberger. This experienced soldier and his almost-as-experienced staff received me warmly. I visited the soldiers of the 41st Division in training, and when I returned in the late afternoon the general himself took a pointer, stood before a map, and explained the strategic situation to me.

"It's precarious," he said. "Here's New Guinea. Its outline always looks to me like a prehistoric monster."

The Japanese had captured tremendous areas – from Korea south, almost all of the Solomons, and half of the northeast coast of the "prehistoric monster." Although General MacArthur had only some Australian forces, two infantry divisions, a few naval vessels, few planes compared to the enemy, and almost no naval transport, he had decided to take the offensive.

On a side trip to the Rockhampton zoo, where General Eichelberger explained the animals to me, he said "Red, are you going to report to General Marshall when you get back?"

"Yes, sir."

"I wish you'd tell him I feel bad that my presence here has not been announced. I want Americans, my family and friends to know where I am."

"I'll do what I can."

In Port Moresby, on the southwest coast of New Guinea, I reported to two other splendid leaders, Major General Ennis Whitehead and Colonel Fred Smith, Air Corps. I knew Fred Smith well; we had been golf partners in Panama, and I had met General Whitehead once or twice. His friendly but gruff manner reminded me of General Lear.

General Whitehead said, "I'm glad to see a baseball player. I'm one, too. Played semi-pro ball in Kansas, where I'm from, and all over the Midwest." We talked about the chances of the St. Louis Cardinals, who were making a run for the pennant.

At breakfast the next morning an aide interrupted the general at his eggs to say, "Sir, there are five observers outside. What shall I do with 'em?"

The few hairs on the general's head seemed to rise. He stalked outside and I with him. "Stand behind me, Red," he said. I did but wished I were back inside.

The five culprits were in every sort of uniform. In the center of the group, wearing a steel helmet on his head and a pistol hanging cowboy-style from his hip, stood the colonel who had occupied the chair all the way from Honolulu while Walsh and I sat on the mail. One observer had so much baggage it required two men to carry it.

"How am I going to run a war bothering with you people?" General Whitehead barked. He peered at the guests over the rims of his specs. "You come in here and eat my chow. I'd like to know: Is my ration going to be increased? You'll pay cash, oh yes, but there's no damned markets around here where we can run out and buy food for you. And I have to bed you down!" The general made it sound as if he personally had to make up the beds. "Each of you people requires special care and I'm not prepared to give it." Then, facing the inevitable, he said, "I suppose you want breakfast. Well, we'll share what we have, only we're not happy." Then he turned to me. "Red, you want to go to Milne Bay? I have a plane for you."

I felt guilty. I was an observer, too, but I was leading a charmed life.

Milne Bay, at the tip of the "monster's tail," was a supply base that had been recaptured from the Japanese, and United States goods of all kinds had been poured in there. If there was any place where the waste of war was on display, it was at Milne Bay. Great piles of everything lay in mud puddles. The place was indescribable. I took snapshots.

The next day General Whitehead sent me over the Owen Stanley Mountains, over some of the most difficult country in the world. These mountains and the courageous Australians had defeated Japanese infantry a month before when they had toiled within twenty miles of the five airfields at Port Moresby. The slopes of the jungle-covered Owen Stanleys looked as sharp as a razor. We flew through gaps in the range just north of Mount Suckling, which rose over eleven thousand feet above the Pacific, and landed at Wanigela airstrip, a lonely field covered with grass about four feet high, which our aviation engineers had carved out of the jungle.

Natives who looked as if they were sponsored by the *National Geographic* magazine rushed up when the plane stopped. Both men and women wore only G-strings or aprons that hung from their waists, except for the more affluent men, who had red blankets for skirts. Here, red cloth served as money. Each native held out his hand for a gift. The only thing I could spare was a mechanical lead pencil that would not work, and I donated that in the cause of United States diplomacy.

A soldier led me along a path bordering a swamp, toward Wanigela Mission. He pointed to a mound beside the trail that had a rude cross fashioned with sticks. "When we were building this airstrip, one of the fellows started playing round with a native's wife. We found him here one morning with a bolo stuck in his back.

These women don't wear hardly anything, but after this murder we keep our eyes straight ahead."

"Did they catch the murderer?"

"Catch him? Why, all these natives look like peas in a pod. The Aussies got one of their Angaus (Australian-New Guinea Administrative Unit) in here as soon as they could, but that was two weeks later. They're like the Canadian Northwest Mounties. As sharp as this Angau was, all he could do was to make notes. None of the natives knew nothin' from nothin'."

Wanigela Mission was a Church of England army post with the grass houses arranged in a small semicircle bordering the beach. With eleven thousand Japanese forty miles up the coast at Buna, the missionary had become alarmed over the safety of his family and had hiked with his wife, their six-month-old baby, and two trusted servants over the Owen Stanley Mountains to the safety of Port Moresby.

The coast lugger *King James*, about eighty feet long, steamed into the Wanigela Bay and tied to the rickety bamboo and sandalwood dock. The boat looked as if it had chugged out of the pages of Somerset Maugham. Almost as soon as I climbed aboard the captain complained of his pay. He was a fat man without angles and a face like dark strawberry jello. He wore a sleeveless undershirt, filthy dungarees, and a dirty yachting cap clapped to the back of his head.

"They pay me a pittance," he said, "and say it's patriotic and all that for me to sail up here and be a target for Nip bombers. This is probably my last trip." He pointed at about fifty holes in the pilot house and smokestack. "Jap bombs done that. That's why I'm creeping up the coast out of here at night. If they fly over, don't you stand up and gawk like my mate done two weeks ago and get a piece of iron through your heart. Lie flat. We buried old Hank at the north end of Goodenough Bay and now my crew is all natives—not a white man who understands. You want Hank's bunk?"

"No, thank you. I'll sleep on the deck."

I was glad to be aboard the lugger as it puffed up the inky coast, happy to feel the breath of a breeze and to escape the clouds of mosquitoes that swarmed out of the jungle at dusk.

Twenty miles south of Buna the *King James* anchored and natives in outrigger canoes paddled the cargo, C rations and ammunition, to the beach. I wondered how MacArthur could ever mount a successful campaign. How could he take even the first step against the Japanese at Buna with this shoestring equipment?

Two battalions of our infantrymen were waiting. Some had been flown over the Owen Stanleys by General Kenney's air forces while others had hiked over the precipitous Kapa Kapa Trail. Both battalions had tried to march up the coast from Wanigela Mission but found the jungle an almost impassable quagmire. Small boats had ferried them to their present position twenty miles from the enemy.

These were splendid men, most of them from the midwestern United States, but they lacked training in jungle warfare. The odds seem stacked against them.

To see as many of them as I could, I followed a trail cut through sword-like Kunai grass six feet high, a path where no air could bother the bugs. At a dirty first-aid station an army doctor from Ohio gave me a cup of tea and I relaxed and listened.

"Nine thousand damned feet up we climbed—up, up, up. It was pure torture and no way to pack my medical supplies without getting them squashed."

The messy layout of medicines and equipment under a tent fly looked as if it had been trampled by a herd of elephants. The doctor read my mind. "When we have wounded to care for I won't be able to give them my best care."

An aid man wearing a beard and a hacked-up khaki uniform filled my canteen cup with more tea. I noticed that no one at the aid station was armed."We're twenty miles from Buna," I said. "Shouldn't you have some weapons here? Suppose a Japanese patrol came down the trail?"

The doctor touched the Red Cross brassard tied about his left biceps. "We're safe. The Geneva Convention."

We had an argument, but he remained convinced that the Japanese would observe the amenities and made no move to become better prepared.

While we were talking, an Australian plane buzzed just over the treetops and pelted us with shoes. Some hung in the tops of the highest trees, others sank in the swamps. Air supply isn't as efficient as the uninitiated think.

"Our men will love these shoes," the physician said. "Our own field shoes were shot after we had been in the jungle three weeks.

These Aussie shoes don't fit us snug under the instep but they are better than anything America's got."

I thought back to my Panama days when I tried to get Lieutenant Colonel Muggins interested in a better field shoe and wished that I had made a definite nuisance of myself.

The infantrymen in the New Guinea jungle were waiting for Australians who were climbing over the mountains, and since no one knew how many weeks would pass before there would be action at Buna, I headed back for Port Moresby.

Hiking down the jungle trail toward the coast lugger, I saw movement through the trees and vines—people coming toward me. It was a tense moment. I had learned in Panama to expect anything on a jungle path. I had a pistol.

In a moment I was face to face with an American colonel and sergeant. "Leif Sverdrup," the colonel introduced himself. He looked like a Norse explorer. "I'm here to hire fuzzie-wuzzies to help an engineer battalion build an airstrip. Where are you from?"

"Washington, sir."

"Washington! I thought they only sent us orders."

When I was back in Port Moresby I said to General Whitehead, "Sir, can you please send me up the Guinea coast beyond Buna and over to New Britain? I'd like to see the country where we're going to fight."

General Whitehead peered at me over his specs. I felt he disapproved, but in the morning he said, "Red, I've got you a volunteer, one of our best men, Captain Ray Petersen.* He's out of West Point three years."

At the B-25 I said to Ray Petersen, "I want to be sure you don't think you *have* to take me."

"Glad to do it. I fly up the coast every now and then."

We heard a yell from a crowd about fifty yards away. When we trotted over to see what the excitement was about, we encountered one of the great natural leaders of the war, General George Kenney. "My buccaneer," MacArthur called Kenney, commander of his air force.

George Kenney was in the center of a ring of about two hundred pilots, navigators, bombardiers and mechanics. Before him stood

*He was killed on an air mission in New Guinea one month later.

a young captain, about Petersen's age—twenty-seven. General Kenney's jaw waggled slightly when he talked. Every eye was on him and you could see the approval on the faces of the group.

"Courage like this fellow has," Kenney said with a tap on the captain's shoulder, "is the stuff that'll beat the Japs. Look at this guy's clothes." Kenney waved his hand at the pilot's spotless coveralls and shined shoes. "He must have known I was coming." The group howled. The Air Corps general reached in his pocket and pulled out the Silver Star medal and pinned it to the heart of the pilot's coveralls. Kenney shook the captain's hand and said, "Boy, if we can keep knocking down Zeros like you did last week we're in." Then Kenney turned to his aide. "Get this man's middle name, serial number, details of time, flight number, and so forth, and when we're back in Brisbane write up the citation."

If this had been infantry, we would have had a formal review for the hero, an adjutant out in front droning canned English, the ranks at attention, eyes front. I wished Kenney were an infantry leader.

When Petersen and I flew in his twin-engine bomber over the Owen Stanleys, rain clouds filled the gaps. The country was startling; back at Port Moresby the fields were burned brown, but on the northeast side of the range everything was a rich dark-green. We flew over Buna and its two airstrips, and you could see why General MacArthur *had* to capture it. The air base at Moresby was all-important; he could not afford enemy airdromes just over the range, and at this time he lacked air bases and naval forces that would let him bypass enemy strongholds. It was now a case of "fight and reduce" every Japanese position.

At Buna a river and two creeks cut through dense rain-soaked jungle. It was almost impossible to see the Japanese positions; only what I took to be a slit trench or two were visible.

The ruggedness of the coast was astonishing. In many places there was no beach, the mountains rising straight out of the ocean. Clouds of steam floated up from some of the valleys, reminders of the almost unbearable climate. When we were 120 miles north of Buna, above Lae, Japanese antiaircraft guns opened up. Dirty-yellow bursts shook the plane, and I did not enjoy it. We were at 8,500 feet. Petersen climbed a few hundred feet more to miss the sprays of iron. I felt as if I were naked on a high-diving platform with someone shooting at me from below.

At the end of four hours we were back at Moresby. General Whitehead, there in his car to meet me, said to us, "You fellows are crowned with luck. Red, do you know about the Coastwatchers?" I knew them, a top-secret Allied organization of civilian volunteers, equipped with tele-radios, who were placed at intervals along the coasts way up into the Philippines. Every now and then a native betrayed a Coastwatcher and the Japanese would capture him and behead him. It took a special brand of courage to be a Coastwatcher.

"Well," General Whitehead said, "A Coastwatcher radioed that five minutes after you fellows flew over Cape Finschafen on your way back, nineteen Zeros zoomed over the place coming in from the Philippines."

I wrote up a description of our flight, but I am sure the report was not worth the risk we had taken. In time I felt guilty about that flight.

Two days later I stepped out of a B-17 "Flying Fortress" at the Brisbane airport. I was retrieving my baggage when a husky master sergeant tapped me. "You Colonel Reeder? General MacArthur wants to see you right away. I've been waiting here for you two days. Get in this car and I'll rush you to *the* general." I recognized his type. The best noncoms in the world are Americans; they weld the United States Army together.

"I have to shave," I said. I knew there was no hurry.

"I don't want you to escape, sir. I'll go with you to the men's room."

The sergeant took me past General Sutherland, in the office that guarded MacArthur, and turned me over to the great general. I saluted. "Sir, Colonel Reeder, one of your old cadets."

MacArthur gripped me on both shoulders—that is, branded me as one of his men. "Old cadet? Comrade in arms!"

He towered above me. I mention this because when he became elderly he lost height. In his prime he was about six foot one.

He motioned me to a settee and remained standing. "Seeing you makes me think of the happy days when I was Superintendent at West Point and Hans Lobert was our jolly baseball coach. I look forward to the day when I can go to a major league baseball game with Hans again, eat peanuts and drink soda pop and yell at the umpire." His mood changed and his dark eyes burned. "I want to hear about New Guinea."

"Milne Bay is the worst supply dump I ever saw, sir. I can't imagine how it could be more wasteful."

"I asked General Blamey, Australian leader, to relieve General Clowes, and he was not relieved because he is so popular with the Australians. I will ask again."

I said, "A Captain Petersen flew me up the New Guinea coast in a B-25 and we went over Lae, Finschafen, Cape Gloucester—"

"You flew into enemy-held territory on reconnaissance?"

"Yes, sir. Captain Petersen took me."

"I am proud of you, proud as I can be. Write up your notes for Chamberlin."*

The general launched into a twenty-five-minute monologue, and the more he talked, the angrier he became. Electricity shot about the room. The couch I was sitting on sagged at the back; I was looking up at him as he paced back and forth. He must have walked a mile, with no ten-minute breaks. At times I felt he was addressing someone who was not in the office. Then the general concentrated on me. "You people in Washington! Don't you read my radios? How am I to defeat an enemy unless I have airfields in the forward areas? When is a combined force of all arms coming my way? Do I always have to lead a forlorn, lost cause?"

I squirmed uneasily. The sofa was uncomfortable. I once heard Hans Lobert say about a ball player, "His play was to keep quiet and he didn't know how to make it." This seemed to fit my case. I coughed; that was the best I could do.

"Did you see our infantry in New Guinea?"

"Yes, sir. Near Moresby and also about twenty miles south of Buna."

"How did you get up the New Guinea coast? Did you ride one of my 'sea transports'?"

"Yes, sir. The *King James*. On it you get a feeling of the day before yesterday."

"How many tons?"

"Eleven, sir."

*Major General Stephen Chamberlin, General MacArthur's expert operations officer.

"See what I mean? An eleven-ton transport! When you go over to the Central Pacific Area near Guadalcanal, you will see cargo ships and transports worthy of the name. As you know, I have some naval support, but not enough—not nearly as much as they have in the South Pacific.

"And another thing." His voice became charged with even more irony. "Marshall sent a lieutenant general all the way here to try to explain why we are a secondary theater." He shook his head and talked on nervously.

I could see the results of the long strain he had been under. He had had no let-up from the terrific pressure, and none was in sight. He doubled back and took a few more cuts at Washington.

The general was making me nervous. I tried to interrupt, but he charged on. A few minutes later I did manage to interrupt. Now he eased up.

"What are you doing at six? Please meet Mrs. MacArthur and me in our suite an hour from now for tea."

At two minutes before six I took the private elevator in Lennons to the MacArthur suite. When I stepped into the L-shaped foyer I heard a thick voice say, "Lady, I'm not movin' a damned hair until I see the greatish general in the world."

A sailor sitting on the floor had his back propped against the wall for badly needed support. He had no hat and no haircut. He was glassy-eyed.

Mrs. MacArthur said, "Colonel Reeder, he says he won't go until the general comes home."

"You're damn' right I wont' go!" He snapped at me, "Listen, mate, you and nobody else's gonna make me. I'm gonna see General MacArthur if it's the last thing I ever do, so hep me."

The elevator boy and I assisted the sailor to his feet and into the elevator. I could hear him howling as the cage descended.

Mrs. MacArthur looked like a debutante. Beautiful. "Red, our tea is postponed. The general may not be home until nine. Tea tomorrow, I hope."

Tomorrow never came. The next morning I became ill and when I woke up I was in a Roman Catholic hospital with good sisters and doctors caring for me. "I think it's dengue fever," a doctor said.

I felt as though I were suspended in a bottle of black ink. Sir William Osler once said, "Humanity has but three great enemies: fever, famine and war; of these the greatest by far and by far the most terrible is fever." I only know famine from hearsay, but I agree with the great Canadian physician.

I was on fire, burning up. People appeared at my bedside and vanished. I never saw the same people twice. The walls and the ceilings tried to crush me. Air? There wasn't any air–just overwhelming blasts from a fiery furnace. A warrant officer popped through the floor and said, "Bad news. I am from General MacArthur's office. A radio. Your father died in Virginia two days ago. General MacArthur said to tell you he is sorry."

I felt a million miles from Virginia and my family. A major glided from his hiding place behind the door–maybe this was the next day or a week later–and said, "General MacArthur sent you this, his photograph." The two messengers seemed like parts of dreams, but when I finally became better there was the signed photo and the sad-news radio from the Pentagon.

In ten days I was able to sit in a swing in the hospital garden near an urn coated with green moss–a quiet spot out of the Middle Ages. My father had died suddenly, of a stroke. I wondered about my mother. I also worried about the war. It seemed to me we were going to lose.

A sister handed me a letter from my wife. Not once during the war years did she write me of her troubles, and with four children there are plenty of troubles. Never once did she complain, but this letter tore my heart out:

> The children and I walked up to the drugstore for an ice cream soda. Russell spotted an officer in uniform seated in one of the booths and ran to him, arms outstretched, crying "Daddy!"

This made me feel bad. I felt such hate for Hitler and Tojo that I almost became sick again. I was not doing my share in raising our children.

When I went back to Lennons Hotel I met Joe Stevenot, reserve colonel, who had been manager of the Philippine Long Distance Telephone Company before the Japanese struck and who had escaped from the Philippines. Stevenot, thin and wiry, showed me a snapshot and asked, "Do you know this guy?"

"Sure. 'Polly' Humber."*

*Colonel Charles Humber died on a Japanese prisoner-of-war ship in 1945.

"Well, here he is—raking weeds in a Jap prison farm. They made him foreman because he knew something about agriculture."

"How far from Humber were you when you snapped this?"

"Oh, twelve feet. I was in the bushes and made a little noise and he looked up. You see, to escape I hung around a while while the Japs ran to the coast and searched for me."

"Can you give me any news of Moe Daly?"

"It's not good. On the death march the only water the Japs allowed our men was in the mud puddles in the road. When the column of prisoners passed an artesian well district, with water spurting out of the ground, two of Moe's Air Corps privates broke ranks to get water and two Jap sentries chased them with fixed bayonets. Moe kept the two guards off, but one of them beat him over the head with his rifle. Before that Moe was a tremendous help to an army officer on the march who had been tortured by the Japs‡—they broke this guy's arm and his jaw because he wouldn't give information."

I still felt weak from the fever and packing up for Guadalcanal was not easy. I wobbled down to the hotel's restaurant, where I was sipping a lemon squash when Lieutenant General Robert Eichelberger and his able deputy, Brigadier General Clovis Byers, walked in. Eichelberger's friendly grin was gone.

"Come up to my room, Red," he said. "I need a drink and something strong." When we three were alone, he sat on the edge of his bed, pulled off his shirt and tossed it wearily aside. "I have just come from General MacArthur. He told me—and Clovis, too—'Take the Japanese fortifications at Buna or don't come back alive.' MacArthur promised me a high-ranking decoration if I took the place and said he would release my name for the newspapers." Eichelberger's humor bubbled through in a grim way. "I never thought that in my old age—I'm fifty-six—I'd get orders like those."

I realized that in this step on the road back to the Philippines Douglas MacArthur was placing the ground leader he considered most capable in command of the attacks at Buna. I had seen the swamps, and I knew of the fortifications. I wondered if General Eichelberger could win.

‡Colonel P. D. Calyer.

(I did not see the battle at Buna. Robert Eichelberger and his Allied forces took the place in a month's campaign, capturing a Japanese field fortification for the first time in the history of the Japanese empire. To win, General Eichelberger went to unusual lengths to rally demoralized troops, even leading small units through swamps, down jungle trails, to overcome the Japanese positions.)

CHAPTER TWENTY-FOUR

Coconut Island

AFTER LEAVING BRISBANE I rested in New Caledonia for two days to try to throw off effects of the fever. When the night plane took off for Guadalcanal, I crept into a berth that would hold a seriously wounded man on the return trip. It was dark. Even the plane's wing lights were extinguished. While the plane droned over the Pacific, the motors were at their tune again, *"Lessons! Lessons! Lessons!"*

The twin-engine C-47 put down an hour before daybreak at Henderson Field in the center of the 9,000-by-5,500-yard perimeter defended by the Marines and an Army regiment. I opened a C ration can marked "Macaroni and Cheese" and diluted an envelope of instant coffee in a canteen cup of lukewarm water. After breakfast I reported to the scholarly-looking Major General Alexander Vandegrift. He was a courtly Virginia gentleman who looked like the principal of a school. He received me as if I were from just out of town, and I liked his warmth.

When I had explained my mission, he said, "I thank General Marshall for asking for my opinion. My message to the troops in training for this type of warfare is to go back to the tactics of the French and Indian days. This is not meant facetiously. Study their tactics and fit in our modern weapons, and you have *a* solution. I refer to the tactics and leadership of the days of Rogers' Rangers."

An hour later I stood beneath a coconut tree and faced some of the best Marine fighters, fifty of them who had gathered in response to my request to General Vandegrift. They were a listless-looking group, sprawling in the shade of the coconut grove. A faint breeze from Lunga Point rippled the tops of the trees. The early November morning on Guadalcanal felt like a June day in the Hudson River valley—there was no hint of the oven-like heat three hours away. But even at midday Guadalcanal had resort weather compared to the dank New Guinea coast. The Marines had their weapons close by.

I took off my steel helmet and addressed the group. "I am from General Marshall's office in Washington. The Army Chief of Staff is very anxious to get any information you can pass on to the United States Army men who are in training. I asked General Vandegrift to send me his best fighters and he sent me you people. Here's your chance to pass on to troops in the United States anything you've learned here."

I readied my notebook expectantly.

No one said anything.

To overcome the inertia of the silent Marines I began again: "When I explained why I was here to General Vandegrift here is what *he* said." I opened my notebook and read his statement. "I'm glad to take that back," I said to the Marines. "I hope you will give me more detail. Who has something to offer?"

No one batted an eye. The fifty Marines looked like fifty graven images. A machine gun chattered up on the scarred crest of Bloody Ridge, and over in the jungle near the Ilu River, where the 164th U.S. Infantry Regiment held a long sector, 81-millimeter mortars coughed. Then it was quiet again. A coconut almost beaned a Marine private just in front of me. With no change of expression he reached for his steel helmet and clapped it on his head. I thought of Private Rodriguez and his helmet when he was attacked by one of William Randolph Hearst's camels. The silence was overpowering.

Finally I beckoned to a rough-looking Marine gunnery sergeant and walked him out of earshot from the rest of the group. We sat on a log. "See here," I said. "I have come a long way. I have to have some of the things you've learned. General Vandegrift said you were one of his best men. Now give me something."

A torrent of words spilled from the sergeant's lips. I took them down, then read them back. "I been in the Marines sixteen years, and I been in three expeditions to China and five engagements since I have been in the Solomons. I will say that this 1942-model recruit we are getting can drink more water than six old-timers. We have to stress water discipline all the time. They don't seem to realize what real water discipline is. We have too many NCO's in the Marines who are 'namby-pamby' and beat around the bush. Our NCO's are gradually toughening up and are seeing reasons why they must meet their responsibilities. Respectfully speaking, sir, I think that when officers make a NCO, they should go over in their minds, "What kind of NCO will he make in the field?" I can't think of nothin' else."

The next Marine on the coconut log with me was Corporal Fred Carter. "I'm in the Fifth Marines," he said, "like Sergeant Beardsley. What do you want?"

"What have you learned here about leadership?"

"Leadership? Why, to me that's knowing your job. Over on the Matanikau River we got to firing at each other because of careless leadership by the junior leaders. We are curing ourselves of promiscuous firing, but I should think new units would get training to make the men careful.

"We learned not to fire unless we had something to shoot at. Doing otherwise discloses your position and wastes ammunition.

"Sergeant Dietrich of Company I of our regiment recently used his head. One night when the Japs advanced, a Jap jumped into Sergeant Dietrich's foxhole. Sergeant Dietrich pulled the pin of a hand grenade and jumped out. There was a hell of an explosion and one less Nip.

"I have been charged twice by the Japs in bayonet charge. Our Marines can out-bayonet-fight them and I know our Army men will do the same.

"A Japanese trick to draw our fire was for the hidden Jap to work his bolt back and forth. Men who got sucked in on this and fired without seeing what they were firing at generally drew automatic fire from another direction."

I had learned something I should have observed long ago: often a virile American is not anxious to stand up and sound off as a hero or an authority in front of his fellows.

After I had worked all morning interviewing the fifty now talkative Marines one at a time, I went up on Bloody Ridge. Here the first battalion of the 7th Marines had withstood the pointed attack of three Japanese regiments and part of a Japanese brigade in the closing days of October. The leader of the defensive stand, one of the great heroes of the United States Marines, greeted me. Colonel Merritt Edson, one of the "best fighters," had told me, "Be sure and see "Chesty" Puller. He's the greatest fighting man in the Marine Corps."

Lieutenant Colonel Lewis Puller had the reputation of being a salty character and he looked it. He had a square jaw and his firm mouth had a grim set to it, yet there was a kindly twinkle in his almond-shaped eyes that carried a glint of green. He stalked along the ridge, plainly in sight of Japanese scouts that must have been in the jungle on the other side of the short field of fire. Chesty was naked except for a steel helmet, white cotton shorts, and field shoes. I wondered why he didn't wear socks.

Puller gave me the "Leif Sverdrup treatment": "From *Washington?* Great day in the morning! This *is* a surprise." He continued in his soft accent, "Course I'll give you a statement, only my higher-ups won't like it, but I don't give a damn." He chuckled to himself. "I been talking out of turn since I enlisted in the Marine Corps in 1918 and I might as well continue." I readied a pencil.

He said, "In handling my companies I take the company commander's word for what is going on. You have to do this to get anywhere. In order to get a true picture of what is going on in this heavy country I make my staff get up where the fighting is. This command-post business will ruin the America Army and Marines if it isn't watched. Hell our platoons and squads would like the command post in the attack if they are not watched! As soon as you set up a command post, all forward movement stops.

"To hell with the telephone wire with advancing troops. We can't carry enough wire. We received an order, 'The advance will stop until the wire gets in.' This is backwards!

"The staffs are twice as large as they should be. The regimental staff is too large. I have five staff officers in the battalion and I could get along with less. The officers have to dress and look like the men.

"It is OK to say that an outfit cannot be surprised, but it is bound to happen in this type of warfare; so therefore your outfits must know what to do when ambushed.

"Calling back commanding officers to battalion and regimental CP's to say, 'How are things going?' is awful."

After I left Chesty Puller I walked toward the army sector past a dugout roofed with coconut logs and buttressed with sandbags. A radio blared static, then I caught the words, "First down, Army . . ." I poked my head in. Two soldiers had their faces pressed to a radio. "Army-Navy game," one of them said. "Come on in."

"What's the score?"

"Navy's ahead by two touchdowns."

No one likes Army-Navy football more than I, but at this time on Guadalcanal it seemed incongruous.

I walked down a jungle path to a board shack, headquarters of Major General Alexander ("Sandy") Patch. The gray boards of the captured weather-beaten shack were dotted with Japanese characters.

The gaunt general lay on an iron bed in the back of the building underneath a mosquito net. He wore a pair of khaki trousers, nothing else. When the aide introduced me, the general waved the mosquito net aside and pushed himself up. He looked all skin and bones, and in a moment toppled back into bed. His watery blue eyes fixed on mine. He was obviously ill. I gave him General Marshall's message and he said, "General Marshall wants *my* opinion? I can't get over it. *My* opinion? Are you sure?"

When I went out, his aide said, "The general has a fever that's eating him up. He won't let us evacuate him because he says to stay here is his duty."

That night, before I stretched out on the floor near the entrance of the general's shack, an aide handed me a mosquito bar and said, "The Japanese bomber 'Washing Machine Charley' usually comes over at about one in the morning and drops a few bombs, a nuisance raid to interrupt our sleep. The orders are, when the alert sounds, everyone gets in a foxhole and stays there. General Patch is very strict on this. I'll show you a hole you can occupy if the bastard comes over."

In the middle of the night the siren at Henderson Field began to moan as if its tail were being twisted. I pulled on my shoes, found my foxhole, and jumped into it. It stank. The ungodly screams of the siren stopped and the night became deadly quiet. Then, in a few minutes, you could hear the faint sound of the Japanese bomber. It sounded miles off and almost tinny, with a faint rhythmic beat.

The aide came through the darkness and said, "Colonel Reeder?"

"Yes."

"General Patch invites you to stand with him. He's under those palm trees near the shack."

When I found Patch, he said, "Reeder, I am the commander and I don't think it becoming of me to hide in a foxhole, so when this darn plane comes over I stand. You are General Marshall's representative and I think—maybe—it's not the thing for you to hide in a hole, either, so I invite you to stand with me. It's up to you, strictly."

"Oh, thank you," I said.

Moonlight made the Ilu River, flowing a few yards behind us, a jagged streak of silver. For a few moments a moonbeam illuminated the general's steel helmet, then the two stars on his shirt. The shadows of the coconut palms cast crab-like patterns on the packed red earth while our own shadows stretched out over twice our length. Mosquitoes hummed almost as loudly as Washing Machine Charley. Suddenly a stick of bombs crashed close to the five-inch guns at Lunga Point. Two more ripped up a metal plank that surfaced Henderson Field and two others roared in the coconut plantation across the Ilu about two hundred yards away. Soon the siren whined again, and we went back to sleep. In the morning we learned that two Marines had died near Henderson Field.

I walked to the tiny command post of Colonel Bryant E. Moore, the 164th Infantry. I had known him slightly when he instructed in French at West Point ten years before. Now he wore army khaki and sat on the side of a jungle-covered hill talking to a bone-tired patrol from his regiment that had been behind the lines for fifteen hours. He handed each of the seven men a miniature bottle of brandy and made them dilute it with water in their canteen cups. After he had interviewed the patrol leader and one or two of the other men, he thanked them and dismissed them.

He said, "No brandy for you, Reeder. To earn this you have to go behind the Japanese lines. You want a statement out of me?"

"Yes, sir."

"The M-1 rifle is a fine rifle. It is doing fine work here."

Then he stopped. He was a state-of-Maine man and not talkative. I once heard his description of a trip on a rich man's yacht from

New York City. All he said was, "We had a splendid trip. When we were out of sight of land we had a mutiny."

"Colonel Moore," I said, "tell me something about leadership."

I had hit a sensitive spot. He forged ahead. "Leadership! The greatest problem here *is* the leaders, and you have to find some way to weed out the weak ones. It's tough to do this when you're in combat. The platoon leaders who cannot command, who cannot foresee things, and who cannot act on the spur of the moment in an emergency are a distinct detriment.

"It is hot here, as you can see. Men struggle; they get heat exhaustion. They come out vomiting, and throwing away equipment. The leaders must be leaders and they must be alert to establish straggler lines and stop this thing.

"The men have been taught to take salt tablets, but the leaders don't see to this. Result, heat exhaustion.

"The good leaders seem to get killed; the poor leaders get the men killed. The big problem is leadership and getting the shoulder straps on the right people."

Sixty-millimeter Japanese mortar shells fell about thirty yards away and attacked a number of coconut trees. I lost interest in taking dictation and the colonel stopped talking. When the salvo was over and things were quiet again, Bryant Moore said, "Where was I? You saw that patrol. I tell you this, not one man in fifty can lead a patrol in this jungle. If you can find out who the good patrol leaders are before you hit the combat zone, you have found out something.

"I have had to get rid of about twenty-five officers because they just weren't leaders! I had to *make* the battalion commander weed out the poor junior leaders. This process is continuous. Our junior leaders are finding out that they must know more about their men. The good leaders know their men."

By dusk on the third day I had filled four large notebooks. I walked to the operations shack at Henderson Field and caught a C-47A that was flying wounded south to Nouméa, New Caledonia. There was only one serious casualty aboard; the rest were walking cases, and maybe the Marine occupying the bucket seat next to mine was a shell-shocked case. He was munching shredded coconut from a can.

"Want some coconuts?" he asked me. "Beats them things with hairy shells on them."

"No, thanks. Where is it from?"

He looked at the label. "I'll be a monkey's uncle! Brooklyn!"

When I was back in the Pentagon, Colonel Bill Ritchie greeted me and asked about my trip. "How'd you make out on those lessons from Guadalcanal the old man told you to bring back?"

"I'm working on them."

"Have 'em typed up, Red. I'm really interested."

I turned my notebook over to Sergeant Lalley to type. I was worried about handing the report in and I had no confidence in it because it was not written in formal General Staff style. I sent a copy to Colonel Jack Whitelaw, an old friend who had served in the English Department at West Point, a literate soldier, and asked his opinion.

Dort and I also went to see my cousin Colonel William McPherson, who lived in Washington with his wife, Daught. Daught and my wife talked about the inconvenience of ration stamps and how to juggle them so you could broil a steak and still eat for the rest of the month while I sat on the floor and read Mac the manuscript.

"I see your problem," he said. "This out-of-line grammar and slang. Wonder what the General Staff will think? They have their own corner on the English language."

"It would do some of them good to be upset."

"If you hand it in the way it is and if it sees daylight, people will read it. It's a brand-new departure."

Jack Whitelaw encouraged me on the phone, then dashed off a note. ". . . This is food for thought for enlisted men and junior officers. The latter will be helped because they will employ it in preparing simple training exercises. Leave it alone! Don't edit it any more. Its punch will be lost with refinement."

I sat on this report for three days, then I told Dort, "I'm going to surrender it just as it is. I think that some of those paperwork hounds will throw a fit because it isn't in General Staff style, but if they don't fancy it they can send me away. I don't like the Pentagon anyhow."

I handed the report to Bill Ritchie at 5 P.M. When I came to work at seven thirty the next morning, there was a strange major sitting at my desk. I thought, *Oh! Oh! Here is my replacement already.*

"Colonel Reeder?"

"Yes."

"I'm from General Marshall's office. He read your report and likes it. He told me to tell you that it will be printed in pamphlet form and will be issued in every place we have troops in training. He's ordered a million copies printed and he says he will try anybody who so much as changes a comma. He says he doesn't want any digests or summaries made. He's ordered it reproduced and studied just as is. He's working on a foreword now, writing it himself."

I sat down on the corner of the desk, too amazed to be elated. I react slowly.

"The general wants to know if you have any objections to the pamphlet being titled 'Fighting on Guadalcanal'?"

"No," I said weakly. "I have no objections."

CHAPTER TWENTY-FIVE

General Marshall

I GAVE GENERAL HANDY the highlights of my trip and he said that General Marshall would send for me when he had time. I went around the Pentagon looking as if I had just stepped out of a military haberdashery. I felt as if I were in cold storage.

A man telephoned from the Government Printing Office. "That report of yours we're working on. We had a bad thing happen. With all this new personnel, we forgot to send you galley proofs and our production people ran off fifty thousand copies. Entirely too many to disregard. What shall we do? This means there may be misspelled words."

"Don't worry about that. It will made some people happy. They'll feel superior discovering balled-up words. Anyhow, General Marshall said he would try anyone who changed a comma."

"Will a light-blue cover be satisfactory?"

"Perfect."

It was ten days before General Marshall sent for me. I found him in a relaxed mood.

"Well, Reeder, glad to see you back. I received the radio from Emmons after you passed through Hawaii." He smiled and his face broke into unusual patterns. "Emmons answered that paragraph you memorized. Splendid report from Guadalcanal. Once when

I was on General Pershing's staff in France I wrote a report in my own style and a staff officer above me suppressed it. I like particularly the thoughts you brought back from Guadalcanal on leadership and weapons. That problem on how to reduce Japanese pillboxes. I am ordering every branch of the service that can assist to study your report. I am anxious to see what they can do. I'm sorry you were ill. How are you now?"

"Fine, sir."

"Now is there anything on your mind? Anything at all that you think I should know? Anything you did not tell Handy?"

I thought a moment. I could see General Eichelberger fighting at Buna. I took a long breath. "Sir, General Eichelberger would like to have his presence in Australia announced. It has never been put out to the press."

A typhoon swept the office. General Marshall jabbed the point of a pencil downward into a scratch pad. He thundered, "If I thought for one minute that Eichelberger asked you to say that I would tear the three stars off his shoulder as I would rip the stripes off a corporal."

I managed to gasp something on a different subject. What it was I do not know.

"That's all," Marshall snapped.

I went back to my desk and sat down. You feel bad when you try to help someone and it boomerangs. I expected a bolt of follow-up lightning to strike, but it failed to dart out of the clouds.

The next day that major handed me a signed copy of General Marshall's 260-word foreword for *Fighting on Guadalcanal*. I liked best his last two sentences, "Soldiers and officers alike should read these notes and seek to apply their lessons. We *must* cash in on the experience which these and other brave men have paid for in blood."

General Marshall sent me to the War College, the Infantry School, and to Fort McClellan, Alabama, to make speeches about jungle warfare and leadership. He ordered each branch of the Army and each section of the General Staff to study the pamphlet, and this was bitter medicine for a handful of weapons experts.

In about a month my mail increased. Someone sent me an order issued at the headquarters of the 88th Infantry Division, Camp Gruber, Oklahoma, which said that the lessons from the booklet *Fighting on Guadalcanal* would be applied in daily training and would be used in officer and noncommissioned officer schools. Then came the awful sentence. "Examinations will be held on the booklet on February 20, 1943." I could see those fellows taking the exams. I never thought I would cause anyone *that* kind of trouble.

Three uncommon notes came. One was written by General Marshall to General McNair, and Colonel Bill Sexton was thoughtful enough to send me a copy. ". . . The British General Sir Harold Alexander told me that this brief pamphlet is the most impressive training instruction he has seen. Alexander referred to it two or three times as the sort of stuff soldiers will read—the ordinary instruction bores them."

Colonel Jack Whitelaw wrote from Army Ground Forces Headquarters, "A sergeant here, not particularly bright, read the pamphlet. When he had finished he thought a while and said, 'Sir, I know now why we train.'"

The third, Sergeant Lalley wrote from England. "I am in the Air Corps now and last Sunday afternoon a mechanic lying in the bunk next to mine was reading *Fighting on Guadalcanal*. Suddenly he let out a yelp. 'Christ! This pamphlet is a lot of crap! No one can tell me that a damn lieutenant colonel is going up to the front to write down what sergeants and privates think.' I told him, 'It's *not* baloney. I know the lieutenant colonel and I typed the manuscript.'"

About three and a half months after I returned to the Pentagon I was at my desk when I felt that something had gone wrong with the heating system. No one else seemed to mind. I put on my overcoat. "I'm catching a cold," I said. "I'm freezing." I went out in the courtyard and sat in the sun—and became very ill. In Walter Reed Hospital the hobgoblins again gathered at my bedside—"the little people," my friend Sergeant Marty Maher of West Point had called the terrors of the night.

Sir William Osler did not lay it on thick enough when he described the tortures of fever. I was stretched out in a dark room that rocked up and down. Water evaporated before I could swallow. My wife slipped in and out. "Reoccurrence of malaria," the doctors said. "We don't think he ever had dengue fever."

I was promoted to colonel, but the silver eagles were not nearly as important as a dose of Atabrine. After I recovered from the illness I had two weeks at home to regain my strength and to be introduced to my children.

Back in O.P.D. top-secret reports coming in from many sources about Americans in the Philippines filled me with mixed feelings. I was proud of Colonel Pete Calyer, Colonel Wendell Fertig, Major Ralph Praeger and other guerrillas who were fighting the Japanese despite great hazards, but I had a hollow feeling when I read dispatches about the prisoner-of-war camps. I could imagine Moe Daly. For news of him I went to see Brigadier General Blackshear Morrison Bryan, whose name, my sister Nardi said, sounded like a chain of hotels. He was provost marshall general for the United States.

"News isn't much," he said. "I saw a note Moe penciled from the Cabanatuan camp: 'I am well. Received Red Cross package.' That was all it said, and it was over two months old."

"What's his address? I want to write him."

"Don't. I think the Japanese have a list of every General Staff officer in the country. If they see your name on a letter to Moe, they'll put even greater pressure on him."*

After I had been on the General Staff about a year, I noticed how many aviators wore the ribbon representing the Air Medal, and I thought it too bad that the ground soldiers did not have a similar decoration. On June 27, 1943, I placed the idea in the form of a letter, stressing that it would be an aid to morale if the captain of a company or the captain of a battery had a medal he could award to deserving people serving under him.

In O.P.D. we had one day off in every thirteen, and on one of my free afternoons I took the paper to Ground Forces Headquarters at Washington Barracks and gave it to General Leslie McNair, commander of Ground Forces. It seemed to me a good idea to carry the paper direct and not send it through channels where it might be harpooned.

I knew McNair slightly and found him interested. "I'll have this staffed—looked into," he said. Then we discussed the war. He had a kindly, informal manner that won your confidence.

Two weeks later Brigadier General Floyd Parks, his chief of staff, telephoned. "General McNair approved your idea. The medal will be called the Bronze Star."

*Colonel M. F. Daly died on a Japanese prison ship in 1945.

About this time, George Marshall encouraged the idea that "lower echelons" should award certain medals rather than have senior officers make the necessary decisions. He abandoned this after a major awarded the Bronze Star to a mess sergeant in Fort Niagara, New York, for inventing a new recipe for stew.

Reading the secret radiograms pouring in from the Southwest Pacific and the important ones coming in from other theaters was like having a grandstand seat in the war, but it made me feel that I was not pulling my oar. You could do the work on an "action radio" but still feel you had done little to help.

One day in mid-March 1944, when Bill Ritchie was away from the section for the afternoon, I received a bolt of electricity. The dreadful intercom squawked, "General Marshall wants to see the top-secret map showing the locations of airfields General MacArthur is using. In a hurry!"

I hauled the map out of the safe, checked to be sure it had a north arrow, and went through a door marked "Secretary to the Chief of Staff, United States Army."

"He's in there waiting." A colonel pointed.

While the Chief of Staff studied the map and made a note or two, I had an opportunity to study him. He was elegance itself in his neat uniform; nails pared and polished, tips whitened. I made a mental note to buy myself some nail whitener. He was sixty-two now and beginning to have a double chin. His reddish-brown hair was thinning. He had a glare he could turn on when he was interviewing slow-thinking staff officers.

He leaned back in his chair, removed his glasses, and rubbed his forehead. I was sitting in a chair at his elbow.

"Reeder, how are you getting along?"

"Fine, sir."

"Can they spare you down in your section?"

"Yes, sir."

"You've been here almost two years now."

"Yes, sir." I wondered what he had in mind.

"Where do you want to go? What do you want to do?"

"I want to fight under General Bradley."

"I should think you would want to go to the Southwest Pacific."

"No, Sir. They know too much about me out that way."

"Well, something may be developing in the 4th Infantry Division in England. I'll keep you in mind. In the meantime Handy is sending you to California to bring back an opinion of the combat effectiveness of the soldiers who are on maneuver at the Hunter Liggett Reservation. I also want to know how realistic the maneuver is. After it's over Handy may send you to the San Francisco Port of Embarkation to check on a supply problem."

San Francisco! I could eat in Bernstein's Fish Grotto. Supply problem? I had no training in supply.

"I don't know when this thing in England will develop, Reeder. You go ahead on the trip to California."

I told Dort about General Marshall's conversation. She picked up the ball quickly. "It looks to me as though you're going to Europe. I think I'll get ready to move to Leavenworth with the children."

A soldier who loves his family and thinks his place is at the front is torn emotionally. I think it was a Bill Mauldin character who summed it up, "War is no damned good."

In order to take our two oldest children to Kansas City, where Grandmother Darrah would meet us and take the children to Leavenworth, I received permission to travel to California by train.

We climbed on the B & O in Washington–Ann, seven, Dodie, five, carrying our luggage and a load of doll suitcases. The trip was easy until we were three hours from Kansas City and Ann began to cry.

"I don't want my daddy to go to war," she sobbed. My feelings sank to my shoes.

A lady across the aisle with a daughter about Dodie's age took care of Dodie, and they played dolls, but Ann knew what was going on. You cannot explain "war" to a seven-year-old child, and that is what I attempted. She held her head in my lap and sobbed. This was a bottom point in my life.

Grandmother Darrah and her beaming face saved a bad situation at the Kansas City station. I slumped in my seat and the train rolled west. I wondered when I would see the children again.

When I stepped off the train near the Hunter Liggett Military Reservation, gray fog was rolling in over the tops of the hills, and I felt grayer when I saw the soldiers who would participate in the maneuver. They looked like sheep, dismayed and lost. By the way they marched down the road I could tell they were only partially trained. It made me angry at our military policy that fostered unpreparedness while wolves and madmen tried to conquer the world. It seemed unfair to even think of sending such raw soldiers to war.

I walked into the circus tent which served as maneuver headquarters and an officer handed me a telegram: YOU ARE BEING REPLACED AT MANEUVER. RETURN TO O.P.D. AT ONCE BY AIR. W. L. RITCHIE.

I felt numb flying east. The trip seemed about fifteen minutes long.

In Washington General Handy showed me a radio signed "Eisenhower." "Red," Handy said, "this vacancy for a regimental commander is in the 4th Infantry Division in the European Theater. It's too bad we sent you to California. Can you leave in three days?"

"Yes, sir." I gulped.

I phoned Dort and said, "I am moving to play the outfield."

There was a pause. "Do you mean what I think you mean?"

"That's right, honey. The lineup is changing in three days. I'll see you tonight."

I ran downstairs to the Pentagon dispensary to take the physical exam so I could go overseas. The doctor was unimpressed and unconcerned. He scanned my medical record. "You can't go overseas because you have had malaria."

I thought I had not understood. "What was that, Doctor?"

"You have had malaria. You can't leave the country."

"This is a damned disgrace!" I shouted.

"What about the scar on your neck?" he said. "Did you ever try to commit suicide?"

I almost swung on the man.

"Hell, no! Listen! We have soldiers fighting under MacArthur who have had malaria eight and nine times, and you tell me I can't go to Europe because I have had it twice! Wouldn't that sound great? A colonel can't fight if he's had malaria, but privates can have it eight or nine times and go straight to the enemy." I was so angry the words shut themselves off.

"I am carrying out orders of the surgeon general."

"Where is his office?"

I grabbed a taxi and sped across the city. On the first floor of a towering office building I ran into a Medical Corps officer who had two stars on his shoulder. I did not know his name but fortunately he knew mine. "What brings you here, Red?" he asked.

I boiled over again.

"I agree with you," the general said. "I'll take care of it. You've passed your physical."

I went back to the Pentagon to fill out dozens of forms, arrange for air transportation, and run final errands. Then I received a note from one of General Marshall's secretaries. "You may invite twelve men to the ceremony in the Chief of Staff's office at eleven thirty tomorrow morning. . . ."

General Marshall stood in the center of the room near his big desk, with the twelve guests lined along the wall. Colonel Charlie Gailey barked out a citation—flowery, and hammered out of the best dead language. I was near the general and felt as though I were getting married again, only there was no bride. I caught phrases, ". . . his understanding of the requirements . . . the result . . . jungle warfare and leadership . . . Allied nations throughout the world."

General Marshall pinned on the Legion of Merit and said, "Photographer, all right." Then he said softly, "Look at me, Reeder, not at the camera." When the photographer was exhausted, the general snapped at the guests, "Right face!" This put Major General Tom Handy and Colonel Jack Francis at the head of the line. Their shoes sparkled. "Come by and congratulate Colonel Reeder."

After the milling around I thanked the general and started for the door. I felt he was going to speak again.

He said, "Reeder, come back. Wait a minute." He concluded some business with General Handy and Colonel Gailey, then, when we were alone, he gripped my hand firmly. "I want you to put your spirit into that regiment. It is important. You can do it. Godspeed."

Down the hall General Handy said almost the same thing. I began to wonder what was up.

I went to see Colonel Royal Lord of the European Section in O.P.D.

"Ikey," I said, "I know that D-Day is June fifth. That's sixty-seven days away. Can you tell me something about the regiment I'm going to lead? What happened to its colonel? Why is there a vacancy?"

"First, get this in your brain, Red. You know that General Eisenhower has set D-Day tentatively for June fifth only because you work here. You've been 'bigoted.'"

GEN George C. Marshall congratulates RR after pinning on the Legion of Merit, March 1944, wishing him God's Speed as he heads for Normandy.

"What's that?"

"That's the code word for the greatest secret in the world—the time and place of the Normandy landings. *Do not let it out!* At this time not even your general in the 4th Infantry Division has been bigoted. They'll bigot people from generals to privates according to a schedule. We have a major general—that is, he *was* a major general before Omar Bradley and Ike Eisenhower busted him to colonel—coming home from London on a slow boat because he talked too damn' much at a cocktail party. Hell of a sad case. I don't know what happened in the 4th Division that turned up a vacancy for a colonel. You may find out when you report. The only particular I know is that the three regiments of the 4th will land on D-Day at Utah Beach, so you're to be a D-Day man. Good luck."

I could feel the pressure already. Sixty-seven days to go—a short space of time in which to learn the ways of a three-thousand-man regiment, to know its people, and to try to make myself an integral part of the unit.

At five that same day I went to an O.P.D. farewell party Bill Ritchie had arranged at the Army-Navy Town Club. General Tom Handy, a natural leader and the official leader of the group, said he wanted to say a few words about bravery. My face burned. Then he said, "This man," he jerked a thumb at me, "will be in the thick of the fight. Red, you have the best wishes of everyone. Now, Red, to put the party on a lighter plane I wish you'd tell about the time you sat up all night working on the radio for General Marshall to send to MacArthur and about how you thought up the phrase, 'Your situation is appreciated.'"

"General, you robbed me of the punch line."

It was a brief party, and at the door some of my friends handed me letters and notes. One read, "You will win a star, as I don't know anybody who can lead a regiment through hell like you can . . . G. Ordway." For luck, I stuck Godwin Ordway's note, along with snapshots of my family, in the wallet that I would carry in Normandy. Another gave me a small package marked "Present from the Asiatic Theater. *Save to read on the plane.*"

That night my wife and I put the two smaller children to bed together. It was a difficult time for us. I set the alarm for 4 A.M., and when it rang Dort scambled eggs and fried bacon for me. They tasted like lead. The toast was raw sandpaper, even when coated with jam. It was hard to swallow anything. A taxi came to the door. I struggled into my new trench coat and kissed Dort good-by. "I will be back," I said.

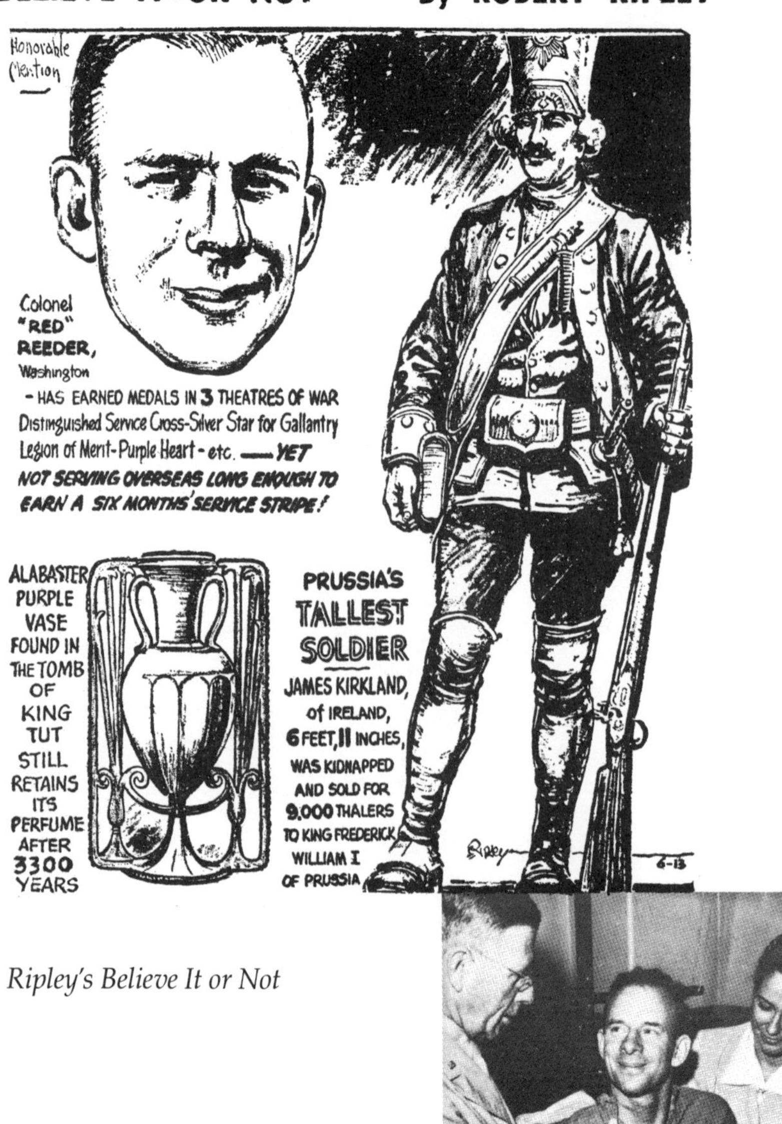

Ripley's Believe It or Not

1944, Dort Reeder watches as General Ben Lear awards the Purple Heart.

1944, Dort Reeder watches as General Ben Lear pins on the Purple Heart

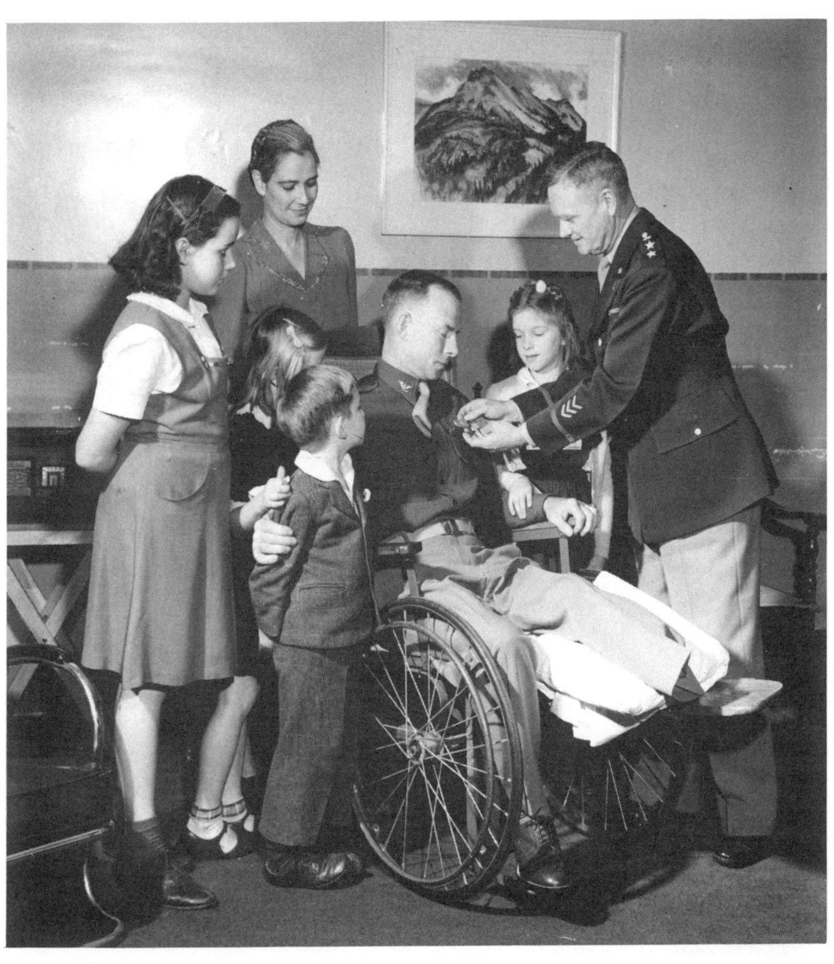

RR's family gathers around at Walter Reed Hospital, 1945, as MG Tom Handy pins on Bronze Star Medal. L. to R.: Ann, Dort, Julia, Russell, RR, Dodie, and MG Handy.

RR and MG Otto Nelson at Army-Notre Dame game in Yankee Stadium, NYC, 1944.

L. to R. Gene Leone, Restaurateur; Red Smith, Sportswriter; Dave Cammerer, columnist; RR; John Martin; Doc Blanchard, W.P. All American "Mr. Inside"; Cappy Wells (standing), PR officer, USMA, at Toots Shor's in NYC, 1954.

CHAPTER TWENTY-SIX

General Montgomery

As THE FOUR-ENGINE PLANE flew over Long Island Sound, I opened the reading material from the Asiatic Theater, O.P.D. It was *Fighting on Guadalcanal* printed in Chinese—an excellent translation, I think.

The plane headed for Goose Bay, Labrador, Iceland, and finally settled at Prestwick, Scotland. It was dark at Prestwick, and I was disappointed because I had always wanted to see Scotland.

Wartime blackout was in effect all over Britain. A guide drove me down the blacked-out street to the railroad station in an automobile that crept along with two tiny parking lights. The gloominess of the darkened station was heightened by people, shadows rather, who moved about without sound. It looked like a station across the River Styx.

The train bore through the night and at daybreak rumbled into London, where another guide picked me up and drove me to General Eisenhower's headquarters. I caught a glimpse of the great general as he hurried down a hall. I was surprised how vigorous he looked, and his grin made me think things were breaking our way.

An adjutant received me. "General Eisenhower will be in conference all morning. If you will go to General Bradley's headquarters, they'll send you to the headquarters of the 4th Infantry Division." I felt like a letter being shuttled through channels.

Part of General Bradley's headquarters on Bryanston Square had been burned out by the magnesium bombs recently dropped by the Germans during the blitz. Already I saw one of the principal differences between the war in the Pacific and in Europe. In the Southwest Pacific the wretched climate was an obstacle; in Europe enemy firepower was far heavier.

I was disappointed not to see General Bradley because I knew him. "He's out inspecting troops," an aide said.

As I was driven to 4th Division Headquarters at Tiverton, fourteen miles north of Exeter, I began to get butterflies in my stomach. I wondered what I was getting into. It was April 1, a dubious day for me to report.

"General Barton is upstairs in his war room," the adjutant general said.

There was a sentry at the general's door, fixed bayonet on his rifle. A sign screwed to the door read: "KEEP OUT—by order Division Commander."

I knocked. The door flew open and on its threshold stood a stocky general, two stars pinned to the collar of his woolen olive-drab shirt. He had a bristly brown moustache that emphasized the whiteness of his skin. His brown hair was neatly parted. I saluted and reported to General Barton.

"Come in. Glad to have you with us." He shook hands and smiled, but almost immediately his attitude stiffened. "Right now I am pressed—tremendously busy." He waved his hand at a table heaped with papers. "I know you want to get to your regiment, the 12th. My assistant division commander, Brigadier General Teddy Roosevelt, will brief you, but come inside a moment."

The walls of Raymond Barton's war room were plastered with maps. I could see the Normandy peninsula down near the floor. The center section of the main wall was the Dutch coast. He introduced me to two officers who were studying the maps, and as he shepherded me back to the door, he said, "Reeder, you've just come from the Operations Division, War Department General Staff."

"Yes, sir."

He said intensely but quietly, "Then you *must know* about the landing. I need to find out when D-Day is, when and where we are going to land. It would help us all in our training if I knew. Do you know?" Barton's brown eyes seemed to bore into me.

I caught my breath and thought of Colonel Lord and his warning. I felt I had to lie. I stared straight ahead. "No, sir."

For a few seconds he said nothing, then he bit off the words, "Well, see Roosevelt. I'll see you in a few days."

I could feel the pressure on General Barton.

On the way downstairs to General Roosevelt's office, I thought, *I am getting off to a swell start, lying to the division commander.* I knew General Barton had a big load on his mind and I suspected that he sensed he had little time to get his division ready for D-Day. Nevertheless his harassed look and the question he asked bothered me.

Teddy Roosevelt was entirely different. He bounced out of his chair, grinned and grabbed my hand. "Well, Red Reeder, where have you been? For a week we've been looking for you. I read *Fighting on Guadalcanal*. What a job! Sit down and relax. Tell me about your trip over. What's going on in the States?"

"Teddy" Roosevelt, Jr., was about five feet nine, with a wiry frame, a nose that had once been broken, and a leathery face. He had unusually small hands and feet, but there was nothing small about his nature. It was expansive. He loved everybody and it was fun to be with him. When I talked about his father and asked about the Roosevelts, he boomed in his raspy voice, "I'm one of the Oyster Bay Roosevelts. We're out of season."Then he beat me laughing at his own joke. I told him that my father had idolized President Teddy Roosevelt and in his understated reply I thought I detected a note of discord. "Ah, yes," he said, "Father was quite a man."

"General, tell me about the 12th Infantry. Why was the colonel relieved?"

"Great bunch. Damn, I like those people. The colonel? I'm a World War I soldier, too, so how can I say he is too old? He is a competent, able soldier but not in good health."

"How many Regular Army officers in the 12th?"

"Oh, six or seven." He picked up a paper from his desk. "Let's see, counting all hands they have a grand total of 167 officers. Right now, Lieutenant Colonel Jim Luckett is holding the fort."

I knew Luckett. He had been a fine hurdler at West Point and had been turned back a year in his studies. "Efficient, and he can laugh," I said. "I am glad he's here. General, what about this regiment?"

"Well, it's the stepchild of the division. The other two regiments receive the praise and the 12th is always close at hand for its share of the hell. I think it lacks confidence. The 12th Infantry has not earned a compliment since the year one. It needs someone who can stand up for it."

I can do that, I said to myself.

General Roosevelt placed a hand on my shoulder. "Red, there'll be problems, yes. You recall Kipling, 'My brother knows it is not easy to be a chief.'" He gave me his wide grin. "If I can ever help you, just get the word to me."

On the drive to Higher Barracks, near Exeter, headquarters of the 12th Infantry Regiment, I wondered more about what I was running into. I felt uneasy about my meeting with Major General Barton. My own problem looked big to me. How could I place my stamp on this regiment as its leader and learn the characteristics of 167 officers and hundreds of noncoms in the two months until D-Day?

Higher Barracks was a small British army post on loan to the United States. The three battalions and some smaller units of the 12th Infantry were billeted in other British posts and in nearby towns. On my second evening, in order to meet the officers, I asked them to assemble in their best uniforms at the gymnasium. When they were lined up in two double ranks, I marched into the building between the ranks followed by the regimental and national colors. I had seen such a formation when I was a second lieutenant at Fort Benning. Then I stood on a small stage, took the regimental colors in my hands, and when the officers were seated made a brief talk about the regiment's background. I was helped by my knowledge of American history, the engraved silver bands on the staff of the colors, the blue-and-gold battle streamers, and a pamphlet I had studied on the regiment.

"This regiment was born in 1799 when a crisis with France threatened our nation. In the War of 1812 it helped smash the British back when they attacked Fort McHenry, near Baltimore, and it was there when the 'Star Spangled Banner' was born. The 12th Infantry served under General Winfield Scott in Mexico, and you can see the names and dates of eight engagements in silver on this staff.

"In the Civil War the 12th fought from 1862 to 1864—thirteen battle rings. It took part in some of the bloodiest battles of that awful war. It was at Antietam. It seized Little Round Top at Gettysburg and held on. It fought under Grant at Spotsylvania, Cold Harbor and Petersburg. . . . Later, in the Indian campaigns, the 12th knew hard, forgotten, lonely warfare. . . It was outstanding in the Spanish American War . . . in the Philippines . . . on the Mexican border in 1915–16 when bandits raided Texas and New Mexico. In World War I many of its men served in Siberia. This is the kind of background we have. The record of our regiment is a story of proud service to the United States. Its motto is 'Led by Love of Country.'"

In conclusion I promised these officers that I would help them all I could, that I was available day or night. After the meeting one officer remained.

"Sir," he said, "I am Second Lieutenant John Everett.* I am not satisfied with the training in my platoon."

"What's the matter with it?"

"It's not good."

I admired the moral courage of this handsome, lanky lieutenant. Few will say that the training they are responsible for is faulty.

I watched his platoon simulate an attack at seven thirty the next morning and it was poor, but the platoon was not typical. Everett lacked experienced noncoms, but there were none available to give him. I worried. *What will happen when casualties hit Everett's platoon?* On the whole the 12th Infantry was far better trained than soldiers I had seen in New Guinea and on Guadalcanal, but it was not as experienced as the Marines of the Pacific.

I soon became acquainted with a worry of the regiment which quickly became my problem: the 12th Infantry lacked four .30-caliber machine guns and eight Browning Automatic Rifles.

I questioned Major Kenneth Lay, the regiment's crack supply officer. "I try every day to get them," he said, "but all I receive are promises. To give our men training we swap guns around, and this wastes time."

"And of course every man wants to train with the arms he is going to use in the fight for his life. I'll go see General Barton."

My conference with the general gained nothing. "I have loads on my mind, too much to worry about this. This is *your* problem."

When I stepped out of my jeep back at Higher Barracks, Major Lay and a lieutenant met me. "Sir," Lay said, "this lieutenant has a boyhood friend in a supply depot twenty-five miles from here.

*This officer was killed in Normandy on D-plus-one.

He called his pal, who's a master sergeant, and if we'll go up there tonight with a truck, he'll slip us those guns. Otherwise we may not get them until about June 1."

"What the hell kind of army is this?" I asked. "*Slip* us the weapons!"

I knew that "cross-country methods," getting supplies through friendship and by other means, ball up a supply system and that it was also against orders.

"Get me Lieutenant Mills," I said.

William Mills, from North Carolina, looked as though he might be nicknamed "Cotton." He was about six foot two, spoke with a drawl, and was one of the best officers in our regiment. He was earnest and mature, and he enjoyed a joke—if he couldn't see one he could think one up. In the regiments of 1944 a colonel was allowed three liaison officers who could be given almost any kind of duty. Lieutenant Mills was one of these.

"Mills," I said, "you'll have to go with this lieutenant and get the weapons. I don't want to send Lay. I'm saving him for a real emergency. And don't get caught or we'll all be hanged."

"I can't go," Mills said. "Tonight's the night of the division commander's map-reading exam."

I had forgotten. Because of the horrible reports that had come in from combat telling of mistakes that officers had made when they tried to read maps under stress, General Barton had ordered additional map-reading courses followed by a test. I was happy that regimental commanders were excused.

"Mills," I said, "I am going to examine you now in map reading. What's the declination of the compass in Nome, Alaska?"

He looked puzzled. "Sir, I don't know."

"Well, what is the exact distance in inches from San Francisco to Brisbane, Australia?"

Mills gave me his wonderful smile. "I don't know, sir," he drawled.

"Can you tell me the exact location of Hitler's headquarters?"

"No, sir."

"Well," I said, "you missed three questions. I know you know all the rest. I am awarding you a grade of 97 per cent. Now go get those guns!"

My West Point conscience bothered me but was salved later when I saw the 12th Infantrymen cleaning Cosmoline from Lieutenant Mills' haul.

A few days after Mills captured the missing weapons. General Barton phoned. "Red, Monty will spend the day with you tomorrow. Your parade ground is too small for a real show, but place the men so he can see them and put a mike on a jeep so he can talk to 'em."

We were lined up wearing steel helmets and field jackets when General Sir Bernard Law Montgomery showed up. With him were Generals Barton and Roosevelt, and ten staff officers. I was at the head of the regiment and Jim Luckett was on my left. Montgomery walked up and I saluted and reported.

Montgomery was wearing his black beret and a long tan overcoat. He was a small alert figure with a perky nose. He fixed his piercing eyes on mine, then turned to Barton and said, "Do you think these two men are qualified to lead this regiment? This man who took six years to graduate from West Point and that one who took five?"

"I'll answer that," I said. "We have more experience than the average."

I was so abrupt I think I spoiled what was intended to be a joke. Monty looked at me in mild astonishment. He turned and went ahead with the inspection and I joined him.

Every now and then he paused to question a man with an attitude bordering on the haughty. "Where are you from, my man?"

"New Jersey, sir."

"Oh, yes. New Jersey. Small state, north of Washington."

When General Montgomery was ready, I gathered the regiment close about him in a huge ring. He climbed up on the hood of a jeep and seized the microphone in a confident manner. It had rained hard the night before and the grass was saturated. "Sit down," said Monty.

Not a man moved. A few looked at the ground and shifted their positions so they might stand in a drier place.

The little general barked, *"Sit down, I say!"*

About six out of 3,220 men carried out his order. General Sir Bernard Law Montgomery was angry. He shouted as hard as he could, "I SAID: SIT DOWN!" The regiment sat down, but I think few heard his speech. I knew of his great reputation but I began to doubt if Monty was the type who could lead Americans successfully in a prolonged operation.

But the free world is indebted to General Montgomery. When Prime Minister Winston Churchill asked him to study the plans for the Normandy invasion, Montgomery reported after working all night. "This is a dog's breakfast. I refuse to approve. The D-Day forces and landings must be increased or the enemy will throw us back into the sea." He was experienced, smart, and arrogant.

Once in Washington General Marshall had sent me with a message across town to Field Marshal Sir John Dill, Senior British officer in the United States. "Stay there and talk to him a little bit," General Marshall said. "I want you to see a real leader." General Dill was a man of great charm with a first-class brain, and his humbleness drew you to him. After I had delivered the message, he said, "Pull up a chair, Colonel Reeder, and tell me about the war. Here I am, an old man, shut off from you young fellows and almost completely ignorant of what's going on." Sir John Dill looked as distinguished as Bocker might have if he were alive and in a general's uniform. You felt as though Sir John were your grandfather, yet you *knew* he was a field marshal.

Montgomery was a far cry from Sir John, yet General Montgomery could be human when he wanted to be. After he had spent about two hours with the regiment on the field, he and his party went to my room to clean up. Teddy Roosevelt pointed at a small silver-framed picture of Dort on my mantel. She was dressed in a white ruffled blouse, with her hair in a braid around her head, and she looked out at you with big dark eyes. Teddy Roosevelt said, "Reeder married above his looks."

Montgomery placed his sharp nose almost on the picture and laughed. "He did, indeed."

A small British major walked in and saluted me. He was the "house keeping officer" at Higher Barracks, relieving us of administrative details. Montgomery had gone to the bathroom down the hall.

The major's voice quivered with excitement. "Sir," he said, "may I please shake hands with General Montgomery? He coached me twenty years ago for my commission."

"Certainly," I said. "Stay for lunch."

So Montgomery would not be surprised, I met him down the hallway and apprised him of the major. He put his chin in his hand and said, "I remember that chap. One eye slightly askew?"

"Yes, sir."

The famous general re-entered the room, ran his eyes over the major and half-faced away from him. The trembling major saluted and thanked him for his help long ago. Montgomery shook his hand briefly and directed his response to me. "Shall we eat? I'm on a schedule."

Monty was loved by his soldiers because he was cautious with their lives. He was vain, caustic with officers, and as the war proceeded, he became controversial with the American high command.

Not long after that one of our outstanding army generals, "Lightning Joe" Collins, a nickname his drive on Guadalcanal had earned him, put us through a difficult three-day maneuver. We were placed on transports and landed at Slapton Sands on the coast of England. The maneuver was more warlike than anyone had bargained for because German E-Boats darted into the convoy and sank one of our transports. When we hit the beach after a realistic bombardment of the coast, the 12th Infantry dashed inland on its mission. One of Collins' staff officers ran up to me as I waded ashore and handed me an entirely different mission. I could see the value. We were practicing confusion and the chances of confusion occurring on the beaches in Normandy were great.

Somehow I turned the regiment and headed it toward its new job. At the end of three hard days I received a message from General Barton. "General Collins congratulates the 12th Infantry on its performance, and so do I."

I seized a jeep and drove to each company of the regiment. From the hood of the jeep I told the men how good they were, and I borrowed a little and added that on, in the manner of Bocker. I did not require a mike like Monty. You could see the looks of appreciation on the faces of the soldiers. I felt the 12th Infantry Regiment was getting ready to pay off the United States.

When I got back to Higher Barracks a motorcycle messenger drove up and handed me a package from General Roosevelt. It was a bottle of Scotch with a note reading, "Congratulations. If you ever do have a staff meeting, serve this. Teddy."

We did have a staff meeting and drank to Teddy Roosevelt's health.

The critique of the maneuver, and a conference on the Normandy landing, were held in a theater in Plymouth. I took with me everyone who had been bigoted, and that now included officers down to the rank of major.

It was great to see old friends at the assembly: James A. Van Fleet; Maxwell Taylor and Matt Ridgway, who would lead airborne divisions in Normandy; Ralph ("Doc") Eaton, who would fly in with the gliders; Colonel George Smythe, famous West Point athlete; and I met Colonel "Paddy" Flint.*

Flint was a character and looked it. He had a weather-beaten face and stenciled on his steel helmet was his "brand," AAA – 0; Paddy said it stood for "Anything, anywhere, any time, bar nothing." This was the motto he impressed on his 39th Infantry Regiment. Smythe told me that some of the generals liked the spirit but not the insignia. "It will tell the Germans that the 39th is in front of them," they said. But Paddy refused to remove it from the helmets of his men. He had it on everything he could think of from the jeeps of the regiment to directional signs. I knew stories about Flint, but I had never met him before.

"Paddy," I asked, "was it true that you were a midshipman and kept bothering the Superintendent at Annapolis for a transfer to West Point?"

"As true as your eyes. If I had come to West Point first, I'd be so high-ranking they'd confine me to a headquarters."

When the large audience was seated in the theater, the curtain went up and revealed a huge map of the Cotentin Peninsula in Normandy. In front of it stood the Corps commander, dynamic Lieutenant General Collins. He talked of the missions of the different units in Normandy. In his hand was a long pointer. "Here is the 4th Division and its job." The pointer swept the map toward Cherbourg. "Here is its 8th Infantry, Colonel Van Fleet commanding. I served in the 8th Infantry. It is a fine regiment of great traditions, and it will accomplish its mission.

"Here is the 22nd Infantry, Colonel Tribolet. I served in the 22nd Infantry. It is a fine regiment of great traditions, and it will accomplish its mission.

"Here is the 12th Infantry, Colonel Reeder Commanding." Then he stopped and talked of the problems of the landing.

*A Vermonter from St. Johnsbury, Harry Flint was killed at the beginning of the St. Lo breakthrough in 1944.

I felt I could not let the general and his talk end there. I had ten 12th Infantrymen with me. When the general paused I stood up.

"Sir," I said, "may I make a statement, sir?"

"Certainly, Red. What is it?"

"The 12th Infantry Regiment is a fine regiment, a regiment of great traditions, and it will accomplish its mission."

After the applause, Van Fleet howled, "Red, you looked like a West Point plebe correcting a first-classman."

CHAPTER TWENTY-SEVEN

"Cast Not Away Your Confidence"

THE TALL MAN on the platform made you feel he was your older brother. I was sitting in the front row with other 12th Infantrymen, engrossed by his every word.

"You Americans who will be first to land in Normandy," General Omar Bradley said in his matter-of-fact, midwestern accent—it was a slightly high-pitched voice that reached the back of the hall—"will some day be proud of your part in ending this war.

"This invasion has had long and careful planning, and that's what it should have, but its success lies with you and your soldiers." He paused. "If things look black on the beaches, hold on! Do your best to move forward. There will be no turning back. More troops and equipment will follow you. . . . *There will be no surrender unless you are wounded and out of ammunition. . . .*"

These were the kind of orders I expected.

General Bradley reminded me of an American version of Sir John Dill, the Sir John of World War I—only taller, more vigorous.

I came out of the building with about six hundred other officers and found Generals Bradley and Barton waiting for me. "What can I do to help you?" General Bradley asked. He had a smile and a warmth that acted like a tonic.

"I am in an excellent regiment, sir, except it lacks experience near the top. If one of our senior officers gets killed or wounded, we have no replacement, and this worries me."

"I'll get you any lieutenant colonel in the United States," General Bradley said. "Name him."

Ten days later Lieutenant Colonel Joe Golden, crack infantryman and former West Point football player, was at my side. Joe Golden was the man I chose because he was dependable and knew his job.

The tremendous task of ferrying 55,000 Americans to two hostile beaches on D-Day was staggering, and the work of high headquarters was felt even down to the squads. To ready the men and to harden them, I was hiking them with the equipment they were to carry: ammunition, weapons, rations, gas masks, life preservers, steel helmets and combat packs topped with raincoats. In addition, each infantry platoon carried two satchel charges: twenty pounds of dynamite, strapped to long two-by-fours, that would be used in blowing up concrete pill-boxes. "You had better stop these hikes," the doctors warned me, "because they are breaking down the men's arches."

I did what I could to toughen myself. When visiting areas where companies of the 12th Infantry were training, I ran behind my jeep. A year and a half at a desk in the Pentagon does not contribute to your physical condition.

The English countryside was beautiful. Hedgerows like those of Normandy, formed by piles of stone that had bordered the fields for centuries, were overgrown with wild primrose, azalea, mountain laurel, honeysuckle, wild cherries, and often briars that cut you when you went through the rows. We were preparing for a battle in a beautiful garden.

I was working the 12th Infantry and myself long hours. I had always wanted to get a glimpse of an English golf course and an authentic pub, but I could not spare the time. A few days after the meeting in the theater in Plymouth, I called a final conference of our three battalion commanders, the officers leading special units of the regiment, and the leaders of five special units who would help us. Some of my own staff were there. Each officer present had been bigoted.

I looked over this group of dedicated officers. "Where is Lieutenant Colonel Jibbs?" I asked. I am awarding this commander of one of the special units a fictitious name.

"I am representing him," a major said.

I asked, "Where is he?"

"I don't know, sir. We haven't seen him since Saturday night at eleven."

When the meeting was over, I questioned the major some more about the missing lieutenant colonel.

The major was nervous. "We had a party at a pub and the last I saw of him was when he got in a civilian car with a barmaid. He's been gone over thirty-three hours."

"Thirty-three hours!" I could imagine all sorts of things. We had been warned of Nazi spies that might be dropped near us by parachute, and I suspected there might be foul play. *Jibbs knows the secrets of the landing,* I said to myself. I called the military police and they, too, were concerned. "We'll put it on the police teletype all over England," they said. Then I telephoned General Barton. "You handle it," he said, "I'm pressed."

Four hours after I had reported him absent, Lieutenant Colonel Jibbs, unsteady on his feet, ashen white and ugly, appeared in my office. "I hear you wanta speak to me." Even the puffiness of his eyes could not hide his antagonism.

"Where have you been?"

"That's my business."

"You've been absent about thirty-seven hours. You are setting a great example, Jibbs. The artillerymen, the navy, the tankers, the engineers and the men from the medic battalion all are working hard to help us and you—"

"I don't want any Sunday school lecture out of you," he interrupted.

There was no use talking to Jibbs. He was still feeling the effects of his prolonged party. "You are under arrest in quarters," I said, "Report to me here at eight tomorrow morning and I will tell you what I am going to do with you."

I thought a while and called General Barton and told him that Jibbs had finally come back and I described his condition.

"Red, I'm busy. Plenty pressure. Handle this man in your own way. His division commander who sent him here to assist you in the landing doesn't expect to be bothered, either. That is the agreement. Jibbs is entirely yours until we reach Cherbourg. I'll back you up 100 per cent. Good-by."

I was tormented all night. We needed Lieutenant Colonel Jibbs' experience-nine years in the Regular Army. If I placed him before a court-martial he would be disciplined, but what help would that be when we faced the enemy? There seemed to be no satisfactory solution. This was undoubtedly one of the most worrisome nights of my life. About two in the morning I rolled out of my twisted bedclothes and walked to my office.

"Halt!" a sentinel shouted.

I identified myself to the 12th Infantryman, chatted a minute, and walked on. It was men like that who depended on Jibbs' experience. But could such an officer be depended upon? I sat down at the adjutant's desk and typed a letter.

When Lieutenant Colonel Jibbs reported at the stroke of eight, he looked almost as if he were still on a binge. He was deathly white and his hands shook slightly. After saluting he stood before my desk. I closed the door.

"What have you to say for yourself?" I asked.

"Nothing, sir. I drank too much, that's all. I'm sorry."

"That isn't all." I handed Jibbs the letter I had written. I knew it by heart and I outlined it. "This letter is addressed to the Adjutant General of the Army, through channels. It starts by describing your responsibility in this landing seventeen days from today. The second paragraph tells how much it means to the United States to have the Normandy landing succeed, and it says that Lieutenant Colonel Jibbs is an expert in his line and we need his help-badly. Then it tells how you failed us. It says, 'If a lieutenant colonel can act this way, who can blame the enlisted men if they act worse?' The next to the last paragraph says you were absent thirty-seven hours without permission and that you missed an important conference about the landing. It ends by requesting that you be tried by court-martial."

Jibbs took a step back. He looked at the letter as if it were on fire. "Colonel Reeder, if this goes through I am ruined. My career, my family—everything."

"What happens to this letter is strictly up to you. What you have is a copy. I talked to General Roosevelt at seven this morning, and he now has the original. If you or your unit fail us on the battlefield in any way, the letter goes through. If you do top work on the battlefield, the letter will be destroyed. I will make the decision, and if I'm killed General Roosevelt will decide what happens to the letter."

"This is unfair," Jibbs snapped.

"You could tell that to the court-martial."

Jibbs shook his head, half snarled at me, shoved the copy in his hip pocket, saluted and left.

I drove to division headquarters to see General Barton and told him about Jibbs's letter. "I hope your solution works," he said, "Listen to this. We have just been informed by our spies in Normandy that the Germans have a trap set for you in the flooded area just beyond the dunes at Utah Beach."

I knew about the flooded area the Germans had made by damming up the streams. The 12th Infantry Regiment, the third regiment to land at Utah, might find the causeways leading inland jammed with vehicles. To hurry on our route to Cherbourg we expected to have to wade one mile of flooded area.

"Our spies," Barton continued, "say that the Germans have a way of setting this flooded area on fire. Maybe they'll dump oil on it from the air and put the oil afire. Tell your regiment what to do if this happens."

"What do you do?" I faltered.

"You bend down like this and splash water over your head." The general squatted like a huge duck and flapped his arms.

"The quicker you get into the woods and head toward Cherbourg, the better," he said.

"Exactly."

Back at Higher Barracks I got the word that Colonel Jibbs was working hard with his unit after hours on a maneuver he had called himself, and that many of the officers wondered if he were going to be punished.

"Put the word out that Colonel Jibbs has plenty on his mind," I said.

Nine days to go.

You could feel the steady increase in pressure. The place of the landing and the approximate date were passed to the junior officers, noncoms and privates. Every squad leader had aerial photos of the Normandy countryside and every platoon a huge sponge-rubber replica of the Cotentin Peninsula. These green rubber maps even had houses in the proper scale. We did not know it, but our mail home was impounded. "Everyone was saying good-by," the censors reported later.

The clock rushed toward D-Day. Attendance at the church services conducted daily by the three chaplains was increasing. I attended the Protestant meetings. When a Roman Catholic chaplain, William Thomas Cummings, said in a sermon on Bataan in 1942, "There are no atheists in foxholes," he could well have added, "or among men on the way to the front lines."

I was frightened, not that I might be killed or wounded, but that I might fail to perform my job well. I admired the Reserve officers who had not been trained for war, as I had, who were carrying on with assurance. Alone in my room, several times a day I was on my knees praying, not that I might survive but that I might lead the 12th Infantry Regiment skillfully and that we would accomplish our mission. I studied the Bible and found help in the tenth chapter of the Hebrews: "Cast not away therefore your confidence which has great recompense of reward."

In the 12th Infantry area, a scholarly-looking officer wearing major's leaves approached me. "Colonel Reeder, I am the division psychiatrist. Just arrived from the States. General Barton sent me to you."

"The what?"

"Psychiatrist. I have checked the other two regiments of the division and now I'm to spend three days with yours. A check on mental health. I'll start with you, if I may. Go right ahead with your work."

After the doctor had been with me for two hours he gave up. "You're normal. Now I'm going down into the companies."

"I don't care what you do, Doctor, but I want you to tell me what you find before you return to General Barton."

At the end of the third day the psychiatrist was back. He was complimentary about the progress of the 12th Infantry and its resolute state of mind. "Excellent. However, in H Company I find you have a splendid example of a psychopath."

"A what?"

"An individual with a personality not well adapted to meet environmental influences. He is malintegrated in a sense of biological inefficiency, a syntonic or cycloid personality."

"How's that again?"

"In your language you might say that this man has the personality of a five-year-old child. You cannot be sure that he will do his part in a fight. I'll tell General Barton that you have increased the esprit of this regiment, but that you have this one man with a personality less adapted than others to meet environmental influence."

When the doctor left I called the "five-year-old's" battalion commander and company commander, and we went to take a look at the cycloid personality. He was a giant, six foot four and built proportionately.

As we walked away, the captain said, "We know all about this guy, Colonel. He gets along fine, a big harmless dummy-never bothers anyone. Strong as an ox—strongest man we have. His job is to carry 81-millimeter ammunition, and he enjoys it. Says it's not real fighting. He never causes any trouble, and the fellows all like him."

"Does he act queerly?"

"Well, only when he gets a letter from home. Then he always cries like a baby."

An adjutant interrupted. "Colonel, General Barton just telephoned that he wants to see you in his office at once."

I found Barton excited. "Reeder, I hear you have a man in your regiment who does not want to fight, a man with the intelligence of a five-year-old!"

"Yes, sir. He's an ammunition bearer."

"Why hasn't he been gotten rid of?"

"Because his captain thinks he can do the job."

"What are you going to do about it?"

"Nothing, sir."

The general's face seemed paler than when I had last seen it. I am not sure he was well. "Reeder, I am holding you *personally responsible* that this psycho—whatever he is—does his job when he hits the beach. I want you with him, and I want him checked on."

I rode back in my jeep in a numb, uninspired frame of mind. I wondered why the general had not mentioned the first part of the psychiatrist's report. I made up my mind to disregard that order. There would not be time on the beach to worry about the H Company giant.

When I dismounted at headquarters, Major Frank Burke, intelligence officer, said, "Colonel Reeder, we just received 167 escape kits."

"What's that?"

He showed me a neat oilskin pouch containing a narrow six-inch saw, a tiny compass about the size of my little fingernail, and a silk handkerchief that had a map of France printed on it.

"Allied aviators carry these, according to the lieutenant colonel from General Bradley's headquarters who brought them. If a pilot has to parachute to safety and is captured, he might cut the bars of his cell with the saw and use the compass and map to find his way across France. The little compasses, he said, are to be secreted in our uniforms."

"Where is this messenger?"

"He's gone, sir."

"I know that General Bradley didn't send these. He wants us in an offensive frame of mind, and so do I. Did these kits come through division headquarters?"

"I presume so. What shall we do with them?"

We can't start talking escape kits, I thought. *We want our minds completely on attack.* "Throw the saws in the trash. Give the compasses to those nice British boy scouts who come every so often to see me, and give each officer a handkerchief as a souvenir."

Violating orders with the invasion at hand, after twenty years or more of carrying out orders, was not conducive to a good night's sleep.

In the last hours there was no time for rest. A myriad of details needed checking. Trucks wheeled in on schedule and carried the 12th Infantry and hundreds of other units to towns and camps near the ports of embarkation. Vehicles were moving in every direction. Every road seem filled with army trucks. On our way to Plymouth we passed acre after acre filled with stacks of war supplies; all England appeared to be a supply base. British citizens lined the curbs and shouted, "Good luck!" but they had done that also when we were going on the maneuver to Slapton Sands. I wondered if the Germans knew the secrets of the landing.

As my car sped toward the front of our column I caught a glimpse of the H Company giant leaning out the back of the truck. He seemed content. We had not had mail in several days.

CHAPTER TWENTY-EIGHT

D-Plus-Five

IN THE TWO-DAY STAY at Plymouth I assembled the noncoms on a hillside and talked to them by themselves.

"Army noncoms helped raise me from boyhood. I owe them a debt. Noncoms can make or break an outfit because they are truly the leaders who are with the men."

It was stimulating to talk to the privates on the same hillside because they were more responsive. "I am with you because there are more of you than anyone else." A great shout. "Here is the straight dope on the landing. You can't fool the troops. I learned that when I was a West Point plebe." I described the landing at Utah Beach as if it were a football play. "The 8th and 22nd Regiments will land ahead of us and will block to the left and right. The paratroopers are our downfield blockers. We will land and plunge through the hole and head for Cherbourg." The privates stood and yelled.

They inspired *me*. "Ordinarily in a battle a colonel goes to a high point called an observation post where he can direct the fight, but we are going to be in flat hedgerow country, and an O.P. is out of the question. To see what's going on, I will be up front with you." The yells startled a flight of sea gulls who banked and flew back toward Plymouth Harbor. "I'm going to carry a bolt-action

1903 rifle because I want the Germans to think I'm a private. Oh, they'll shoot at you fellows, but they'd much rather hit a noncom or an officer."

I have never had a better response.

Plans of the high headquarters were working perfectly. LCVP's, clumsy-looking but practical motorboats, ferried us to larger craft in Plymouth Harbor. With two hundred other 12th Infantry soldiers I climbed aboard an LCI (Landing Craft Infantry) that looked like a small destroyer, and was greeted by efficient U.S. coastguardsmen. The captain gave me his bunk and I rolled into it, exhausted.

The wind outside the Plymouth mole was kicking up huge whitecaps. "We can make it," the skipper said, "but it's going to be a rough passage."

I was delighted when word was flashed over the Navy command net that because of the bad weather General Eisenhower had postponed the assault for twenty-four hours.

When we finally set sail on the afternoon of June 5, 1944, I thought of the Pilgrims and John Reeder. Probably the weather had been just as gray when the *Mayflower* sailed for America over three hundred years ago; John Reeder, the first of his breed in America, followed the Pilgrims a few years later from this same port.

Lines of landing craft and small boats steamed out of the bays and rivers along the English coast and took their places in the procession headed for Normandy. The whole movement looked like a well-rehearsed play. A U.S. destroyer raced by us and dropped a depth charge about a hundred yards away, and I thought we were headed for Davy Jones' place because our LCI rattled and shook as if its plates were coming apart. Seeing this destroyer was reassuring. I was happy that the United States Navy was responsible for our safety in crossing the treacherous Channel; in an emergency there is nothing like your own people.

About an hour before sunset the five thousand landing craft were in two lines a half mile apart, stretching back as far as you could see, and floating above almost every one of them was a barrage balloon anchored by a cable. Americans, British and Canadians were heading for Normandy in the greatest invasion in history.

The flagship for the operation, U.S.S. *Augusta,* cut by us. Her knife-like prow made her look like a racing yacht. I knew that General Omar Bradley was aboard and wished that he would hang around closer instead of rushing off over the horizon. Three men-of-war who would support the 12th Infantry by firepower steamed into view, the cruisers H.M.S. *Black Prince* and U.S.S. *Tuscaloosa* and the battleship U.S.S. *Nevada*. The *Nevada,* the farthest away, was a faint gray shadow, but I felt she was a friend, salvaged from the devastation of Pearl Harbor. I had visited my brother, Fred, on her when he was a midshipman.

The captain of the LCI said, "Colonel Reeder, you're senior officer aboard and the orders are for the top man to read this order to the men. It's from General Montgomery, D-Day assault commander." (We did not receive Ike's message.)

I looked it over and asked that all soldiers assemble either on the forward or after decks. This message came at the right moment; it hit exactly the right key:

21 Army Group
PERSONAL MESSAGE FROM THE C-IN-C
To be read to all troops

The time has come to deal the enemy a terrific blow in Western Europe. The blow will be struck by the combined sea, land and air forces of the Allies-together constituting one great Allied team, under the supreme command of General Eisenhower.

On the eve of this great adventure I send my best wishes to every soldier in the Allied team. . . . (We are) striking a blow for freedom which will live in history. . . .

I want every soldier to know that I have complete confidence in the successful outcome. . . .

As we enter the battle, let us recall the words of a famous soldier spoken many years ago:

"He either fears his fate too much,
  Or his deserts are small,
Who dare not put it to the touch,
  To win or lose it all."

(Signed) B.L. Montgomery
General

The Earl of Montrose, who wrote that verse to inspire his fierce Highland clansmen, could not have been more successful with it than was General Montgomery. I read the verse twice to each group. The hour was approaching when our lives and the fate of the invasion would be put to the touch.

Almost everyone on our LCI was up at six thirty, which was really four thirty, because we were using "Double British Summertime."

In the early mists the low-lying Normandy coast looked like a gray watercolor. Through my field glasses I could see two church spires, the only landmarks that stood out-but what spires were they? I joined a group of soldiers on the forward deck and ate ten-in-one rations with them. People were polite and helped one another.

Suddenly there was a roar. The *Nevada*, cruisers, and destroyers began to blast German defense positions. In the gray light the explosions of the guns formed fearful orange patterns. The invasion fleet covered the sea—boats everywhere.

We knew that Colonel James Van Fleet and his men were landing on Utah Beach, but from four miles out it was impossible to tell if they were successful. The hands on my watch would not move. The time from six thirty until we landed at ten thirty was the longest four hours I ever spent—including Colonel Echols' four-hour math exams.

Just before we left the LCI to clamber down into the smaller LCVP's that would rush us ashore, General Barton called me on the voice radio. "Cactus to Cargo, come in."

"Come in, Cactus," I answered.

"Good luck, Red—*static—static*. Cabbage reports—*static*—Give 'em hell. Out."

"Cabbage" was the inelegant name for Colonel Van Fleet. What it was he had reported I never learned.

When I climbed down the cargo nets into the bucking LCVP, a young sailor said, "Colonel, sit up here on our perch with the coxswain and me. You can see better."

"No, thanks," I said. "I read in a book that a leader is supposed to be up front. I'll stand at the front ramp with Colonel Montelbano, battalion commander,* so I can be the first one out of this thing."

That decision saved my life. When the boat grated on the Normandy shore I stepped into waist-high water and ran up the beach while light artillery sprayed the sands with iron. A shell hit in the LCVP and killed the young sailor, the coxswain, and the last 12th Infantryman leaving the boat.

*Lieutenant Colonel Dominic Montelbano was killed on D-plus-5.

All along Utah Beach 12th Infantrymen were wading ashore and running to the top of the dunes.

"Mills," I said, "things don't look right to me. Where the hell are we?"

Lieutenant Bill Mills took my map and in a moment justified his grade of 97 per cent on the map-reading exam. He said, "They've landed us about two miles south of where we're supposed to be."

"It don't matter. We know where to go! Get the word out we're two miles south of where we ought to be."

At the top of the dunes I passed General Roosevelt, who had landed with Van Fleet's first wave. "Red, the causeways leading inland are all clogged up. Look at it! A procession of jeeps and not a wheel turning. Something wrong." Roosevelt looked tired and the cane he leaned on heightened the impression.

"We are going through the flooded area!" I yelled as loud as I could. Down the dunes I saw Lieutenant Colonel "Chuck" Jackson, of the first battalion, and I gave him an arm signal. I knew the rest of the regiment coming ashore in the the next wave would follow us.

A mile across the flooded meadow lay the village of St. Martin de Varreville. Rising above it was a church steeple that looked like a friendly beacon. We waded through water in the German-made lake which varied in depth from waist to arm pit and in a few spots was over our heads. We had the non-swimmers paired with the swimmers, and even so I was proud of the non-swimmers around me who were holding onto their weapons. The large groups of men in the water made a perfect target, but we waded the water safely.

We walked through the village, past amazed groups of French women, children, and old men, and formed in attack formation. Soon after the regiment moved into the wood, the leading battalion halted. Lieutenant Colonel Jackson and I walked up to the two front scouts.

"What's the trouble?"I asked.

A scout said, "All you have to do is walk up that little bank and get fired on."

"How many Germans do you think there are?" I asked.

"Two."

"Where are they?"

"I don't know. You can't tell, sir."

"Three thousand men are behind you and two Germans are holding us all up. Any suggestions?"

No answer.

"Well," I said, "under the rules we can go in any direction but back, so let's sideslip and leave these two Germans for the division commander."

We walked through the wood to the left, swung around the two Germans and headed once more on our course.

Late in the afternoon we were in a battle with the Germans a hedgerow away—about two hundred yards—both sides kneeling like minutemen at Lexington. Bullets were whip-cracking overhead. I radioed for artillery help. In a few minutes it crashed down just behind the Germans with an unbelievable roar, and a splendid barn with a red tile roof went up in smoke. It was a close-up of the awful waste of war.

Shells from German nebelwerfers howled in the darkening sky. These strange chemical mortars were now throwing high explosives, but fortunately the shells passed overhead. "Screaming meemies," the soldiers called these hounds of hell.

At twilight, on schedule at nine o'clock, sixty American gliders flew over us, just above the treetops, and headed for the German lines. They looked like huge weird birds in silent flight. Across the field I could see Germans raising rifles and automatic rifles, pumping bullets into the gliders. I yelled and signaled, "fire faster!" to help the glider soldiers, and volleys of musketry spat at the Germans. Then it got dark.

I walked back toward the flooded area to the regimental headquarters that had been set up in an ancient Norman castle. With its turrets, battlements, and walled courtyard the castle looked like a stone fort that still might hold knights of William the Conqueror. I walked beneath a pointed arch into the courtyard that held a plowhorse in a stone stable, a manure pile, and 12th Infantry jeeps; then I ran up stone steps into the castle.

Its first floor was a beehive of staff officers, communications experts, message center clerks, and messengers. I was so elated from the success of the 12th Infantry I felt intoxicated. In the main hallway at the foot of a stone stairs I yelled at the top of my voice, *"Vive la France!"* It was great having at last a place in which to employ the language that I had studied under Colonel Thiers and at West Point.

An old Frenchman appeared at the top of the stone steps and poured French at me. I called back the only thing I could think of, *"Puis-je effacer, monsieur?"* a classroom expression for, "May I erase, sir?" The Frenchman disappeared.

Lieutenant Colonel Jim Luckett said, "Things are going great. A few shells hit near the courtyard, otherwise OK. What time shall we attack tomorrow?"

"When do you recommend?"

"Six thirty in the morning."

"Right. Get ahold of Major Gorn and we'll work out the attack order."

Major Lay, supply officer, gave me a report on ammunition and food that had come ashore, then a sergeant major said, "We just got a radio from division that General Barton wants to see you at his headquarters at Audouville la Hubert."

"Where the hell is that?"

"Back down the road three or four miles."

I hunted a jeep driver, and when I found one he was unenthusiastic.

"I'll drive you anywhere, Colonel, in the daytime. I just drove in here without lights from Huberts. Look at this." He took my finger and placed it on a bullet hole through his windshield. "I don't want to win the Medal of Honor. What I want to do is get this damned thing over with and get back to Sadie in Salinas. How could that bullet have missed me?"

It *was* hard to see how the bullet could have missed him by more than a few inches.

"We have to go," I said. "General Barton wants me."

We crept along the rough, dark country road, no lights showing, my rifle cocked and ready. The trees along the road were gaunt arms silhouetted against a blue-black sky. In a half hour I found General Barton sitting beneath a tree outside his headquarters with Colonels Tribolet and Van Fleet. "I called you back here, Red," the general said, "to tell you that the 12th Infantry did a magnificent job, to congratulate you, and to give you a canteen cup of champagne so you can drink to the health of the best division in the army."

In fifteen minutes the jeep driver and I started inching through the night back to our part of the beachhead.

Next morning when we moved to the attack, we discovered that the Germans had pulled back. Evidently they had been frightened by the gliders that had landed behind them. The tremendous field before us, bound by hedgerows, looked like a junk yard for gliders; their wreckage was everywhere, and casualties had been heavy. Men who survived had joined the fight.

On the third day of our advance I walked to the flank where Lieutenant Colonel Jibbs's unit was helping us beat the Germans. Jibbs had a streak of dirt across his jaw that made it look as if it had been slashed. Defiance still dominated his brownish-green eyes as it had ever since his binge at Exeter.

"Jibbs, you've done an immense job and I came to thank you. This morning I sent a motorcycle messenger back to General Roosevelt to get this." I handed him the letter.

Jibbs grinned. "Is this all the copies?"

"Yes, sir. You have the only other one."

"Good. I tore that up."

"Well, tear this one up."

It was an awkward moment and Jibbs relieved it by showing me his situation on a map. His unit was operating like a model from a school of war.

Late that afternoon our third battalion was surrounded. It was hard to tell how many Germans were around them. It sounded as if it were a regiment. At daybreak I sent the rest of our men to rescue them. The turmoil and noise were unbelievable. The confusion of battle was rampant. Units were intermingled in the scattered woods, and it was difficult to tell exactly where our soldiers were and where the Germans were.

I was standing near a hedgerow where there was a radio. German artillery was crashing trees around us as if by magic. In the field over which we had just come lay about ten dead 12th Infantrymen. Nearby seven dead Germans lay in a neat line, sightless eyes staring at the sky. I do not know what killed them. Lieutenant Mills and I were studying the map to see what was the best route for reserves if they had to be used.

A hand grenade exploded in the pocket of a paratrooper sergeant who wore the 82nd Airborne patch and who had been fighting shoulder to shoulder with us. In his form-fitting jump suit he looked like a fullback. His olive-drab uniform became red and he fell down. Two other paratroopers assisted him.

A harassed-looking doctor ran out of the hedgerow and tore for me."Colonel! If you get me a jeep right away I can save the lives of three men."

"The road is over there," I yelled above the crack of the artillery bursts. From his face I knew that he was disappointed that I was not more helpful, and I knew how he felt.

A staff officer ran up and screamed, "Colonel, E Company can't go on. All their officers are killed."

"Yes, they can. Their noncommissioned officers can lead them."

There was blood on the radio, and I do not know where the blood came from. A tree crashed and almost hit it. There was no radio operator. I yelled, "Runner!"

A private stood before me, Eugene Narduli. Back in England he had cut my hair, and when his barber shop was empty he had confided in me, "I do not want to fight. I want to go home to my family and my barber shop in the Bronx. I don't like war."

I had talked Narduli into believing that the best and quickest way for us both to get back home was to win. Now I shouted a message at him. He was trembling like an aspen leaf. I wanted to tell Narduli I admired his courage but there was no time. I yelled my message above the crescendo of the shells, and he spouted it back as proof he understood.

When he had gone, I yelled, "Runner!" again, and when another man stood in front of me, I started to send the same message by a different route. A bullet cracked over my shoulder and struck the messenger in the face. It went crimson and he collapsed. (I learned later that the bullet tipped the runner's helmet and that he survived.)

I ran from him as fast as I could along the hedgerow, and thirty yards away I met a first-aid medic who passed me running to help the stricken messenger. I circled back like a base runner who has been surprised by a shoestring catch and who has to get back to his base fast.

When the regiment cut away the ring of Germans around the third battalion, its leader, Lieutenant Colonel Thad Dulin,* of Washington, D.C., ran out of the forest. He was so boyish-looking he seemed like a high school cadet. Dulin was on fire with love of his men. It was his battalion that had been surrounded. "Colonel

*Killed on D-Plus15 leading a bayonet charge.

Reeder, you should have seen them! The greatest men I have ever seen anywhere! Why, Sergeant–"

It was a hard thing to do but I had to stop this marvelous person from talking. I told him the new plan of attack and told him to get his men in the new position fast.

The situation toughened, and it appeared that the reserve unit would have to be employed. Mills and I studied the map again to determine how to reach them. We expected to have to hike back about 1,000 yards, but when we pushed our way through a hedgerow, there–125 yards away–stood the reserve unit. It was far too close. They were spread out in a huge rectangular field as if they were about to pitch pup tents. German artillery started to bombard a church steeple in Emondeville about 300 yards away, and I knew what that meant. We would be next; the artillery was checking the range.

It swung into our field and a burst killed a man.

To rush this reserve unit out of danger and to move it in a direction where it might be used, I yelled above the sharp crack of the artillery, "Move your men by the left flank!"

"I can't do it," the commander shouted back. "They are not in the right formation."

Another shell burst near us. I ran through the field yelling, "By the left flank, double time!" and waved my arm in that direction.

The large unit ran out of the field, plunged through a hedgerow, tumbled into a sunken road–and streaked for the rear. The bursts of the shells in the field beside the road sounded like claps of thunder. I thought, *If the artillery catches them here, these men will be in a meat chopper.* I was running in the center of the unit, and to turn them I scrambled up a red dirt bank, waved my map and shouted, "Follow me!" About twelve men within sound of my voice responded.

In the field at the top of the bank we twelve men ran face to face with an equal number of Germans. The enemy scrambled back into a hedgerow, some of them started firing at us, and you could see the rest working feverishly to set up a machine gun. They were at a distance of about thirty-five yards.

The twelve Americans hit the dirt in the open field. The man on my right was Bill Mills; on his right was a man who had strapped to his back a radio so powerful it could talk to Eisenhower. The soldier on my left was hit in the leg by a German bullet. He screamed. The excitement was something like almost drowning. I thought, *Are my legs in the right position to shoot?* Then I realized this was a silly thought. I was squeezing the trigger working the bolt of my rifle smoothly, and pumping bullets into the hedgerow. Old Major Cadwalader, back on the Fort Benning range, would have been proud of me. Suddenly I remembered a maxim cavalry officers had taught us cadets on the dirt roads across the Hudson from West Point: *In a meeting engagement the side that acts first wins.* I rose to my feet with my rifle and yelled, "Follow me!" and we charged the Germans. The cavalrymen were right.

I was disgusted. In ten minutes I had gone from regimental commander to squad leader. The reserve unit had scattered like quail, and it took three hours to round them up.

I talked on the voice radio to Jim Luckett, who was taking care of things at the regimental command post, and my message seeped through the code. He understood generally there would be a delay and the reason. I was thankful for Luckett's help and for the loyal way he ran things for us.

About the time we were set and ready to move again, Colonel Van Fleet came over for a moment and said, "I want you to know that we caught up to you. We're on your left flank." Having this rugged leader at hand was like being supported by the U.S. Treasury.

On the sixth straight day of our organized attack the German resistance increased. They were on the high ground near Montebourg and tanks failed to help us budge them. I called for air support, and we spread out little orange panels of cloth so the aviators could see our front lines. In about forty minutes the B-17's roared over our heads, a dozen of them, maybe four thousand feet high. I felt proud that they would respond so quickly. Suddenly, their bottoms opened and objects that looked like trunks started to fall. I wondered what they were.

The bombs dropped on us with a horrible crash. One man was killed. It was too terrible even to become angry.

The private carrying the radio said, "Call for you, sir."

I took the receiver and recognized Luckett's voice. "Barge to Bayonet, Barge to Bayonet. Come in."

In this radio net "Bayonet" was my code name. "This is Bayonet," I answered.

"*Big* Bayonet is here at headquarters and wants to see you."

I knew he meant Barton.

Mills, nine riflemen who were protecting us, and I started back. I stopped to talk a moment to some replacements sitting behind a hedgerow, who had just arrived from England. I felt sorry for them because they looked frightened. I said, "Great to have you fellows with us. You're joining a winning outfit. The 12th Infantry has been beating the Germans for six days."

When we walked across an open field, a single shell cracked over my head, and I went down. My left leg was on fire. I sat up and looked at it. It was horribly mangled above the ankle. My left elbow was torn open. I screamed and could not help it. Bill Mills, who was wounded and stunned in the same explosion, recovered quickly and placed a tourniquet on my leg. His blood splashed on me. He gave me a shot of morphine from his paratrooper's first-aid kit. I was thankful for Bill Mills.

I lay there in the dirt maybe fifteen minutes. A jeep rolled up carrying six wounded on stretchers and I saw the top man being removed for me. "Oh, no, you don't," I called. "Take those men to the aid station, then come back for me."

"Sir, this is a German."

"Lay that son of a bitch in the shade," I said.

When our pitiful load of wounded rolled into a rambling Norman fortress that was serving as a command post, as the castle had back at the flooded area, I reported to General Barton on a stretcher. It was a hard time. He was shocked, as were Jim Luckett and other friends. I gave Luckett the situation up front as I saw it. Father Fries, Roman Catholic, prayed over me, and with more morphine taking hold, I relaxed—some.

General Barton shook my hand. "I am so sorry, Red. I wanted to tell you to stop until we get help to crack Montebourg."

"We shouldn't stop."

When I woke up I was in a huge black tent. The wounded on stretchers lay in neat rows. Two shadows appeared. One I recognized in the dim light as the head of the beach hospital. The other, who wore a steel helmet, knelt on one knee.

"Red, this is General Collins." He fumbled with my shirt. "I am pinning on you the Distinguished Service Cross. Brad—General Bradley—said to tell you he was sorry that he could not come himself, and he wants you to know he sent an aviator to London to get this. This is the first DSC to be awarded in Normandy."

General Collins stood up. "Red, is there anything I can do for you?"

"Make Van Fleet a general."

"The recommendation is already in. What can I do for you?"

"Tell the regiment it won the first DSC, and that I will be back."

He hesitated and looked at my leg. "I hope so, Red. But you have to get well."

CHAPTER TWENTY-NINE

New Horizons

WHEN OUR amphibious vehicle, a DUKW (or "duck") motored through the blue water, I was lying on the top stretcher. It was very nice up there. You could see all around.

The LST we were heading for lay about a mile offshore. Other LST's were unloading supplies of war, and ducks were chugging them toward the Normandy beach. There were six wounded men stacked like cordwood in our duck. Beside me stood a soldier who was also being evacuated to England. "What's your name?" I asked.

"Colonel, I'm Private Jackson."

"What's the matter with you, Jackson?"

"Sir, I've got eczema."

This burned me up. We had a medical officer in the 12th Infantry who had been wounded in the leg and who refused to be evacuated because he was still able to help others.

"What kind of job did you have, Jackson?"

"Sir, I'm one of these amphibious-duck drivers. We come over three days ago in one of these ships that opens its mouth. Our cap'n said to me, 'You country boy. Crank up your duck and drive it out with the rest and make little circles in the water.' Bye 'n' bye the cap'n drove his duck out and we headed for the shore. Then in

President Eisenhower and RR fishing at Delafield Pond, West Point, about 1953. RR is angry. He was told to shield Ike and a photographer jumped out of the bushes.

the weeds we built the cap'n a bomb-proof dugout. In the morning it was scary with the dead paratroopers hanging from the trees in their shrouds.

"The cap'n told us, 'Boys, crank up.' I was right behind him when we clanked down the road, in Number 2 duck. You could hear the guns off to the right yelpin'. When we got to a crossroad there was an M.P. Us boys lost a lot of confidence in that cap'n because he had to *ask* that M.P. which way to go."

The man on the stretcher beneath me started to talk. "Colonel Reeder, I'm a paratroop doctor. I jumped on the night of D-plus-one, broke my leg, and the Germans captured me. The German doctors operated on me, and I wish you could have seen the nurse in the operating room. Blond, blue eyes, and the prettiest figure you can imagine. I can't get her off my mind. She was French and wouldn't have anything to do with the doctors, who were absolutely crazy about her. I'm a New York City boy, and I've seen all the famous shows on Broadway, the Follies, the Vanities—but I've never seen anything like that girl. I can't get her off my mind."

A shell exploded in the water about 150 yards away. Private Jackson said, "I don't see how you people can talk about women smack in the face of death."

I said, "Jackson, I guess you want to get your eczema cured and get back to your unit, *Don't you?*"

"No, sir. I'm from Chicago, the Windy City, and I want to go back there and give 'em the benefit of my 'sperience."

Our duck roared up the ramp of the LST and they laid us out in rows in the cavernous main compartment. A salty-looking naval captain, cap on the side of his head, said, "Colonel Reeder, I'm Jack Ford. I have a bottle of brandy for medicinal purposes, and I'd like to buy you a drink."

I did not recognize the famous movie director, but it made no difference. "Thanks, I am craving pineapple juice."

"Pineapple juice!" John Ford stepped forward as if he had been insulted. "Are you in your right mind?" Ford did the best he could; he brought me a tumbler of tomato juice.

When we landed in England, stretcher-bearers carried me to a tent that had a sign near its entrance: SHOCK.

"No, you don't, " I said. "Put me down."

A doctor came up. "What's wrong?"

I said, "I'm no mental case. I'm just humbly normal and I don't want mental treatment."

"'Shock' refers to your physical condition," he said.

"Take me in," I said.

Later, after an ambulance ride to a temporary hospital, a doctor examined the repair work on my leg and cut off the right leg of my trousers. I think maybe ten days had passed since I was wounded. The surgeon showed me a gap in my right leg, about five inches by two, above my knee. "Look at this. I can see the femur. Amazing. This slash is healing nicely in spite of a coat of grass, cloth and dirt." After looking me over, he said, "I'm going to take out of your shoulder a cube of iron, about the size of a die. Your left leg will require treatment in a United States hospital. What will happen, I'm not prepared to say."

The temporary hospital was an unhappy place. I was in a ward with twenty-nine second and first lieutenants and nothing suited them. Eisenhower was using the wrong strategy, their company commanders were stupid, the food in the hospital was awful, and the treatment inefficient. I have never heard such a fire of complaints.

One hideous night, about two in the morning, the officer in the bed next to me woke me up yelling.

"What's the matter?" I asked.

"The man next to me is bleeding to death."

I started yelling for help, and soon every patient who could yell joined in. No one answered. It was the most helpless situation imaginable; no one could get out of bed. Finally the corps man who was supposed to be on duty responded, and he summoned a nurse and a doctor who saved the man's life.

Later my friend Bill Mills was brought in suffering from head and leg wounds, but he was too groggy to be of much comfort. (In action later he lost his leg from the explosion of a mine.)

You heard snatches of conversation from other incoming patients. "Lieutenant Colonel 'Spike' Nave was killed." I had known Nave—West Point quarterback for Biff Jones.

"I was in Colonel Nave's regiment," a lieutenant said. "He's not dead. I'll bet on it. The Germans couldn't kill a man like Nave."

"I saw him killed."

Another badly wounded newcomer said, "The guy next to me on the stretcher coming across the Channel was Major Hal Smith of the 12th Infantry. He was shot in the stomach."

I said, "How is he? Where is he?"

"I don't know."

When the Germans sent flights of V-2 rockets carrying one-ton warheads to England it was hard to lie in the temporary building, but there was no alternative. The hospital quivered with each nearby blast, and I felt helpless and frightened. The army nurses, who acted as if they had heard rockets in the next field all their lives, gave me strength. Nothing seemed to bother the marvelous nurses except patients who were unconscious.

After we were flown to Prestwick, Scotland, the wounded were placed in every available shelter because bad weather prevented overseas flight. I was happy to be in an enlisted men's ward with other 12th Infantrymen, and it was quiet there, a relief after the complaining lieutenants.

The flight to Washington over the Atlantic was smooth. When I heard we were over Ireland, I raised myself from my bunk and looked out the tiny window. The ground was a hazy light-green. I could see why they called it "the Emerald Isle." When the plane put down in Newfoundland, a girl wearing a Red Cross uniform came aboard and called out to us patients. "You have your choice of a drink: Coca Cola, Pepsi Cola, three kinds of whiskey—Scotch, bourbon or rye—ginger ale, milk or beer."

She took a tally and said to our nurse, "Nineteen milks. Same as the last plane. I told my boss that if this keeps up, we'll have to have more cows."

In Walter Reed General Hospital in Washington my first caller was Colonel Jack Francis, Ground Forces Liaison Officer with OPD. "You have to live," he said. "You have to get well because of your family." At another time he said, "Red, you have to think about a new horizon."

But when you were left alone and your family and friends had gone, a new horizon seemed like a mirage.

General Marshall sat patiently by my bedside when I was full of morphine. I was talking nonstop and couldn't quit. I gave the Chief of Staff instruction in how to lead a platoon, company, battalion, and was on my way to the higher units when corpsmen wheeled me to the operating room.

On one of his visits General Marshall said, "We are handicapped in this country by some of our laws. In the British Army they retain the wounded if they want to stay in the service and if they can

In above photo, Dr. Wells (center) presents Freedom Foundation Award to RR and astronaut John Glenn, 1963.

Vince Lombardi and RR closing up Bear Mt. Inn, about 1950.

still help. I was talking about this to Anna Rosenberg, Director of the New York War Manpower Commission, and used you as an example. I can think of a dozen positions in the army in which you can produce, but under the law you will have to be retired in a year or two."

I could not bring myself to think about the future; my mind was occupied by an apparatus the doctors had erected about my bed that looked as if it had been invented by Beowulf. I was rigged to it with a system of ropes, pulleys and weights that compensated one another, the doctors said. It was painful being in bed with this scaffold, and to make matters worse a retired colonel used to pay me regular visits and shake the rigging when he wished to emphasize a point in his endless stories.

Dort brought our four children to Washington and rented a home near the hospital. How she found time to care for them, run the house and visit me, too, I don't know. She brought the children to me frequently. The two smaller ones, Julia and Russell, six and four, were tiny. They were about as concerned as if I had a bad cold. My mother and others in my family came, and my brother Fred even flew Oysters Rockefeller twice from Antoines in New Orleans. My family was a tremendous aid to my spirits.

Lying in bed day in and day out is hard. I had been in bed over two months when I said to a doctor. "You know, I'm uncomfortable in my right hip. I may be getting a bed sore."

They unhitched me from the rigging, X-rayed the fleshy part of my hip, and then removed a jagged piece of iron—a fragment of shell measuring ⅞ by ½ by ¼ inches.

After this journey to the operating room I felt terrible. My body burned and throbbed. The outlook was dismal. How could my dedicated surgeon overcome a four and a half inch gap in my shinbone, just above the ankle? Dort, my steadfast and beautiful wife, came in. She did not unload her troubles: stretching my pay to meet expenses; raising four young children in wartime Washington. To the contrary, she buoyed me. When I said, "It looks like I'm going to be an amputee. How do you feel about being married to one?" she kissed me and said, "I married a man, not a leg."

In October, after four months of trying to save my leg, the doctors were forced to amputate. The moment an amputee never forgets is that instant when he regains consciousness and sees only one foot at the end of his bed.

But friends helped keep up my morale. General Marshall, looking tired and showing the strain he was under, sat by my bed for two more visits. He sent staff officers to show me top-secret maps of the war situations, but to me the pictures seemed as unreal as if they were in the movies. I could not bring myself to any sense of identification with war anywhere.

General Tom Handy, with my family and wounded men gathered about, hung the Bronze Star Medal on me, and General Lear pinned the Purple Heart to my pajamas.

General Otto Nelson, a West Point classmate, lined up ambulances, wheelchairs, an airplane, doctors and nurses, and took me to Yankee Stadium to see Army beat Notre Dame 59-0. Coach Red Blaik came to my wheelchair after the game and offered me the football, but it was too unusual a trophy for me to accept. The crowd and the excitement of the game made me glad to return to Ward Five.

Then a visitor came to see me who, according to John Ford, could have been one of the great character actors of all time if he had had the training and the opportunity: Sergeant Marty Maher, of West Point. This Irish storyteller had ridden day coaches from West Point, and Marco Polo's travels paled beside his.

"A beautiful lady"—(all of his ladies were lovely)—"took me into the diner, and while she sipped a bellywash drink she begged me to have two shots of Old Bushmills. The conductor rushed in and said, 'This diner's being cut off for Harrisburg. 'And where's Harrisburg?' I said. 'Well, it isn't near Washington,' the dear lady said. 'My suitcase is in the day coach.' I cried. 'You'd better get with it,' the conductor said. I found a sailor sitting on my suitcase drinking a bottle of beer. . . ."

A nurse interrupted to place a thermometer in my mouth. Marty bowed and brushed back his silvery-white locks. "Miss," he said, "up at West Pint the first time Doctor Howard Snyder put one of those things in my mouth at the cadet hospital I thought it was some kind of cure. He went off and left me sitting there sucking that glass tube while he got interested for three hours in deliverin' me niece Margaret."

I had no inkling that old Sergeant Marty Maher would provide me with a springboard into a new career, one that led my friend John Kieran to give me the title "King of the Literary Frontier." Seven years later my sister, Nardi Campion and I wrote articles

RR on movie set of The Long Gray Line *at Battle Monument with director, John Ford, 1955.*

on Marty for *The New York Times* and *Collier's* magazines, which led to a book about him, which led to the movie *The Long Gray Line,* directed by the old pirate, John Ford.

A train of infections made my leg a torment. During one hemorrhage I took a sixth trip to the operating room. When I was wheeled in, there was a brigadier general whom I had met in Australia on the adjacent operating table. He greeted me, then continued his conversation with the surgeon.

"I can tell you," the brigadier said, "MacArthur's way overrated. Supposed to be a great strategist—baloney! He has a bad habit of announcing a victory before the place is actually captured. Civil War stuff! This will catch up on him one of these days, you watch. Dugout Doug!"

I bristled. "General," I said, "how much pay do you get a month?"

He told me. "Why?"

"You keep on talking like that and the Japs and Germans will pay you twice as much."

A nurse clapped an ether mask on my face.

Some months later expert leg makers worked to fit me with an artificial limb, and I started taking walking lessons. General Marshall's aide came to my room in the hospital. "The general wants to see you as soon as you feel up to it."

The next day I laced on my leg, pulled on my uniform and went to the Pentagon. George Marshall was in his office with Lieutenant General Larkin and Major General Stephen Henry. General Marshall grasped my hand. "Reeder, I want to thank you for what you did for the United States and to tell you if you had not been wounded you would have been a one- or two-star general."

I know he meant that as a compliment but it put me in a blue funk. By coincidence—I guess it was a coincidence—I received a letter the same week from General Bradley in Europe. ". . . If you had not been wounded you would have been a two-star general."

The help of friends kept me on an even keel.

Horace Stoneham, president of the New York Giants, sent me a telegram: "Please help Hans Lobert run a baseball tryout camp for boys at Erie, Pennsylvania, for three days. Your terms." I went, and came back to the hospital feeling younger.

Colonel Jack Francis brought to my room a set of Freeman's *Lee's Lieutenants.* "You're interested in leadership," he said, "and these books are crammed with it, good and bad."

General Ben Lear, now commanding the Army Ground Forces, came on the evening of a day when a contemporary of mine had visited me to show trophies he had picked up in Europe: over-and-under shot guns, field glasses, and Nazi weapons.

I moaned to General Lear about it. "I don't have anything," I said.

He snapped, "What are you complaining about? You got back with your shirt, didn't you?"

I felt better immediately.

There was a lot of talk and there were a lot of letters about what I was to do—not an easy decision to make after a year and a half in a hospital. Major General Maxwell Taylor, West Point Supe, wrote offering me an opportunity in the West Point Tactical Department "as leader of a regiment of our cadets."

Dort and I discussed it, and I wrote my old friends, the Gatchells, at West Point.

General Taylor wrote again, "You can help the cadets. . . ."

Then a friend sent me a scrawl on brown scratch paper from Brigadier General George Honnen, Commandant of Cadets, "I'll take him in a wheelchair."

This clinched it. It meant almost as much as my West Point diploma. New horizons lay ahead.

CHAPTER THIRTY

Extra Innings

WHEN I DROVE DORT, our four young children and our dog, "Hivey," through the Thayer Gate of the United States Military Academy at West Point, New York, clouds raised from the horizon. Julia, age seven, sitting on the crowded back seat, set a happy mood when she pointed across a field and asked, "What are those big things?"

"Barracks," I answered. "Soldiers who teach the cadets live in them."

"No," she said, "those *big* things."

Everyone was interested.

"Those big things that have trees on them," she persisted.

Dort unravelled the mystery. It was the Hudson Valley Highlands she was asking about. She had never seen mountains before.

A delightful time was starting for our family, but I faced a hard transition. A year and half in a hospital makes you self-centered. The daily course of business on your ward seems to revolve around you. Even pain becomes your routine. Taking my mind off myself and thinking of others was not easy.

I needed a change of pace, a refuge, and I got one when I took lessons in oils from my cousin Charles L. Wrenn, distinguished artist in Connecticut. Landscapes in the Hudson River Valley are beautiful and challenging. I hoped to make the hobby pay, but I sold only six paintings. After a two-year drought, I realized that I was not an artist.

What lifted me into an acceptable orbit was my work with the Corps of Cadets.

The Superintendent, Major General Maxwell D. Taylor, gave me command of the cadet Second Regiment, twelve companies (half the Corps of Cadets) and a small staff, at the cadet summer training center at Camp Buckner, in the hills five miles west of West Point, on Lake Popolopen. Twelve hundred cadets during the academic year, nine hundred in the summer. We in the Tactical Department were responsible to the Superintendent and Commandant for the cadets' military training and discipline, and as Private Pete Dussen might say, "for growing them up." I faced new situations each day.

One evening at Camp Buckner, a senior cadet, of Puerto Rican descent, upset himself and me. He was riding in a truck returning to camp after a field problem when his brown felt campaign hat sailed off. The driver ignored his plea to stop. The cadet's solution to retrieving his hat was to go to the motor pool, take a jeep without permission and, furthermore, without a driver's license. In turning the vehicle around, he put it in a ditch and a wrecker had to be sent to the rescue. I referred the matter to the Commandant's Disciplinary Board, and he was confined to limits for four months.

The cadet appeared in my office almost in tears. "Sir, I am in deep trouble. This weekend my entire family is having a reunion in New York City to honor my grandmother who is coming from Puerto Rico. I am her favorite grandson. She left New York in a sailboat ninety-five years ago and has never been back. She is one hundred and six years old."

"I'll see what I can do," I said.

I phoned General Higgins, the Commandant. "Please excuse me for calling you at your home, but this is about a grandmother who is one hundred and six years old." I told him the story.

"What do you recommend?" he asked.

"Let him go," I answered.

"That's approved," he said.

West Point cadets, carefully selected and continually tested, along with midshipmen and cadets at sister academies, are among the finest young people produced in our country. They inspired me. These alert youngsters are most interesting because they are half grown up. Just about the time you think that everything is all right, suddenly it isn't. In my job I was assisted by fourteen outstanding officers, one "Tac" officer for each company, with two working in our headquarters.

On a trip with my excellent boss, Brigadier General Higgins, to interview prospective Tacs, I said, half in jest, "I think we should select one eight ball . . . having cadets continually exposed to our top officers gives them the wrong impression of life in the army."

"No,"Higgins said. "We'll get one of those without trying."

He was right. One of the new Tacs commanded no respect from cadets in his company. They talked back to him. He experienced difficulty in getting orders carried out. And he violated a cardinal rule: he criticized senior cadets in front of their juniors. Higgins solved the situation by asking me to give this officer a staff position where he would control one clerk and mounds of paper. Not everyone can lead people.

During summer training at Camp Buckner, I had contact with two unusual cadets, Mr. Anastasio Somozo who later became the cruel dictator of Nicaragua and was assassinated in 1980, and Mr. Alexander M. Haig, Jr. Because of his arrogance, Somoza caused headache problems that were difficult to solve. The antithesis of Somoza was Al Haig. Haig's Tac, Lieutenant Colonel James Keller, called my attention to him, saying, "If this cadet gets a break in life, he will rise to high places." He did indeed, becoming Chief of Staff to the President of the United States and Secretary of State.

Among the many outstanding cadets was Doc Blanchard, Glenn Davis' running mate. Blanchard's Tactical Officer said to me, "Doc won't shine his shoes, and all the cadets are following him."

I called Doc in and said, "Doc, I wish you'd shine your shoes."

He did. And they did.

To try to keep abreast of the cadets, I got up early. I inspected reveille formation in the North Area of barracks at five-fifty one crisp fall morning and found the cadets milling around in excitement. A raiding party had stolen the Navy goat and had transported it from the Naval Academy at Annapolis. I went to the nearest phone and called our "winningest" football coach, Colonel Red Blaik. It gave me pleasure to awaken him at such an hour. I could almost see him rubbing his eyes. When I gave him the news, he

Brigadier General Harvey R. Fraser at 4th Inf. Div. Monument, Utah Beach, Normandy, 1993.

moaned, "Jez-is Cady! What did they do that for? It only makes my job harder."

General Taylor called me to his office in 1946. "I want you to start a leadership course for cadets.* Something basic that the cadets can bite into. Topics like how a lieutenant motivates his platoon, handles his relationship with the first sergeant, and so on. Have your excellent, combat-experienced company Tacs help you develop the course outline and bring it to me in five weeks for aproval. The course will start in three months. Figure on thirty one-hour sessions per cadet. Your Tacs are to be your instructors. Any questions?"

Cadet interest ran high. In the forty some years since, we instructors have relished remarks from our former students: "This course helped me face my first platoon," "It saved me and gave me confidence in Korea," etc. However, the course was unpopular with

*It took me two years to discover that the originator of the new idea was General of the Army Eisenhower.

the faculty. It was held during academic time, and none of us instructors held Master's Degrees or Doctorates. Retired Brigadier General Douglas Kinnard, professor at the University of Vermont, summed it up. "You were just a bunch of guys teaching leadership."*

When the army was reduced in 1947 by the removal of all retired officers from active duty, I tugged my uniform off for the last time. I had worn it for twenty-one years and felt very sad. Fortunately I was employed. Colonel L.M. (Biff) Jones, Graduate Manager of the Army Athletic Association at West Point and one of the giants in the athletic world, hired me as his assistant. "You will be responsible for the operation and maintenance of our athletic facilities," he said, "and I'll call on you occasionally to make speeches about West Point." (I made 250 in the next twenty years.) I was starting a new career at age forty-five.

My family would remain at West Point, and I would move about the post in civilian clothes. I felt as uncertain as a novice climber facing the Matterhorn.

I was braced on my new job by an agronomist who advised me about turf on the athletic fields and golf course, and by three unusual foremen whom I liked: retired Engineer Sergeant John (Casey) Willis, Mr. Tony Congiglere, and retired Engineer Sergeant Joe Daniels all three smart, dedicated, and unusual.

Casey bossed twenty-one laborers. Once when our beautiful Kentucky Blue turf in Michie Stadium was flooded, Casey made a sage remark: "Water is always in the wrong place."

Tony Congiglere, an old-fashioned handy man, fast disappearing from the American scene, was an expert electrician, mechanic, plumber, tile and stone mason, climber and, in the winter, operator of the hockey rink. Tony told me at the start, "If you have emergencies, don't hestitate to call me, even if I'm home. I *like* emergencies."

When I interviewed ex-first Sergeant Daniels for the position of foreman in Michie Stadium, I knew that at the close of World War II he had commanded a force that removed 13,000 Japanese mines from Philippine beaches without a fatality, winning the Silver Star.

*In 1947 this course took a giant leap forward. Today's formal and erudite course offered by the Department of Behavioral Sciences and Leadership may trace its birth to our primitive but effective beginnings.

We agreed on hours and pay, and after I described his work, he said, "I'll take it provided I never have to boss over two men. I am sick of leadership."

Colonel Red Blaik, now our Director of Athletics as well as head football coach, asked me if I would volunteer to coach the plebe baseball team in addition to my other duties. Though a late-in-the-afternoon job, I was delighted because it gave me contact with cadets, the real pay for anyone working at West Point.* The Plebe team played on the windswept diamond down by the Hudson River. Spectators were scarce. Often the only fan huddled on the cold five-row bleachers was my faithful Dort.

During the Korean War, we endured a most difficult time. At least once a week we went to the cemetery to the funerals of boys who had been in our home or whom I had coached in baseball, or who had participated in our leadership course.

On vacations I organized canoe trips to the scenic Racquette River in the Adirondacks and in Canada. I learned that you cannot win over a portage, especially if you are an amputee; and if you insist on trying, it is wise to take along a daughter. To a campout on an island in Blue Lake in the Adirondacks, I invited our thirteen-year-old "Dodie." She built the fire, cooked and served the meals, washed the dishes, fluffed the sleeping bags, caught fish, and brightened the day.

Having long since given up painting, I was interested when Dort's sister, Miss Jane Darrah, a children's librarian, wrote me, "There is a need for books for children about West Point, Why don't you fill the gap? You wrote a 'best seller' in World War II. I think you can do this." I decided to give it a try. I took a correspondence course in writing and worked hard at it. I had an incentive: my retired pay, plus my salary in the Athletic Association, was not enough for the education of our children.

For the next twenty years, I got up at four-thirty to write, then went to work at eight. Dort became my typist, and developed amazing skills as an editor and copy-editor, while running our home and working as the troop leader for the West Point Girl Scouts. I published thirty-five books, counting two co-written with my sister, Nardi Reeder Campion.

*I coached there for five seasons, and then helped with the "veracity," as Philadelphia outfielder "Mule" Haas called it, for the next thirteen.

Nardi's and my biography of old Sergeant Marty Maher, *Bringing Up the Brass,* was made into the movie *The Long Gray Line* by Columbia Pictures.* This company descended on West Point for five trying weeks and its requests were innumerable. The director, John Ford's, real name was an almost unpronounceable Gaelic one, and his leadership with actors was harsh and difficult. With his black patch over one eye, felt hat pulled down to try to conceal it, he seemed like an old pirate, a far cry from the LST† skipper who cared for a deck full of wounded sailing from Normandy to England. When I inquired about an actor, he snapped, "Actors are dirt under my feet! They do what I tell them, when I tell them." Only Marty escaped his verbal lash. "Marty reminds me of my father back in Ireland," he said.

He gave me the bit part of the Commandant of Cadets addressing new cadets at Battle Monument. When I told him that Commandants do not talk in such a stilted manner, he said, "You're just like all the actors, complaining about your lines. Well, how would you have them changed?" I responded. In a moment he said, "Okay, have it your way."

Ford was feared by many actors. But he was one of the best directors of all time.

My acting career was brief, but my writing was catching on. My paperback, *The MacKenzie Raid,* about Colonel Ranald MacKenzie leading 1,200 cavalrymen into Mexico in 1873 on unwritten orders from General Sheridan to punish marauding Lipan Indians, was also made into a TV series. On the screen Colonel MacKenzie commanded about twenty horsemen. John Ford would never have put up with that.

My six fictional books about "Cadet Clint Lane" and his friends were successful and attracted boys to West Point. On the football field, "Clint" was modeled after Cadet Pat Uebel, star Army fullback, but after me when he was playing baseball or in trouble.

I also enjoyed writing non-fiction books for young people: *Omar N. Bradley—The Soldier's General* and *Dwight David Eisenhower—fighter for Peace.* Both leaders agreed to correct the manuscripts. When

*For the record, we divided all proceeds from our book and the movie equally with Marty. Nardi and I divided our share with the telephone company, or so it seemed.

†Landing Ship Tank

COURTESY OF BO GILL, *NEWBURGH NEWS*

Friends at Doubleday Field, L. to R.: LTG Willard Scott, Mrs. Douglas MacArthur, RR, and Mrs. Priem, receiving the scoop from Carl F. Ullrich, about 1986.

General Bradley was ready to comment, Dort and I drove to the Bradley's suite in New York City. "I have only one comment," General Bradley said in his quiet voice and modest manner, "and that is about the French General LeClerc. On the smash toward Paris in '44, you have me saying that I gave him orders to go there. Please change it to *'I issued him orders through military channels.'*"

I asked if he would write the Foreword, and he said, "Certainly."

His wife Kitty spoke up, "I have a comment. You have my husband saying to a large group of officers before the Normandy invasion, 'There will be no surrender unless you are wounded and out of ammunition.' He wouldn't say such a thing."

I countered, "That's exactly what he said and what we expected him to say."

She turned toward her husband. "Did you say that?"

The general said softly, "Well, if he says I did, I guess I did."

Long before, in interviewing Omar Bradley about his cadet baseball days of fifty years ago, he had talked about his famous throwing arm. "I guess you'd say I over-developed my arm when I was a boy in Missouri by unloading gondola coal cars—at $1.21 an hour. The second summer they raised me to $1.31. I was a left fielder. Once on a play at home plate, I threw the ball over the back stop. Our coach Sammy Strang Nicklin was disgusted."

I knew that he had not distinguished himself in an Army-Navy contest. I said, "How did you happen to get picked off first base in the 1915 Navy game?"* The result was electric. He jumped out of his chair and shouted, "I WAS SAFE! HE NEVER TOUCHED ME!"

He sat down and moved back to the present. He dabbed his forehead with his handkerchief and asked, "Will you join me in a cool glass of water?"

Later, when preparing to write a biography for young people, I interviewed General Eisenhower in his office at his Gettysburg farm, I made no mention of his baseball days. He had talked before of his play in Abilene. "One of the biggest disappointments of my life—the disappointments of your youth may be your greatest—was in not making the West Point baseball squad. I was a good choke hitter, but Coach Sammy Strang was looking for 'cowtailers,' batters who swung from the handle, and who might bang the ball over the fence."

His batting days behind him, General Eisenhower kept his arm limber with occasional fly casting. Once when he was Chief of Staff, he had visited West Point, and General Taylor had asked me to take him fishing. I drove him to lovely Bull Pond, a crater-like lake atop Bull Pond Mountain, on the secluded western edge of the reservation. We were casting for bass from a rowboat when he stood up and said, "I've got the bottom."

I maneuvered the boat to free his lure. "I don't want to lose this bait," he said. Suddenly, the biggest bass I had seen in that lake shot out of the water and tossed the lure loose. "I am embarrassed," he said, shaking his head. "I'm fishing like an amateur."

*I am amazed at my bravery asking such a question.

President Reagan welcomes RR and Jim Young, head coach of the Army team, to the White House, 1988.

We drifted into lily pads, enjoying a tasty basket lunch, big enough for a squad, that Dort and Dodie had put up. Suddenly he said, "They're trying to get me to run for President. Do you think I should?"

I almost fell out of the boat.

I took a deep breath. "No, sir. General Grant was a great general, but he became a poor President. We are trained to be soldiers, not politicians."

He gave me his wonderful smile, "You sound like my brother, Milton."

Now at Gettysburg my work lay on his desk. We chatted about my research. I said, "I was amazed to discover that as a boy you 'rode the rods' under freight cars. The danger."

President Bush enjoys his campaign pin in RR's lapel, White House, 1989.

He nodded, "Boys love an exciting challenge. They're not famous for thinking." He picked up my manuscript. "I have penciled in changes. Editorial license. Now I'm not so naive that I don't realize I've made your manuscript more valuable. Promise me that you will always keep it."

I do not know why he said that, but I have that manuscript in a safe place.

"Yes, sir," I said, and then added, "Sir, will you please write the Foreword?"

He grimaced. "No, I won't do that. I'm deluged. I don't know how many requests I get to do that. I made an exception and wrote the Foreword for dear old Sergeant Marty Maher, the book you and your sister wrote on him."

RR presenting Red Reeder Trophy for the "best football player" to Cadet Mike Mayweather, 1988.

We said goodbye. He showed me a mahogany, glass-enclosed cabinet crammed with mementos and souvenirs.

In a week, unexpectedly, his Foreword *did* arrive.

Before I retired from the Army Athletic Association, I had the honor of escorting our three daughters at their beautiful weddings down the long aisle in the inspiring Cadet Chapel, beneath battle flags that had been carried in the Civil War. Dort managed and staged each wedding. Ann married Captain T. Scott Riggs, Jr.; Dodie, Second Lieutenant Dale E. Hruby; Julia, Mr. Hugh L. McCutchen. Russell III, after his divorce from Susan Millard, married Miss Deborah Rothman. The result of these unions was eleven wonderful grandchildren.

In 1967, Dort and I moved across the Hudson to rural Garrison, dubbing our dwelling Home Plate. It is guarded by a towering copper beech, almost-as-tall Norway spruces, evergreens, maples, oaks, black birches, dogwoods, a sycamore. Japanese maples, lilacs, a Japanese Scholar, an euonymous, and huge black walnuts.

People at West Point were nice to us. After our family's twenty-two year stay, we felt we were part of the institution. I received honors from various factions of the Academy, but the ones I cherish most came from the Cadets.

I established an office in nearby Cold Spring and worked on my writing at decent hours.

Fortunately one cannot see life ahead. It can change without warning.

CHAPTER THIRTY-ONE

Home Plate

ONCE AGAIN American boys were giving up their lives in the name of freedom. This time in Vietnam.

Dort and I worried about our two sons-in-law, Scott Riggs and Dale Hruby, who were fighting with Armor-Cavalry units. Also, our son, Russell, was a technician for General Electric instructing G.I.s in Saigon on the use of the intricate mini-machine gun, "Puff-the-Magic-Dragon."

Our three returned, but sadly thousands weren't so fortunate.

The war finally over, new dawn broke. When Russell III came home he graduated from Richmond College on Long Island and entered Columbia University. In May 1975 we proud parents drove from Home Plate to see him receive his Master's degree in Student Personnel Administration. It was warm at the Morningside Heights exercises. I felt raging hot. I saw no connection between my fiery furnace condition and an anti-tetanus inoculation that I had received three days before.

In a week my legs felt weak. I drove to West Point and consulted the football team's doctor. He laughed at my complaint, and remarked, "Any amputee who can walk as good as you can has no problem." In a month and a half I was back to see him. He pooh-poohed my complaint again and gave me anti-inflammatory pills.

One would think, with my legs weakening, that I would consult a different doctor, but in late September I went to see him again. He increased the dosage of anti-inflammatory pills.

By mid-November I was laboring to move, and I could only go upstairs by sitting down, backwards, using my hands to lift my body one step at a time. Later that month I collapsed, and could not get up. Finally I said, "Dort, please call the ambulance."

The Cadet Hospital tested me for two weeks and then moved me to the U.S. Naval Hospital in Philadelphia, where during the next three weeks I received thirty-nine tests, not including the "test" of sitting in a wheelchair in a hallway outside the x-ray room while its machine was being repaired for three hours.

I puzzled a team of doctors. They could not discover the cause of my weakening, semi-paralyzed condition. Eventually, they listened to the pleas of the young neurologist to "tap his spine." This disclosed that I had contracted the rare Guillain-Barre. The team vanished. There is no medicine for this syndrome.

LTG Russell V. (Slim) Vittrup with RR at the Fairfax Retirement Community, 1993.

In checking me, the neurologist placed a dime on my bedside table and handed me a pen and pad. "Pick up the coin," he said, "and let's see your signature." I picked up the coin easily, and he admired my signature. But two years later, I could not pick up a thin coin and my signature looked like Methuselah's in his final year. I developed a tremor. The disease damaged my gait and balance. All cases of Guillain-Barre may not be the same.

At the end of my twenty-one day testing ordeal, I was moved back to Home Plate, and Dort worked long hours taking care of me while running our home. I became so weak that in trying to transfer from a straight back chair to a wheelchair, in spite of her help, I slipped to the floor and could not get up even with her assistance. She phoned the Garrison Volunteer Rescue Squad, and two of its members lifted me to bed. I returned to spend almost a month in the Cadet Hospital.

For the next nineteen months I lay at Home Plate, bedridden. Family and friends rallied me by visits and by mail. Egon Weiss, U.S.M.A. Librarian, brought me the newest books every two weeks. Major Leslie M. Burger, a dedicated physician, set what must be a record for this age: for eighteen straight months he drove to Home Plate from West Point to check me.* There may not be medicine for Guillain-Barre, but *morale is medicine.*

Among visitors sliding into Home Plate was the incomparable sportswriter Red Smith. He wrote in his column in *The New York Times: "Red Reeder was not at the Parade at West Point to greet returning Army football stars: Doc Blanchard, Glenn Davis and Pete Dawkins. He was across the Hudson . . . in the house that he and Dort call Home Plate. – The middle flagstone in the doorstep is a pentagon measuring 24 by 6 inches, and the figure of a right-handed batter stands aside the sign marking the driveway. – Outside the window, wooded slopes plunge down to the river, with Highlands of the the Hudson rising beyond . . .*

"Red attends Army games when he can but lately his doctor warned him to slow down. He is in his third year of recuperation from the Guillain-Barre Syndrome, a paralysis caused in his case by an anti-tetanus shot. He is proud of the way he and his artificial leg get around the house and grounds now . . .

"Saturday Red took it easy at Home Plate. He used his single aluminum crutch only to demonstrate Ty Cobbs' batting style . . ."

*In 1989 Leslie M. Burger was promoted to brigadier general.

RR receiving Doubleday Society Distinguished Service Award—Nov. 1991. L. to R.: Rod Vitty, '55 Pres. of Doubleday Society; COL (ret.) Ric Ordway, '58; and Dennis R. Haydon, '69.

I was learning to walk for the third time. Most mortals have to learn to walk only once.

In April, 1985, the Devil sat cross-legged at Home Plate. Dort had devoted a morning to shopping, and after lunch took a long nap. When she was fixing supper for us and three visitors, I noticed that she was limping. I asked about it. She said, "I think I had a stroke while I was sleeping."

Most people would have remained in bed and cried. She was stoical. After supper she went to bed and slept for most of the next thirty-two hours before entering the hospital.

When I visited her there in her bed she looked so small and pitiful it wrenched my heart.

Our daughter, Ann Riggs, expert registered nurse, helped Dort to compensate for her disability.

Her expert physical therapist, from Cold Spring, was Julie Burggraf, who not only treated her professionally but befriended her.

Julie's gift of laughter sustained Dort, and our homemaker's helper, Myra Holmes, made it possible for us to remain at Home Plate.

As Dort and I began to rally from our respective illnesses, Carl Ullrich, now Director of Intercollegiate Athletics at West Point, buoyed me. He had us transported to Michie Stadium for football games. This unusual former Marine infantry captain had experienced fighting in temperatures thirty-five below zero at Chosin Reservoir in Korea. Problems in the athletic association are many and varied, but after experiences at Cornell, M.I.T., and Columbia, where he was a champion crew coach, this Korean War veteran dominated the situation.

In 1988, with the approval of General Dave Palmer, Superintendent, Ullrich included me in the party of Head Coach Jim Young's senior cadet football players when they flew to the White House

RR's grandchildren and spouses gather at Vee and Ken Kilgour's wedding, 1986. L. to R. (rear): Brian Champigny, Dale Hruby, Ken and Vee Kilgour, Scott McCutchen, Russ Reeder, Alan and Audrey McCutchen. Front row: Wendy Reeder, Kristan Hruby, Dorothea Riggs, Elizabeth Hruby, Taya Champigny, Heather McCutchen.

Dedication of Red Reeder Room, Washington Hall at West Point. RR at Bat, 1985. R. to L.: appreciative friends, Kathleen Boylan, LTG Willard Scott, "Dusty" Scott, Dort Reeder, and BG Peter Boylan.

to receive The Commander-in-Chief's trophy from President Reagan. When I was introduced to Mr. Reagan, he said, "We are the only two of our generation in the room."

The next year Ullrich included me again with senior football cadets when they received the same trophy from the new President. He pushed me down the hallowed halls of the White House, past rows of Secret Service men, to the Theodore Roosevelt Room, where General Carl Vuono, Chief of the General Staff, and General Palmer received us. Mr. Bush walked in looking sharp after a vacation in Maine. After a brief ceremony, he moved the group into the Oval Office where he shook hands with each of us.

When I met him, I said, "Sir, I am Fred Reeder's brother."

He cracked, "What a hardship!" Then he said softly, "I love Fred."

Mr. Bush and my brother have common bonds: dogs, politics, and naval aviation. Like President Bush, Fred was a naval pilot in World War II.

Thank God my brother and I did not have to fulfill our pledge to die fighting rather than be taken prisoner by the Japanese.

While most of the action I saw was in Europe, Fred's focus was in the South Pacific.

An Early Naval Aviator, he trained over a thousand pilots to fly and for combat. He formed and trained the Navy's pride: Air Group One, a 90-plane carrier unit. As Chief Staff Officer, he developed the air plan for the attack on Kwajelein and other Japanese strongholds. Unfortunately, he suffered stomach ulcers, and his sea duty was interrupted by massive hemorrhages. Later, he grieved over the loss of 46 of Air Group One's 125 pilots, killed in action.

After hospitalization, he became restless; while commanding the New Orleans Naval Air Station, he wired naval headquarters in Washington: I DEMAND INSTANT COMBAT WITH THE JAPANESE.

The spirit propelled him into action as executive officer on the *U.S.S. Bataan* After ninety days at sea, he became ill again. He received promotions to Captain and, on retirement, to Rear Admiral. Ironically, Fred and I held our post-war reunions in a hospital, Walter Reed, when he twice flew to see me after I was wounded. The Reeder brothers were happy to face peace and to return to our families.

Back at Home Plate in Garrison, I responded to West Point and cadet invitations to talk at their company meetings and dining-ins. I asked for transportation and escorts. One captain, assigned to pick me up, disregarded directions and got lost. He was a map reading instructor. When the cadets learned of this, they were very happy.

Gradually I got better, but in the long stretch of bedridden months, while I fought Guillain-Barre Syndrome, I experienced no pain. I indulged in introspective thinking. My mistakes stood in bold relief. I am not listing them. The publishers have established a word limit.

Unless you are a super person like Matthew B. Ridgway, who staved off defeat by turning a war around, or like Frank Borman and his fellow astronauts who flew fiery capsules to conquer outer space, you need family and friends to help win your daily battles. And I suspect that the super people do, too.

My sister Nardi Reeder Campion moved me with a quote from Marianne Moore, who set the tone, "If you will tell me why the fen appears impassable, I will then tell you why I think that I can get across it if I try."

If I were to start over, I would set the same course, but I would strive for a better education in prep school, as a cadet, and beyond. I am aware of my debt to West Point.

An individual receives many lessons. You could almost call them directives. An invaluable one I gained from my mother, and from those dedicated and demanding coaches on playing fields of long ago, is *never quit but to press on and on.*

RR with Dort and their extended family at Liz and Terry McKerrick's Wedding, West Point, 1988.

APPENDIX

"*The Factor X in Victory*"

by Wesley Price

Editor's Note: Soon after Colonel Reeder was wounded, the Saturday Evening Post *published a story about him written by Wesley Price. Parts of it are reproduced here with permission of Wesley Price and the Curtis Publishing Company, ©1944, 1964, by Wesley Price and the Curtis Publishing Company.*

SOMEBODY OUGHT TO put in a word for the infantry colonels. They've got themselves lost to public view in this war, somewhere between the pearl-handled generals and the correspondent's love, G.I. Joe. And yet, in a sense, it's a colonels' war; an appalling number of them have been killed and wounded.

Their casualties came up for discussion in the Pentagon the other day, and the talk drifted to leadership, and how it is more important than all the secret weapons in the world. And that brought up the name of Red Reeder, who is a colonel, a casualty, and famous throughout the Army as an unexampled leader of men. His impact on his regiment is vividly remembered by Lieutenant Robert B. Kay, of Richmond, Virginia, who was present when Reeder was introduced to the regimental officers. "He struck us as a sharp character," Kay says. "He had a hard voice when he zeroed us in. Every spot of brass on him shone. When he hit you with his eyes, he gave you a clean, once-over look, a straight-on look."

The grapevine worked at top speed from the day Reeder moved in. Let any infantry regimental commander get out on the wrong side of bed in the morning, and by noon the 3000 men and the 167 officers of his command know all about it. And they conduct themselves accordingly. In Reeder's case, his every move was of life-and-death interest, foreshadowing how he might act in battle.

Item, reported by a private, "We worried about the new colonel, but when we saw that he ran along behind his jeep more than he rode in it, we were satisfied."

"Why?"

"It showed us he was a strong man, didn't get tired. He could keep up with us in the fighting—be up front, where we wanted him."

The automatic riflemen liked him because he was an expert in their specialty, and he had a way of taking them aside for serious talks about it. The noncoms respected him because he really understood the responsibilities of squad leadership. As for the privates—well, the Old Man gathered them round one day and asked, "Who's going to win the war?"

"We are!" they shouted.

"Wrong," he said, "The privates are—let's hear it." They gave it back to him roaring.

He earned the tribute that good leaders get, an Army cliche: "Hell, he's easy to work for. He just expects results."

In Normandy Reeder led his regiment ashore on a sandy beach three thousand yards long and seventy-five yards deep. There was a sea wall, then sand dunes, and beyond that a wide, flooded area fifteen hundred yards across. They had casualties before they reached the wall, but there, in contrast to what went on at other and bloodier beachheads, the operation went pretty much according to plan.

One regiment of the division fanned left, another went right, and Reeder's, the 12th, plunged through the center. By nightfall of the first day, the division's command post was two or three miles inland, and the regimental C.P.'s were even farther. From then on, it was savagery in the hedgerows.

Almost every man in the 12th Infantry saw Colonel Reeder in person in those first days. He had a command post—three or four officers and some communications equipment in a ditch—but he wasn't there for long at a time. Mostly he did his coloneling at point-blank range, in the forwardmost hedgerow. There was no bravado about it. All good colonels do the same. It's the quickest way to get battle information, and it's good for morale if the leader has the knack of radiating confidence.

Everywhere Red Reeder went he was hailed by enlisted men, "Say, Colonel, how's things going?"

Reeder had an answer that delighted them: "We're so damn' far ahead of the Eighth and Twenty-second that our patrols can't even locate them."

Brigadier General Henry A. Barber says that Reeder's smile was the broadest in Normandy. His whole bearing suggested strength. A lieutenant said, "He was like a stallion," and a Browning automatic rifleman, Private Walter Mills, of East Lynn, West Virginia, said, "He took steps that were thirty feet long."

If Reeder is remembered by the 12th as a great leader, he has his own memory of the regiment as a spirited outfit. Symbolic to him is the grimy infantryman who waved his rifle from a bloody hedgerow and called in pride and triumph, "Hey, Colonel, whatta you think of E Company now?"

The 4th Division's first big objectives were St. Martin de Varreville and Ste. Mere-Eglise. On the way, one of Reeder's battalions was stopped in front of a fortified town, while another battalion was grinding out an advance through hedgerows on the flank. A reserve battalion that Reeder wanted to reinforce the successful flanking movement got in the wrong position and found itself pinned down by artillery fire. Colonel Reeder joined the harassed battalion and moved it on the double into what seemed a safe hedgerow.

The hedgerow turned out to be a sunken road. Men were packed into it shoulder to shoulder. If German artillery found them there, it would be a massacre. Without waiting to find the battalion commander, from whom he had become separated, Reeder shouted, "Follow me!" and scrambled up the forward bank. Everyone within sound of his voice followed him into a level field and spread out. At the same moment, German infantrymen poured from a hedgerow thirty-five yards in front.

Both sides were surprised. Reeder and his men fell prone on the grass and opened fire. The Nazis popped back into their hedgerow and from its security rained bullets on the exposed Yanks.

Reeder stood up in that leaden storm and shouted, "Come on! Surround them!" He ran forward into the gun flashes.

Time and again in this war, high-ranking officers have led assaults on entrenched enemy forces. From a military standpoint, their personal courage is less significant than the fact that their strength of character impels men to follow them. Colonel Richard A. Legg put it this way, "When you tell a guy to break up a machine-gun nest, he doesn't do it because you're an officer. He does it because you're a leader."

When Reeder's men got off the ground at his urging and went with him through gunfire to the hedgerow, they were obeying a leader. Some Germans held their ground and died. The rest fled in panic. Reeder swiftly developed the flank, and his battalions took the fortified town that had been holding them up.

He moved about the front lines constantly, day after day, carrying an M1 rifle and a map, keeping in touch with his command post by radio and runner. He carried five talismans, including a four-leaf clover and a rabbit's foot, and he acted as if he were immune to gunfire.

But even the best of luck can be pressed too far. On the sixth day, an enemy artillery observer spotted him crossing an open space with four runners and a lieutenant. A single 88-millimeter shell screeched over and exploded. Reeder went down with a great hole in his left leg below the knee. His foot dangled by a pulp of bone and muscle, and he might have died there if the lieutenant hadn't been a fast man with a tourniquet.

He came finally to Walter Reed Hospital in Washington. So many well-wishers called on him that corridor traffic in Ward 5 was snarled. Walking wounded enlisted men from the 12th shuffled over from other wards to see him. Sergeant Marty Maher, the trainer in the West Point gymnasium, who has known every cadet since '96, traveled down to spend five minutes with Red and give him a shake of the hand. There was a squad of generals, led by the Chief of Staff himself, and enough majors and colonels and sergeants to form a platoon.

Reeder's army friends are uncountable. He is, as the saying goes, an army brat; he was born at reveille just as the saluting gun boomed at Fort Leavenworth, Kansas, March 4, 1902, a son and the namesake of an officer who died a colonel after making a distinguished record in two wars. He grew up at army posts, and he had a way with him even as a small boy. When grownups couldn't persuade his little sister to eat her soup, he held out a rare inducement: soup would grow hair on her chest, eminently desirable for all right-thinking little girls. She ate. That was one form of leadership.

He was eleven years old when he dived into Casco Bay, in Maine, and rescued the six-year-old son of a sergeant from drowning in deep water. For that he got his first decoration, the Treasury Department Silver Life-Saving Medal. Red says his mother should have got the medal, because she commanded, "Go get that child, Russell!" Mrs. Reeder refuses the credit. She says she remembers saying nothing of the sort.

He was bat boy and mascot for a soldiers' baseball team at Fort McKinley. Enlisted men who played ball were his heroes. When his father enforced military discipline on one of these glorious characters, young Red squirmed with shame and embarrassment. He thought his father was too stern, too tough. Why bawl out a star infielder for failing to salute? Nowadays, Reeder thinks his father was easygoing. "If a man can't carry out a simple order about saluting, what kind of an order can he carry out?"

At West Point, Reeder's talent for leadership found expression in sports. He was captain of the baseball team and an outstanding drop-kicker in football. He played water polo and helped manage boxing, but textbooks were dull headaches. It took him six years to graduate.

As far back as 1931, a foresighted superior, weighing him for the record, reported, "Especially desire to have him in a command job during war, because of his dash and vigor."

The Reeders have three girls and a boy, whom Red named Russell Potter Reeder, III. They are being raised in an atmosphere of intense family loyalty, just as Red was—Red, who prayed at his father's grave in Arlington before going overseas in this war.

When the war came, Reeder was a major with fifteen solid years' experience as an infantry officer. He had his bedroll packed an hour after the Pearl Harbor flash, expecting active duty. Instead of getting it right away, he went to Washington on orders to report to the General Staff, while his regiment headed for Attu. His first big action job was an assignment to get first-hand information about the fighting in the South and Southwest Pacific. He flew on reconnaissance missions over enemy territory and attached himself to jungle patrols. He returned to Washington with a malaria hangover, a Silver Star for gallantry in action and a notebook that set a new standard for military reporting.

One of his departing instructions from General Marshall had been: "Go to Guadalcanal and bring back the lessons our soldiers have learned." Victory on Guadalcanal was still in doubt. We were learning about jungle warfare and paying for the lessons in blood, but the men who knew most were too busy fighting to put their knowledge in writing for the home office. Reeder hunkered down in the mud with the marines and soldiers, asked questions and compiled their bitter wisdom. It's recorded today in a famous blue-covered booklet, *Fighting on Guadalcanal.* A million copies have gone to Army and Marine training commands, and the Chinese use it in translation.

Fighting on Guadalcanal changed training methods and thereby saved many lives. Reeder won the Legion of Merit for it. General Marshall pinned on the decoration just before the colonel went to England, saying, "I am certain that you will win more honors with your regiment." Reeder came back this time with the Distinguished Service Cross.

And today, despite the recent amputation of his shattered leg, Reeder still has the compelling glance and the voice with jump in it. It's the old follow-me, strong in him. An Air Force colonel said, "I never saw a redhead with a big grin who couldn't get people to do anything he wanted." He was groping for Factor *x* in the anatomy of leadership, the mystic spark which enlivens the whole body of soldierly virtues.

Without it, our titanic mass of weapons is useless. The generals know that when the last ship grounds on the last beach in this war and opens its iron jaws, we shall still not have won; not until some resolute man, some leader, steps ashore saying, "Come on. Come on, follow me!" It could never end, otherwise.

Index